ETHICS AND THE ACCOUNTANT

TEXT AND CASES

ETHICS AND THE ACCOUNTANT

TEXT AND CASES

Floyd W. Windal
University of Georgia

PRENTICE HALL, Inc., Englewood Cliffs, New Jersey 07632

Library of Congress Cataloging-in-Publication Data

Windal, Floyd W.

Ethics and the accountant : text and cases : by Floyd W. Windal.

p. cm.

Includes index.

ISBN 0-13-290255-9

1. Accountants—Professional ethics—United States—Case studies.
2. Accounting—Standards—United States. I. Title.
HF5616.U5W57 1991
174'.4—dc20 90-44987
CIP

Editorial/production supervision
and interior design: *Robert C. Walters*
Cover design: *Lundgren Graphics*
Manufacturing buyers: *Trudy Pisciotti/Robert Anderson*

Printed in the United States of America

10 9 8 7 6 5 4 3 2 1

ISBN 0-13-290255-9

Prentice-Hall International (UK) Limited, *London*
Prentice-Hall of Australia Pty. Limited, *Sydney*
Prentice-Hall Canada, Inc., *Toronto*
Prentice-Hall Hispanoamericana, S.A., *Mexico*
Prentice-Hall of India Private Limited, *New Delhi*
Prentice-Hall of Japan, Inc., *Tokyo*
Simon & Schuster Asia Pte. Ltd., *Singapore*
Editora Prentice-Hall do Brasil, Ltda., *Rio de Janeiro*

To

Robert N. Corley

Whose encouragement and advice provided
the impetus for my initial writing in
the area of ethics and professionalism.

CONTENTS

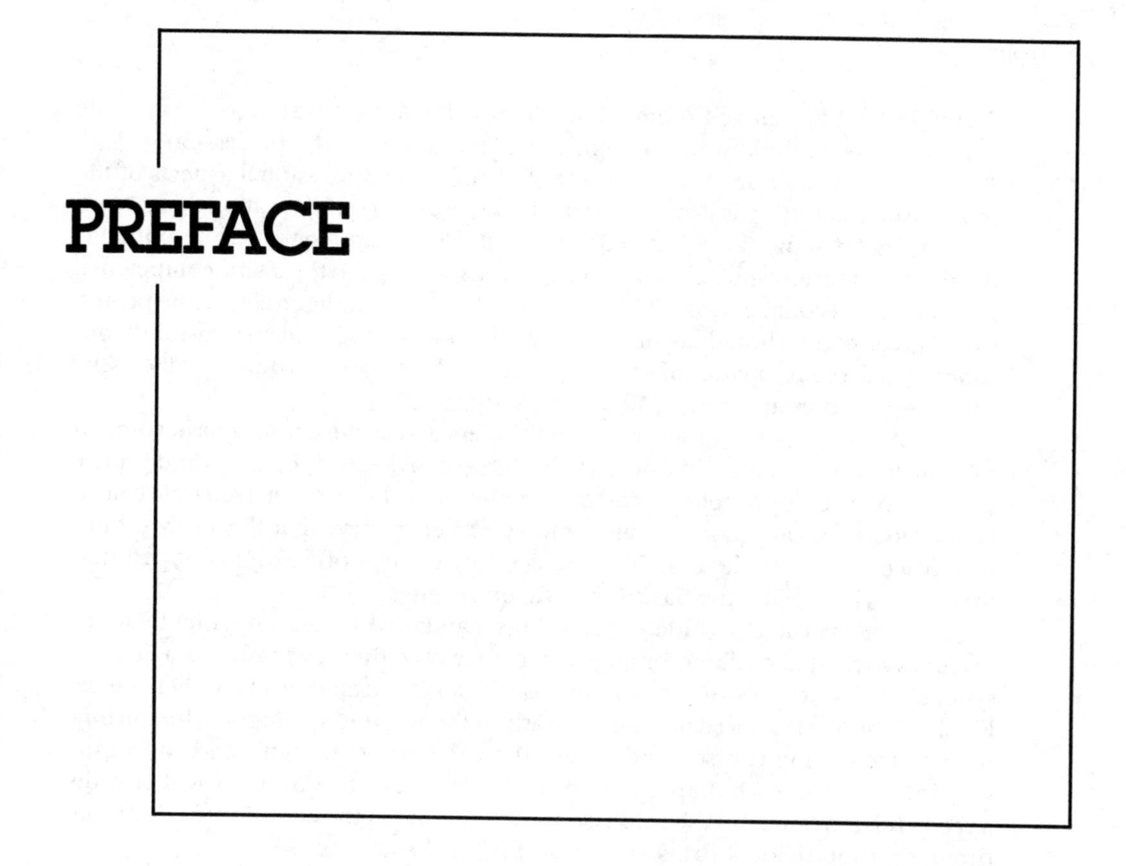

PREFACE

"Auditors in the Dock," "The Hill's New Assault on CPAs," "Accounting Firm Settles Fraud Suit for $2.9 Million," "State Jury Awards $30 Million to Firms in (X) Accounting Firm Case," and "Two Auditors Are Convicted of Stock Fraud," are examples of newspaper headlines dealing with contemporary problems facing the accounting profession. Members of Congress, the Securities and Exchange Commission, courts, attorneys, and clients are often critical of the "accounting establishment" and of the quality of service being rendered by many professional accountants. Many members of the profession are also concerned about the ethical standards of the practice of accounting. This book has been prepared to assist the student of accounting and the practitioner in developing an understanding of the ethical standards and professionalism required of accountants.

For many years it has been assumed that individuals would somehow just know what was right and what was wrong, that there was no real need for an in-depth study of ethics and profesisonalism as they relate to accountants. As the foregoing headlines attest, that assumption is false. Too often, accountants in industry and public practice are guilty of not seeing the obvious wrong, are not aware of an accepted standard of practice, are not living up to the moral code expected of professionals. Civil and criminal liability suits, injunctive and enforcement proceedings by the

Securities and Exchange Commission, congressional investigations, and possible additional regulation by government are a fact of life for the profession.

It is the author's belief that the study of these professional aspects of the practice of accounting is just as essential to the professional education of accountants as similar topics are to the education of doctors and lawyers. The public is demanding more responsibility and higher standards of ethics and competence from all professional persons. Therefore, all who consider themselves to be professional accountants should not only study professional ethics and responsibility, but should make them a matter of ongoing concern. This work was developed to assist with these studies and reviews.

Accounting educators and practitioners across the country have come to the conclusion that more time needs to be devoted to the study of ethics and professional responsibilitiy in colleges and universities. Some believe that a separate course is needed as a focal point for these studies. Others believe that the study should take place in each of the individual accounting courses offered. It is hoped that this book will provide the basis for both approaches.

The instructors' guide and solutions manual, which accompanies this text, provides suggested outlines for an ethics course on either a semester or a quarter system. The text may also be used as the basis for an ethics module in another course. Finally, if the text is utilized in a module early in the accounting program, instructors in later accounting courses could draw upon the many questions and cases provided at the end of each chapter. For those already in practice, the book will provide a ready reference work. It should also prove valuable in the continuing education programs of individual firms and of professional societies.

In the chapters that follow, the world of the professional accountant will be explored in great detail. The organization of the profession, its challenges, and its opportunities will be examined in chapter 1. The next five chapters will provide a detailed look at the profession's ethical code and at many of the day-to-day questions that must be answered within its framework. In each chapter, the ethics and responsibility of the auditor, the management consultant, the tax practitioner, and the internal professional will be examined. The chapter headings parallel the subject matter in the American Institute of Certified Public Accountants (AICPA) Code of Professional Conduct. Throughout the book, the discussion is enhanced by excerpts from published articles and by the reproduction of pertinent accounting and auditing standards.

It is the objective of the book to provide the reader with an understanding of professional ethics and responsibility and of what it means to be an accounting professional. The appendixes provide ready access to the *AICPA Code of Professional Conduct* and its interpretations; the *AICPA Statements on Standards For Management Advisory Services;* the *AICPA Statements on Responsibilities in Tax Practice;* the *Standards of Ethical Conduct for Management Accountants;* the *Code of Ethics* of the Financial Executives Institute; the Institute of Internal Auditors' *Code of Ethics, Statement of Responsibilities of Internal Auditing,* and *Standards for the Professional Practice of Internal Auditing;* the *Code of Ethics of the Association of Government Accountants;* and the *Summary of*

Statement on Government Auditing Standards by the Comptroller General of the United States. In addition, the American Bar Association's *Statement of Policy Regarding Lawyers' Responses to Auditors' Requests for Information* is reproduced.

Appreciation goes to the American Bar Association, the American Institute of Certified Public Accountants, the Association of Government Accountants, the Financial Accounting Foundation, the Financial Executives Institute, The Institute of Internal Auditors, the National Association of Accountants, The United States General Accounting Office, and to other publishers for the generous permission to quote from their publications.

The author is very grateful to those students who originated cases included in the Questions and Cases section that follows each chapter. Although rewritten and modified in many instances, permission to use them is very much appreciated. Recognition is given at the beginning of each case originated by a student.

Thanks also go to the able reviewers of the manuscript for the book: Edward E. Milam, University of Mississippi; Thomas H. Oxner, University of Arkansas at Little Rock; John T. Ahern, DePaul University; and Thomas D. Hubbard, University of Nebraska. Finally, I am grateful to my daughter, Jodie L. Windal, who provided valuable assistance in the preparation of the manuscript.

Floyd W. Windal

1

THE ACCOUNTING PROFESSION

INTRODUCTION

What is it that impels one person to live by a high moral code and another to disregard such values? Is it true that those engaged in certain human endeavors are, by the very nature of those endeavors, motivated to a higher standard of conduct? It has certainly been true over the centuries that an especially high standard of behavior has been expected of those engaged in one of the learned professions.

Too often, however, those in such positions of trust have disappointed us! Time and again, instances of illegal and immoral activity are brought to our attention, leading us to distrust codes of ethics and professional oaths. Is it not true that in the final analysis the man makes the job, rather than the job the man? Only from within can the motivation come to be an honest lawyer, a trustworthy physician, or an objective accountant.

The late Albert J. Harno, for 35 years Dean of the College of Law at the University of Illinois, shared his great insight on these issues in a graduation address in 1961. The following excerpts from that address show that it is as valid today as when it was given:

Life for most people is a day-to-day affair; it is "numbered by years, daies and hours."* Men live, seek diversion and comfort, have fleeting glimpses of happiness, are touched by sorrow, and pass from the scene. A few stop to contemplate and to wonder. But now and then there rises from the multitude a prophet, a Plato, an Aristotle, a Jesus of Nazareth, a Beethoven, an Abraham Lincoln, to fashion for us in words, in poetry, in music, and in song, some lasting conception of the eternal verities of life—of the good, the true, and the beautiful—and to formulate for us directives and precepts to guide us on our way.

We live in an age in which materialism and, in many parts of the world, crass materialism prevails. It is a technical age in which men put their faith in mechanized force, in atomic power, missiles, earth satellites, and space ships. We look for guidance and hear only a bable of voices as men give expression to guile, deception, hate, greed, and prejudice. . . .

There is a clash as to the meaning and place of law as a governing force in society. We Americans subscribe, at least outwardly, to the idea and to the ideal that ours is a government of law—that no individuals, no not even our highest governing officials, are above the law. . . .

But law is not the only force that regulates human conduct. I wish to speak about three areas or domains, of human action. I am indebted to an Englishman, Lord Moulton,† for this classification. The development is my own. The *first* is the area of free choice; the *second*, the domain of obedience to the unenforceable; and *third*, the domain of law.

The first, the domain of free choice, is a limited area. I sometimes wonder if we really appreciate how little freedom of choice we have in making decisions; we are constantly under one pressure or another. If we have an evening to ourselves, we may have a choice of reading . . . or of going to a movie. We may be able to choose whether we will or will not take sugar in our coffee. But even that choice may be denied to us by doctor's orders.

The second domain, that of obedience to the unenforceable, is difficult to define. In it there is no law which determines our course of action, and yet we feel that we are not free to choose as we would. It is a very broad area. It covers those actions which we are not compelled to perform but which some inner voice directs us to discharge. It is the realm of kindliness and conscience—the domain of manners, ethics, and morals. It is the realm which recognizes the sway of duty, of fairness, of honest dealings between men, of sympathy, of taste, and of the spirit. It covers all those things that make life beautiful and a good society possible. What other than a call of conscience is it that makes us willing to take part in community enterprises and in matters relating to the public welfare?

It is the realm of courtesy. There is no compelling reason other than the inner voice that prompts us to speak kindly to our fellowmen. It is the domain of good manners and honest dealings with others. Manners signify good breeding—and more. Manners are the outward expression of an intellectual and moral conviction. Manners are based in that true and deepest self-respect, and they originate in a respect for others. Manners do not make the man, but they reveal the man.

What is it that causes men to maintain self-restraint and consideration for others in the face of danger? Instances come to mind in which many people were faced with impending disaster and death—a shipwreck, fire, or exposition. The way to escape was open to but few. While this has not always been true, often the physically strong have resisted the temptation to fight their way to safety and have permitted

*Bartas, Guillaume De Salluste du, *Divine Weekes and Worker*, second week, third day, part two.
†"Law and Manners," *The Atlantic Monthly*, I (July 1924), 134.

> the weaker members, the women and children, of the group to escape. Why was this? Law did not require it. Force at that time was not a factor.
>
> It is the realm of tolerance. When men have lost their tolerance for the views and practices of others, they have lost something that is precious to a good society. Tolerance is the premise for some important provisions that have been written into our Constitution—freedom of speech, freedom of worship, freedom of the press.
>
> It is the realm of truth, of ethics, morals, aesthetics, the spiritual, and of those great precepts: Love they neighbor as thyself; do unto others as you would have them do unto you.
>
> Truly, the full measure of a man can be gauged by the extent to which he gives obedience to these guides to human conduct that are unenforceable. The extent to which its members give credence to these standards is also the measure of the greatness of a people, of the greatness of a nation. It is through obedience of the people to these precepts that a democratic society is made possible. . . .
>
> Observe how closely the last two domains, that of obedience to the unenforceable and that of obedience to law, are interrelated. They intertwine and complement each other. Obedience to law in a free society is of the essence, but law observance would come to naught unless the members of that society were also deeply devoted to the precept of obedience to that which they cannot be forced to obey. . . .
>
> The issue before us is one of values. There are those among us who assert, and with reason, that we have lost our sense of purposeful direction; that we are a drifting people in ideas and ideals; that we are "paralyzed in self-indulgences"; that the impact of technology upon self-government is subjecting "the processes of democracy to a complete change of scale" . . . it is imperative that we do not permit ourselves to be deflected from the supreme and enduring values. We must fortify our lives and all of our actions with these values and make them a fighting faith.
>
> We must never waiver in our support of the democratic process, in our adherence to the rule of law, and in our fidelity to the enduring values of life. Thus accoutered, the individual can rise above the confusion of the day. To live by these values marks the supreme measure of a man, of a people, of a nation.

The emphasis which Dean Harno places on an "inner voice" or a "call of conscience" which speaks to individual men and women, is far more satisfying than the other possible justifications for ethical behavior which we sometimes see advanced. The motivation for ethical behavior must be more than just duty or cost effectiveness, for example. An accounting professional must have a higher justification for preparing accurate financial statements than the need to fulfill his duty as an employee or as a member of a learned profession. And he or she must not prepare those same financial statements accurately just because discovery of inaccurate statements would be too costly to his or her reputation in the financial community or the company.

Akin to the duty and cost effectiveness justifications are what might be called long-run ethics and situational ethics. The former might argue that unethical behavior should not be countenanced in the short run because it would hurt the individual or the company in the long run. The latter might argue that unethical behavior might be all right in certain situations, but not in others, as for example when a so-called lesser evil would allow one to accomplish a greater goal—the ends justifying the means.

All of these suggested justifications must be rejected in favor of the one advocated by Dean Harno. Each individual must listen for the voice within to direct them to the higher road—to the establishment of their own personal set of values which will hold them to the very highest standard of behavior and obedience to the unenforceable.

THE NEWEST PROFESSION

Certified public accountants have for many years regarded themselves as professionals, equal in every respect to the more uniformly recognized professions of law, medicine, and theology. In recent years, furthermore, they have come to be regarded by society as deserving of that appellation. As the subject matter with which they are concerned has increased in volume and complexity, in accordance with similar changes in society, their services have become more critical and more in demand. Our industrialized world of today could not get along without this newest member of the learned professions.

Although those in the public practice of accounting are now generally regarded as professionals, it is just becoming recognized that many accountants practicing within an organization are also worthy of that title. Just as many lawyers work for private business and government, so professional accountants can be found in industry, with a governmental agency, or with a not-for-profit organization. Many hold the CPA certificate and are members of the professional associations of those similarly recognized. Others hold the relatively new CMA certificate and refer to themselves as certified management accountants. Still others are certified internal auditors (CIAs). All of these people, if true to their calling, have the objective outlook and the high standards of performance attributed to professionals.

One outward sign of the increasing stature of accountants is the establishment at some universities of schools of accounting. These new administrative units have the potential to do for the accounting profession what schools of law have done for the legal profession. Those schools already established and the faculties at universities with similar goals and standards have organized a Federation of Schools of Accountancy to further their aims and speed their progress.

THE STRUCTURE OF A PROFESSION

Just what is it that entitles a particular discipline or calling to be referred to as a profession? There are many pretenders to the title, but few are generally so regarded. A profession might be likened to a building, all parts of which are needed in order for it to be complete and ready for occupancy.

The Foundation

Underlying any profession must be a solid foundation consisting of a recognized body of knowledge essential to the well-being of society. Certainly, the subject matter of accounting meets this criterion. The most widely publicized and accepted statement of this foundation of the accounting profession is *Horizons for a Profession,* by Robert H. Roy and James H. MacNeill.[1] A further validation of the existence of a large and at times very technical body of knowledge in accounting can be found in the accounting programs of the many universities offering courses and degrees in accounting.

That this body of knowledge is needed by society can also be easily confirmed. The myriad accounting reports and filings required by the various agencies of municipal, state, and federal governments would be sufficient in themselves to establish society's need for accountants. The requirement by the Securities and Exchange Commission (SEC) that financial reports filed with it be certified by an independent public accountant is also clear evidence. And, of course, the widespread continued demand for college graduates with training in accounting is further proof.

The Framework

The framework erected on a building foundation also has a parallel in the structure of a profession. Three elements comprise this framework: (1) an educational process to acquire and maintain the body of knowledge, (2) an examination and licensing process to test whether individual practitioners have a firm grasp of the subject matter, and (3) a sense of responsibility to society with regard to the use of this knowledge. All three of these elements are essential.

In accounting, the educational process is well established. Schools and programs of accounting are widely available at colleges and universities. In most states, certain minimum formal educational requirements must be satisifed before an individual is allowed to sit for the CPA examination. Those sitting for the CMA examination must hold a baccalaureate degree from an accredited college or university, achieve a satisfactory score on a recognized graduate school admission examination, or already hold a CPA or comparable certificate from a foreign country. Candidates for the CIA examination must hold a baccalaureate or its equivalent from an accredited college-level institution.

After the year 2000, those wishing to become members of the American Institute of Certified Public Accountants must have 150 semester hours of education. An increasing number of states have also set this as a prerequisite to taking the CPA examination.

Most states now have continuing education requirements for continued practice as a CPA. Furthermore, all members of the American Institute of Certified Public Accountants must satisfy a continuing education requirement as a condition of membership. Holders of the CMA certificate must also meet a continuing education requirement in order to maintain their certificate, and one of the standards of the Institute of Internal Auditors is that technical competence should be maintained through continuing education. In addition, government auditing standards set by the Comptroller General of the United States require continuing education of those

[1]Robert H. Roy and James H. McNeill, *Horizons for a Profession* (New York: American Institute of Certified Public Accountants, 1967).

involved in government audits, including a specified amount on subjects directly related to the government environment and to government auditing.

As pointed out earlier, a very formal examination and licensing process does exist in accounting. Each state has laws for the examination and licensing of CPAs. A uniform national examination is given, with some states adding sections on subject matter of particular interest in their area. Boards of Accountancy in the various states normally are charged with monitoring the practice of accounting. The National Association of State Boards of Accountancy is an association of these boards. Although no licensing is involved, formal examination procedures also exist for awarding the CMA and the CIA certificates.

Finally, the sense of responsibility to society certainly does exist. This is particularly true of the CPA who is practicing as an independent auditor. He is well aware that his opinion on the fairness of financial statements will be relied upon by third parties, and he acts accordingly. The CPA practicing as a management consultant or as a tax practitioner, and the CPA, CMA, or CIA practicing internally are also becoming increasingly aware of their public responsibility. The trial and conviction in recent years of lawyers and accountants working in government and industry, as well as in public practice, have brought these responsibilities to the attention of all.

The Finish

Just as the walls and roof must be attached to the frame to complete a building, so the professional structure needs some additions for its completion. Three elements are needed: (1) professional associations, (2) codes of ethics, and (3) technical standards.

Professional associations abound in the accounting field. The most important of these is probably the American Institute of Certified Public Accountants. Although primarily an organization of individuals, it also has a Division for CPA Firms, with an SEC Practice Section and a Private Companies Practice Section. The CPAs in each of the various states are also organized into state societies, which normally cooperate with the AICPA in the discipline of members and the monitoring of quality standards, although they are autonomous.

One of the leading associations for management accountants, those internal professionals working primarily in industry and government, is the National Association of Accountants. The Financial Executives Institute is an association of internal professionals who hold senior positions in the accounting and finance area. Other important organizations of practicing professionals are the Institute of Internal Auditors, the Planning Executives Institute, and the Association of Government Accountants. In the academic world, the American Accounting Association is the leading organization.

The American Institute of CPAs has long had a code of professional conduct. The principles and rules established under this code and their interpretations are reproduced in Appendix 1.

The Institute of Internal Auditors has had its own code of ethics and statement of responsibility for many years. The code is reproduced in Appendix 6 and the Statement of Responsibilities in Appendix 7. In addition, the National Association of Accountants (Appendix 4), the Financial Executives Institute (Appendix 5), and the Association of Government Accountants (Appendix 9), all have codes.

The technical standards of the profession come from many sources. The primary sources for financial accounting standards are the Financial Accounting Standards Board (FASB) and the Governmental Accounting Standards Board (GASB). These private sector bodies, which the Financial Accounting Foundation oversees, are assisted by an advisory council. Pronouncements made in prior years by the AICPA Committee on Accounting Procedure and the Accounting Principles Board are also considered authoritative unless expressly superceded by the FASB. Accounting principles are also promulgated for defense contractors under federal contracts by the Cost Accounting Standards Board, an official governmental body. First established in 1970, the CASB was reestablished by the Congress in 1988 after a brief period when it was not funded. Finally, the Securities and Exchange Commission, through its rulings and persuasive power, also establishes and influences the establishment of accounting principles.

In the auditing area, accountants must adhere to generally accepted auditing standards which have been approved and adopted by the membership of the AICPA and which are continually interpreted in Statements of Auditing Standards issued by the Auditing Standards Board. The Comptroller General of the United States has also issued a set of audit standards to be applied to audits of all government organizations, programs, activities, and functions, and of government funds received by contractors, nonprofit organizations, and other nongovernment organizations. A summary of these standards is reproduced in Appendix 10.

The Institute of Internal Auditors has also approved a set of standards for the professional practice of internal auditing. A summary of these standards is reproduced in Appendix 8.

THE SECURITIES AND EXCHANGE COMMISSION

Of great significance to the professional accountant is the authority and activity of the Securities and Exchange Commission. Established in 1934, this commission has the authority to define the content and form of financial statements and other reports submitted to it, as well as the methods of accounting used in deriving them. It can also require disclosure of all information it considers necessary for investor decisions. Because virtually all large companies must file reports with the SEC, this gives the commission effective control not only over accounting principles, but also over the auditing procedures necessary to insure proper reporting. Certification of financial information by an independent accountant is required by the securities laws.

Fortunately for the accounting profession, the SEC has delegated to the private sector the general responsibility for the establishment of accounting principles. Its Accounting Series Release (ASR) No. 150 reads in part as follows:

> . . . Various Acts of Congress administered by the Securities and Exchange Commission clearly state the authority of the Commission to prescribe the methods to be followed in the preparation of accounts and the form and content of financial statements to be filed under the Acts and the responsibility to assure that investors are furnished with information necessary for informed investment decisions. In meeting this statutory responsibility effectively, in recognition of the expertise, energy and resources of the accounting profession, and without abdicating its responsibilities, the Commission has historically looked to the standard-setting bodies designated by the profession to provide leadership in establishing and improving accounting principles. The determinations by these bodies have been regarded by the Commission with minor exceptions, as being responsive to the needs of investors.
>
> The body presently designated by the Council of the American Institute of Certified Public Accountants (AICPA) to establish accounting principles is the Financial Accounting Standards Board (FASB). . . the commission intends to continue its policy of looking to the private sector for leadership in establishing and improving accounting principles and standards through the FASB with the expectation that the body's conclusions will promote the interests of investors.
>
> In Accounting Series Release No. 4 (1938) the Commission stated its policy that financial statements prepared in accordance with accounting practices for which there was no substantial authoritative support were presumed to be misleading and that footnote or other disclosure would not avoid this presumption. It also stated that, where there was a difference of opinion between the Commission and a registrant as to the proper accounting to be followed in a particular case, disclosure would be accepted in lieu of correction of the financial statements themselves only if substantial authoritative support existed for the accounting practices followed by the registrant and the position of the Commission had not been expressed in rules, regulations or other official releases. For purposes of this policy, principles, standards and practices promulgated by the FASB in its Statements and Interpretations will be considered by the Commission as having substantial authoritative support, and those contrary to such FASB promulgations will be considered to have no such support.
>
> In the exercise of its statutory authority with respect to the form and content of filings under the Acts, the Commission has the responsibility to assure that investors are provided with adequate information. A significant portion of the necessary information is provided by a set of basic financial statements (including the notes thereto) which conform to generally accepted accounting principles. Information in addition to that included in financial statements conforming to generally accepted accounting principles is also necessary. Such additional disclosures are required to be made in various fashions, such as in financial statements and schedules reported on by independent public accountants or as textual statements required by items in the applicable forms and reports filed with the Commission. The Commission will continue to identify areas where investor information needs exist and will determine the appropriate methods of disclosure to meet these needs.
>
> It must be recognized that in its administration of the Federal Securities Acts and in its review of filings under such Acts, the Commission staff will continue as it has in the past to take such action on a day-to-day basis as may be appropriate

to resolve specific problems of accounting and reporting under the particular factual circumstances involved in filings and reports of individual registrants. . . .[2]

As pointed out in the release, the delegation of authority by the SEC is not absolute or complete. The basic rules for the form and content of financial statements filed with the commission are included in its Regulation S–X, and Financial Reporting Releases often set forth required accounting and auditing procedures, as well as disclosure requirements. The SEC has fulfilled its promise in ASR 150 to "continue. . . to take such action on a day-to-day basis as may be appropriate to resolve specific problems." As detailed in Accounting Series Release No. 253 (now codified in Financial Reporting Release No. 1, Section 406), for example, the commission overruled a decision of the FASB on the controversial issue of accounting and reporting practices for oil- and gas-producing activities. As a general rule, however, frequent consultation and communication between the SEC and the FASB have avoided such results.

Regulation S–X is also the vehicle for stating the SEC rule on auditor independence. Rule 2–01, dealing with the qualification of accountants practicing before the commission, states in part:

> The Commission will not recognize any certified public accountant or public accountant as independent who is not in fact independent. For example, an accountant will be considered not independent with respect to any person, or any of its parents, its subsidiaries, or other affiliates (1) in which, during the period of his professional engagement to examine the financial statements being reported on or at the date of his report, he, his firm, or a member of his firm had, or was committed to acquire, any direct financial interest or any material indirect financial interest, or (2) with which, during the period of his professional engagement to examine the financial statements being reported on, at the date of his report or during the period covered by the financial statements, he, his firm, or a member of his firm was connected as a promoter, underwriter, voting trustee, director, officer, or employee. A firm's independence will not be deemed to be affected adversely where a former officer or employee of a particular person is employed by or becomes a partner, shareholder or other principal in the firm and such individual has completely disassociated himself from the person and its affiliates and does not participate in auditing financial statements of the person or its affiliates covering any period of his employment by the person. . . . the term "member" means (i) all partners, shareholders, and other principals in the firm, (ii) any professional employee involved in providing any professional service to the person, its parents, subsidiaries, or other affiliates, and (iii) any professional employee having managerial responsibilities and located in the engagement office or other office of the firm which participates in a significant portion of the audit.
>
> In determining whether an accountant may in fact be not independent with

[2]Securities and Exchange Commission, "Statement of Policy on the Establishment and Improvement of Accounting Principles and Standards," *Accounting Series Release No. 150,* December 20, 1973. Accounting Series Releases were discontinued on April 15, 1982 and this release is now contained in *Financial Reporting Release No. 1,* Section 101. FRS No. 1 is a codification of all ASRs dealing with accounting and auditing matters of general interest that have not become obsolete or been previously rescinded.

respect to a particular person, the Commission will give appropriate consideration to all relevant circumstances, including evidence bearing on all relationships between the accountant and that person or any affiliate thereof, and will not confine itself to the relationships existing in connection with the filing of reports with the Commission.[3]

Various Accounting Series Releases have provided interpretations and guidelines for the implementation of this rule. In Chapter 2, some of these are noted as the issue of independence is explored in great detail.

The SEC has also adopted certain rules of practice applicable to proceedings before the commission, and Rule 2(e) has become the basis for the suspension and disbarment of accountants who fail to meet the commission's standards. That rule reads in part:

The Commission may deny, temporarily or permanently, the privilege of appearing or practicing before it in any way to any person who is found by the Commission after notice of an opportunity for hearing in the matter (i) not to possess the requisite qualifications to represent others, or (ii) to be lacking in character or integrity or to have engaged in unethical or improper professional conduct, or (iii) to have willfully violated, or willfully aided and abetted the violation of any provision of the federal securities laws. . ., or the rules and regulations thereunder.[4]

THE CONGRESS

On occasion, an accounting issue has become so controversial and its outcome has been of such importance to the affected parties or the economy that congress has intervened. For example, legislation reinstating an investment credit for federal income tax purposes in the early 1970s included the provision that companies should be free to choose from among alternative methods of accounting, thus precluding the prescription of a particular method by the profession, as had been attempted earlier. In the late 1970s, the Congress as a part of Public Law 94–163, *Energy Policy and Conservation Act* (452 U.S. Code, Sec. 6383), empowered the Securities and Exchange Commission either

to prescribe rules applicable to persons engaged in the production of crude oil or natural gas, or make effective by recognition, or by other appropriate means indicating a determination to rely on accounting practices developed by the Financial Accounting Standards Board, if the Securities and Exchange Commission is assured that such practice will be observed by persons engaged in the pro-

[3]Securities and Exchange Commission, "Qualifications of Accountants," *Regulation S-X, Article 2–01.*

[4]Securities and Exchange Commission, *Rules of Practice,* Rule 2(e), par. 201.2.

duction of crude oil or natural gas to the same extent as would result if the Securities and Exchange Commission had prescribed such practices by rule.[5]

The effect of this provision was to require that an accounting question, over which there was great disagreement, be resolved by a specific date. The Congress was unwilling to allow the private sector to proceed at its own pace with resolving the issue.

Congressional Investigations

Congress also became directly involved with the accounting profession in the late 1970s as the result of a variety of national concerns. Some of these are detailed in the following introduction to a report of the Subcommittee on Reports, Accounting and Management (Metcalf subcommittee) of the Committee of Governmental Affairs of the United States Senate. The report itself is entitled "Improving the Accountability of Publicly Owned Corporations and their Auditors."

> During the past several years, serious questions have arisen concerning the activities and accountability of publicly owned corporations operating in the United States and throughout the world. These questions have arisen in large part from a series of unexpected failures by major corporations, as well as disclosures of widespread questionable and illegal activities by the managements of many publicly owned corporations. Such problems have contributed to a severe decline of public confidence in the integrity of American business.
>
> Public confidence in the integrity and efficiency of the business community must be restored because such confidence is the key element in making the Nation's economic system function effectively. The Federal Government has certain public policy responsibilities in helping to assure the accountability of publicly owned corporations as set forth in the Securities Act of 1933 and the Securities Exchange Act of 1934. The Federal Government also has an important direct interest in understanding and correcting problems in the business sector. Those problems can lead to substantial Federal assistance programs, as in the cases of Penn Central Corp. and Lockheed Aircraft Corp.
>
> Congress has attempted to meet its responsibilities in this area through various initiatives, both in the enactment of legislation deemed necessary and in the increased oversight activities by appropriate committees.
>
> The Subcommittee on Reports, Accounting and Management is responsible for assuring, among other things, that accounting and financial reporting practices promulgated or approved by the Federal Government are responsive to the needs of the public. Accordingly, this subcommittee has devoted substantial time and effort over the past two years to evaluating the role of such accounting and financial reporting practices as a means of improving the accountability of publicly owned corporations.

[5]"Financial Accounting and Reporting by Oil and Gas Companies," *Statement of Financial Accounting Standards No. 19* (Stamford, Conn.: Financial Accounting Standards Board, 1977), par. 75.

The CPA Letter, a semimonthly news report published by the AICPA, summarized the report of this Senate subcommittee as follows:

> Accounting and auditing standards relating to publicly held companies should be set by the accounting profession with close oversight by the SEC. This is the thrust of the report of the subcommittee on reports, accounting and management of the Senate Committee on Governmental Affairs.
>
> Heading the list of recommendations is the establishment of a self-regulatory organization with disciplinary powers similar to those of the New York Stock Exchange or the National Association of Securities Dealers. All firms that audit publicly held companies would be required to join and meet the organization's performance and behavioral standards. A quality review program would be an essential element. The SEC would have an oversight role to evaluate and determine whether the standards and policies meet established public policies.
>
> The following are among the subcommittee's other recommendations:
>
> Broaden the basis for representation on standard-setting bodies to include members from small businesses and accounting firms.
>
> Require all firms with publicly held clients to disclose financial data and important operating information.
>
> Require that the profession or the SEC mandate corporate audit committees composed of outside directors.
>
> Limit management advisory services by accounting firms to areas directly related to accounting. The report states that these related activities "are confined to the limited area of providing certain computer and systems analyses that are necessary for improving internal control procedures of corporations.
>
> End artificial professional restrictions against advertising and talking with another firm's clients. Also, employment offers to employees of other firms should be permitted without first consulting with the present employers.
>
> Auditors should be liable to private parties who suffer damages as a result of the auditors' negligence.
>
> Rotate personnel assigned to a specific audit within an accounting firm, pending more study by the profession and the SEC on the desirability of the rotation of firms among publicly held corporations.[6]

In the House of Representatives of the Congress, a similar investigation was undertaken by the Subcommittee on Oversight and Investigations (the Moss subcommittee) of the Committee on Interstate and Foreign Commerce. The outcome of that investigation was the introduction of a bill to further regulate the accounting profession through the establishment of the National Organization of SEC Accountancy (NOSEC). The bill, which did not pass, also called for the establishment of an SEC-appointed board which would be authorized to review and investigate auditors registered with NOSEC. Economic sanctions, fines, and other disciplinary actions were provided for in the proposal.

[6]"Metcalf Report Calls for Prompt Private Sector Action," *The CPA Letter, Vol. 57*, No. 20, November 28, 1977, p. 1. Copyright © 1977 by the American Institute of Certified Public Accountants, Inc.

Again in the 1980s, Congress became concerned with the accounting profession. The House Committee on Government Operations, chaired by Congressman Jack Brooks, became concerned about the quality of CPA audits of federal financial assistance funds. In addition, the Subcommittee on Oversight and Investigations of the House Energy and Commerce Committee, chaired by Congressman John D. Dingell, began looking into the performance of independent auditors, particularly in connection with the detection and disclosure of fraud.

Response of the Profession

Many of the recommendations and concerns resulting from the congressional investigations of the 1970s and 1980s have been addressed and resolved. The following actions are all a response, at least in part, to the issues raised by Congress and by other concerned individuals, inside and outside the profession.

1. The AICPA Division for CPA firms was established to provide a private sector mechanism for disciplining and monitoring the standards of firms. Both Senate and House subcommittees had raised the question of a governmental body to perform that function.
2. Increased attention was given to the problem of standards overload for small companies; the concern of small CPA firms were given greater attention by the establishment of the Private Companies Practice Section of the Division for CPA Firms.
3. Members of the SEC Practice Section of the Division for CPA Firms were required to make available for public inspection specified information about their firms; peer review was required.
4. Artificial restrictions against advertising and talking with another firm's clients were ended: employment offers to employees of other firms were permitted without first consulting with the present employers.
5. Members of the SEC Practice Section were required to rotate audit partners on SEC engagements everu seven years, unless the firm had less than five SEC clients and less than ten partners.
6. The AICPA's Code of Professional Conduct was completely revised and restructured to set forth more clearly and to more effectively enforce the ethical standards of the profession.
7. The AICPA established a practice-monitoring program, required continuing education of its members, and increased its education requirement.
8. A series of new and revised audit standards were issued to respond to a perceived expectation gap between what the profession was doing and what the public expected them to do.
9. A National Commission of Fraudulent Reporting studied and issued a report calling for specific action to deal with the prevention, detection, and reporting of fraud.

In summary, the accounting profession is still under intense congressional scrutiny. Although many of the concerns expressed by the Metcalf, Moss, Brooks, and Dingell committees have already been addressed, the burden of proof is still on the profession to prove that its own self-regulatory legislation is effective and adequate. Otherwise, new regulatory legislation is likely to be forthcoming.

THE COMMISSION ON AUDITORS' RESPONSIBILITIES

Concurrently with the congressional investigations discussed in the preceding section, a comprehensive study of auditors' responsibilities was conducted under the auspices of the AICPA. An independent commission, chaired by the late Manuel F. Cohen, former chairman of the Securities and Exchange Commission, devoted about three years to the project.

The conclusions and recommendations of the commission, some of which have already been adopted, are complex and do not lend themselves readily to summarization. They deal, however, with the following subjects and are worthy of separate study:

1. The independent auditor's role in society.,
2. Forming an opinion on financial presentations.
3. Reporting on significant uncertainties in financial presentations.
4. Clarifying responsibility for the detection of fraud.
5. Corporate accountability and the law.
6. The boundaries of the auditor's role and their extension.
7. The auditor's communication with users.
8. The education, training and development of auditors.
9. Maintaining the independence of auditors.
10. The process of establishing auditing standards.
11. Regulating the profession to maintain the quality of audit practice.[7]

Specific recommendations of the commission will be mentioned throughout the text as various topics are considered.

THE TREADWAY COMMISSION

From October 1985 to September 1987, the National Commission on Fraudulent Financial Reporting, chaired by James C. Treadway, Jr., studied the financial report-

[7] *The Commission on Auditor's Responsibilities: Report, Conclusions, and Recommendations* (New York: AICPA, 1978), pp. xvii–xxxiv.

ing system in the United States. This Commission, referred to in the previous section, was a private-sector initiative, jointly sponsored and funded by the American Institute of Certified Public Accountants, the American Accounting Association, the Financial Executives Institute, the Institute of Internal Auditors, and the National Association of Accountants.

The mission of the six-member Commission was to identify causal factors that can lead to fraudulent financial reporting and steps to reduce its incidence. The Commission appeared twice before the House Committee on Energy and Commerce's Subcommittee on Oversight and Investigation, referred to earlier, as part of that Subcommittee's inquiry into the adequacy of auditing, accounting, and reporting practices under the federal securities laws. Its final report is very extensive and contains recommendations for the public company, the independent public accountant, the SEC and others to improve the regulatory and legal environment, and for education.[8]

EDUCATION STANDARDS

In 1969, the AICPA Committee on Education and Experience Requirements for CPAs concluded that at least five years of college study were needed to obtain the common body of knowledge for CPAs, set forth in *Horizons for a Profession.*[9] In 1978, the AICPA Task Force on the Report of the Committee on Education and Experience Requirements for CPAs reaffirmed that conclusion, although restating it in terms of 150 semester hours. This task force, in addition to revising the curriculum proposals of the 1969 report, reviewed and reevaluated the recommendations made by that committee. In October 1978, the following ten statements of policy recommended by it were approved by the governing council of the AICPA:

STATEMENTS OF POLICY ON EDUCATION REQUIREMENTS FOR ENTRY INTO THE ACCOUNTING PROFESSION

1. The CPA certificate is evidence of basic competence of professional quality in the discipline of accounting. This basic competence is demonstrated by acquiring the body of knowledge common to the profession and passing the CPA examination.
2. *Horizons for a Profession* is authoritative for the purpose of delineating the common body of knowledge to be possessed by those about to begin their professional careers as CPAs.
3. At least 150 semester hours of college study are needed to obtain the common body of knowledge for CPAs and should be the education requirement. For those who meet this standard, no qualifying experience should be required to sit for the CPA examination.
4. The scope and control of the educational program should approximate what is

[8] *Report of the National Commission on Fraudulent Financial Reporting,* October 1987.

[9] *Report of the Committee on Education and Experience Requirements for CPAs* (New York: AICPA, 1969), p. 6; and Robert H. Roy and James H. MacNeill, *Horizons for a Profession* (New York: AICPA, 1967).

described in "Academic Preparation for Professional Accounting Careers," and should lead to the awarding of a graduate degree.

5. At the earliest practical date, the states should adopt the 150 semester hour educational requirement. The date by which implementation of this policy may be practical may be dependent upon the following factors: (1) the current education requirement in each jurisdiction; (2) the availability of graduate accounting education in each jurisdiction; and (3) appropriate lead time to permit individuals to meet proposed education requirements.
6. Candidates should be encouraged to take the CPA Examination as soon as they have fulfilled the education requirements, and as close to their college graduation dates as possible. For those graduating in June, this may involve taking the May examination on a provisional basis.
7. Student internships are desirable and are encouraged as part of the educational program.
8. The AICPA should encourage the development of quality professional programs of accounting (or schools of professional accounting) and participate in their accreditation.
9. Educational programs must be flexible and adaptive, and this is best achieved by entrusting their specific content to the academic community. However, the knowledge to be acquired and abilities to be developed through formal education for professional accounting are proper and continuing concerns of the AICPA.
10. The AICPA should review periodically the standards of admission requirements for CPAs.[10]

"Academic Preparation for Professional Accounting Careers," referred to in statement 4 above, is an Appendix to the report and includes a sample program.

In 1986, the Education Executive Committee of the AICPA decided to review the 1978 report and in 1988 issued a revision.[11] The committee concluded that no changes should be made in the ten policy statements, but updated the sample or illustrative program contained in the report. The revised illustrative program is shown in Table 1.

Another AICPA-appointed group, the Board on Standards for Programs and Schools of Professional Accounting, completed its work in 1977. Its charge was to "identify those standards that, when satisfied by a school, would justify its recognition by the accounting profession." The board acknowledged in its final report that "professional careers in accounting can be pursued in either the private or public sector, that the professional accountant can function as a member of management or as a practicing certified public accountant, that such a person can serve as either an internal or an independent auditor, and that recognition of professional com-

[10]Task Force on the Report of the Committee on Education and Experience Requirements for CPA's, *Education Requirements for Entry Into the Accounting Profession: A Statement of AICPA Policies* (New York: AICPA, 1978). Copyright © 1978 by the American Institute of Certified Public Accountants, Inc.

[11]*Education Requirements for Entry into the Accounting Profession: A Statement of AICPA Policies*, Second Edition, Revised, (New York: AICPA, 1988). Copyright © 1988 by the American Institute of Certified Public Accountants, Inc.

TABLE 1 An Illustrative Program

	Semester hours
General Education	60–80
Ethics	
Communication	
Behavioral sciences	
Economics	
Elementary accounting	
Computers	
Mathematics and statistics	
Other general education (for example, history, philosophy, literature, languages, arts, humanities, and sciences)	
Electives	
Education in Business Administration	35–50
Economics (theory and monetary system)	
Legal and social environment of business	
Business law	
Marketing	
Finance	
Organization, group, and individual behavior	
Quantitative applications in business	
Communication skills	
Business ethics	
Electives	
Accounting Education*	25–40
Financial accounting	
Financial accounting theory	
Applied financial accounting problems	
Managerial accounting	
Accounting for decision making	
Cost determination and analysis	
Management accounting controls	
Taxes	
Tax theory	
Tax problems	
Auditing	
Audit theory and practice	
The computer in auditing	
Audit problems and case studies	
Information systems	
Professional ethics and responsibilities	
Internships and cooperative programs	
Electives	
Total education program	150

*Elementary accounting is included in General Education; schools with AACSB accounting accreditation should refer to the required accounting hours specified in the curriculum standards.

petence and attainment can be achieved by successful performance on an established examination, such as the CPA examination."[12]

The report goes on to identify certain environmental conditions that are essential for a professional program, as well as specific standards dealing with such things as admission and retention of students, curriculum, faculty, financial support, physical plant and equipment, library, computer facilities, and the performance of graduates.

The Committee on Accounting Education of the American Accounting Association also prepared a statement of standards for a professional accounting education. This report is very similar to that of the AICPA and, in fact, borrows freely from it. It goes one step beyond the AICPA report, however, and sets forth standards for a four-year baccalaureate program and for Master of Business Administration programs with an accounting concentration. It points out that while these are not professional programs, they do provide a comparative advantage in accounting-related activities.[13]

Accounting programs for many years did not receive separate accreditation, but rather were viewed as one of the components in the accreditation of a school of business by the American Assembly of Collegiate Schools of Business. Separate standards are now developed for accounting, however, and are applied as part of the overall AACSB examination of a business school. Included on the committee responsible for setting the standards are representatives from the American Accounting Association, the American Institute of Certified Public Accountants, the National Association of Accountants, and the Financial Executives Institute.

Finally, as mentioned earlier, the AICPA has now strengthened two aspects of its education requirement. By membership vote in 1988, those applying for membership after the year 2000 must have obtained 150 semester hours of education at an accredited college or university, including a bachelors' degree or its equivalent. In addition, in order to retain their membership, members must complete prescribed continuing education requirements. These new requirements grew out of the report of the Special Committee on Standards of Professional Conduct for Certified Public Accountants (referred to as the Anderson Committee, after its chairman, George Anderson), issued in May 1986. Other recommendations of this committee, including a restructured Code of Professional Ethics and a quality review program were also adopted.

The 1990s will doubtless be characterized by a fundamental reevaluation of accounting education—what subject matter should be covered in the new 150 hour programs, and how it should be delivered. A major study by a Committee of the American Accounting Association[14] and a white paper issued by the managing

[12]*Final Report, Board on Standards for Programs and Schools of Professional Accounting* (New York: AICPA, 1977), preface.

[13]Committee on Accounting Education, *Standards for Professional Accounting Education* (Sarasota, Florida: American Accounting Association, 1976), p. 1.

[14]The American Accounting Association Committee on the Future Structure, Content, and Scope of Accounting Education, "Future Accounting Education: Preparing for the Expanding Profession," *Issues in Accounting Education*, Spring 1986, pp. 168–195.

partners of the eight largest public accounting firms[15] both call for such a reevaluation. Greater emphasis will certainly be given to teaching students how to think, and they will receive greater exposure to ethics and professionalism, to oral and written communications, and to the liberal arts.

THE EVOLUTION TOWARDS GREATER PROFESSIONALISM

Although given in the late 1970s, the following excerpts from a speech by Wallace E. Olson, then president of the American Institute of Certified Public Accountants, are still relevant and provide a useful perspective on the progress of the accounting profession and its possible future development:

> It is not uncommon these days to hear expressions of grave concerns within our profession about excessive competition, unrestrained solicitation, concentration and a general decline in intraprofession courtesy. At the same time, representatives of our federal government are criticizing our profession for not being sufficiently independent of corporate management, failing to recognize fully our responsibilities to the public and engaging in practices designed to restrict competition and entrance into the profession.
>
> These concerns have led some to worry that our professionalism is either already dead or teetering on the brink of extinction. There are yearnings among us to return to the good old days when the firms were small, there were leaders of great stature, and camaraderie, rather than competitive rivalry, was the rule. We would prefer to forgo the critical commentary about our profession, which has become commonplace in the print media. And few of us are overjoyed by the attention being given by Congress to our professional affairs.
>
> Even though we all have a natural tendency to resist change, such a course is rarely productive or successful. A more constructive approach involves paying careful attention to the social trends that are playing a part in shaping our future and devising ways to meet changing public demands. To do this, it is necessary to look back at what has been happening during the past 30 years within our profession and the business community.
>
> Following the Second World War, our profession went through a transformation that largely paralleled the rapid expansion of the economy. It was during the next 15 years that the growth-by-merger movement took hold in the profession. The large firms became even larger by absorbing local firms and by establishing operating offices in an ever-increasing list of cities. The scope of services was expanded by employing members of other disciplines to meet the demands for a widening array of consulting assistance. Also, to meet the needs of clients that were becoming international in scope, the larger CPA firms devoted a great deal of effort toward establishing affiliations on a world-wide basis.
>
> Out of these developments grew the substantial gap that exists today between the eight largest firms [reduced to six in the late 1980s by mergers] and the remainder of the profession. To be sure, a number of other national firms with international affiliations emerged during this period. But they started from a much smaller base

[15]Big Eight Managing Partners, *Perspectives on Education: Capabilities for Success in the Accounting Profession,* April, 1989.

of publicly held clients, and their practices were built primarily by serving smaller and medium-sized companies.

It was also during this period that pressure arose to establish more extensive accounting and auditing standards, and concerns emerged about preparatory education and aggressive programs for recruiting college graduates.

In short, it was a time when a segment of public accounting was becoming a big business to meet the needs of users of financial statements of publicly traded companies that had grown to become corporate behemoths. The larger CPA firms could no longer operate efficiently as professional partnerships in the traditional sense. They adopted many of the operating characteristics of the large corporate enterprises that they served. Partners delegated board management powers to executive committees and managing partners, which resembled boards of directors and chief executive officers in the corporate world. Thus, central management that involved national office staffs and line divisional officers (managing partners of operating offices) became the normal organizational structure of the national firms.

In the meantime, a large segment of public accounting chose to continue to practice as local or regional firms. These firms were also prospering as a result of business expansion, and some grew to considerable size by serving smaller and privately held business enterprises. Generally, however, such firms continued to be operated as true partnerships and their managements were shared by their partners.

Out of these developments grew the two-tiered profession that exists today, chaacterized by sharp differences in organizational and management structure and the general nature of clientele that is served. The large national firms adopted all the commercial traits that their size required. Their practices became more commercial in tone. Their chief executive officers became subject to pressures from the owner-partners to achieve annual increases in gross fees and net earnings. Aggressive tactics to sell more services and attract new clients beame commonplace. If such activities did not violate the letter of the profession's behavioral rules of conduct, they certainly did damage to their spirit.

The smaller firms were also becoming more aggressive, but it is probably fair to say that they were more restrained and more inclined to abide by the intent of the rules of conduct. Perhaps this reflected the fact that their practices were still being conducted on a more personal basis and in the form of traditional professional partnerships.

The changes in attitudes that emerged during this era are at the root of the uneasy feeling that the traditional notions about professionalism are in danger of becoming extinct. It had long been accepted that one of the main characteristics of a true profession is a dedication to putting unselfish service to clients and the public ahead of income considerations. The size, structure and operating methods of the largest firms seemed to run counter to this ideal. Partly because of this perception, local firm practitioners have become increasingly critical of the larger firms, whose activities they regard as turning their profession into a commercial business.

The fundamental changes in approach to the practice of public accounting adopted by the larger firms were carried into the 1960s. It was during this decade that the merger movement within the profession began to subside and a period of consolidation took place. At the same time, however, the corporate world was embarking on a spree of mergers and acquisitions, which culminated in the birth of many new large conglomerates.

Some of the people responsible for assembling the conglomerates were a new breed of management who had discovered how to take advantage of alternative accounting principles to reflect earnings on financial statements before such earnings had actually been realized. Others used a similar approach to capitalize on the widespread speculation that was taking place in the securities markets, particularly in such fields as franchising and real estate development.

Because the profession had just come through a period of rapid expansion it was ill-prepared to deal with these new developments. The firms were often inclined to view their responsibilities as running primarily to management, and they generally felt justified in expressing unqualified opinions on financial statements—as long as the statements conformed to one of the alternatives permitted under generally accepted accounting principles. Ultimately, the combination of abuses in the application of accounting principles and the rampant speculation in the securities markets culminated in a series of spectacular business collapses followed by a rash of class action lawsuits against the auditors involved.

Meanwhile, as a result of the collapse of such major corporations as Penn Central, the financial press began to discover that the work of auditors was newsworthy. The importance of accounting principles was quickly identified, and the cry went up that the setting of accounting standards was too important to be left solely to the accounting profession. Members within the profession were also calling for reforms in the standard-setting process, thereby reflecting the differences in views that existed between the national firms. It was in this context that the Study on Establishment of Accounting Principles (the Wheat committee) was set up, which led to the establishment of the present Financial Accounting Foundation and the Financial Accounting Standards Board.

Initially, the profession was slow to realize the full implications of the mounting public concern about accounting principles and the outbreak of lawsuits against auditors. However, as the lawsuits multiplied and the claims for damages assumed monumental proportions, the national firms began to take steps to protect themselves. Extensive training programs were developed, defensive auditing procedures were adopted and intensive systems of quality controls and compliance reviews were installed. The large firms rapidly were becoming acutely conscious of legal liability, and they began building in-house legal departments to cope with the growing volume of litigation.

By the mid-1970s, the pressures of civil liability suits and Securities and Exchange Commission injunctive and enforcement proceedings had brought about significant changes in attitudes within the national CPA firms. Responsibilities to investor and creditor interests came to be more fully recognized, and every precaution was taken to assure that audited financial statements were not based on accounting measurements that reported earnings prematurely. The forces of the marketplace and existing institutions had resulted in correcting the abuses of the 1960s—and they have had a profound and lasting impact on the practice of public accounting as it relates to publicly traded companies.

Not to be overlooked during this period was the combined impact on accounting principles of an aggressive and activist chief accountant of the SEC and the emergence of the FASB. Beginning in 1972, the SEC issued a steady flow of accounting series releases, which greatly increased the amount of disclosures required in financial reporting and which pressed auditors to assume new responsibilities. Reviews of interim financial statements, expressing preferability with respect to alternative accounting principles, disclosures of replacement costs of productive plant and inventories, and reconsideration of the desirability of publishing financial forecasts were among the many issues that were addressed.

Meanwhile, the FASB was shifting into higher gear. It issued standards on such long-standing problems as accounting for research and development costs, leases, translation of foreign financial statements and segments of a business. The standing of the FASB's pronouncements was greatly enhanced by the issuance of ASR 150, which acknowledged the SEC's willingness to rely on standards established by the FASB.

In the space of less than five years, these developments caused an enormous growth in both the volume and complexity of financial accounting and reporting standards. This upsurge in activity was a direct result of the demands for better accounting and disclosure that arose from the abuses and business failures of the late 1960s.

Despite the impressive progress achieved in making financial statements more informative and reliable, events occurred that aroused the interest and concerns of congressional committees. Congress discovered that economic data used for establishing national policies was only as reliable as the financial statements on which it was based. This fact became painfully clear when, as a result of the energy crisis, Congress found that financial reports of different oil and gas companies were not comparable because various methods of accounting measurement were used. Congressman John E. Moss (D–Calif.) promptly introduced an amendment to the 1975 energy legislation to mandate the establishment of uniform accounting standards for the petroleum industry. In the process, he raised anew the question of whether accounting standards should be established by a government body instead of relying on the private sector.

Hard on the heels of this development came the disturbing revelations of improper political contributions, illegal bribes and offbook slush funds of hundreds of the nation's largest corporations. The shock waves from disclosures of these practices are still reverberating, and they have raised questions about the performance of independent auditors—questions that have damaged the credibility of the profession.

Out of these and other related events has come the . . . investigations by various government bodies into the role and performance of our profession. Subcommittees of both houses of Congress, the SEC, the Federal Trade Commission and the Justice Department . . . all engaged in deliberations about what should be done to make auditors more effective and financial reporting more reliable. Among the concerns . . . addressed are

1. The establishment of accounting and auditing standards.
2. The independence of auditors.
3. Regulation of independent auditors practicing before the SEC.
4. Anticompetitive practices and concentration within the profession.

Although the profession did not anticipate much of what has happened, it was sufficiently concerned about its growing loss of credibility that an independent commission was appointed in 1974 to study the role and responsibilities of auditors. The final report of this Commission on Auditors' Responsibilities, chaired by the late Manuel Cohen, . . . contained over forty recommendations that, if fully implemented, will have a far-reaching effect on how independent auditors discharge their responsibilities. . . .

Clearly, the profession had to respond to these calls for changes or it ran the real and imminent risk of losing a voice in the shaping of its own destiny. The possibility of federal legislation to impose new layers of regulation on the profession was too serious to be ignored.

Starting in June 1977, the American Institute of CPAs formulated a comprehensive program to respond to criticisms and recommendations that had been made. The key features were

1. Establishment of a division for CPA firms and also to deal with the problems relating to differences in the size of firms and nature of clients served in public practice.
2. Improvement in the effectiveness of the disciplining of individual CPAs.
3. Steps to enhance the independence of auditors.
4. Changes to improve the auditor's report, the selling of auditing standards and corporate accountability through expanding the role of auditors, based largely on recommendations of the Cohen commission.
5. Modifying the profession's rules on advertising, solicitation and other behavioral prohibitions that might be regarded as anticompetitive.
6. Providing for greater public participation in the affairs of the profession by adding public members to the AICPA board of directors and opening meetings of other policy-making bodies to the public. . . .

The establishment of a division for CPA firms composed of two sections, one for SEC practice and another for private companies practice, has given formal recognition to the long-standing differences involved in serving clients that are publicly traded and those that are not. Fears have been expressed that institutionalizing these differences will aggravate the competitive problems of the smaller firms and result in a divided profession. . . .

The fact is that no amount of pretending that differences in practice do not exist will make them disappear. . . It is clear that the vast volume of complex accounting and auditing standards appropriate for SEC registrants has become excessively burdensome when applied to smaller and privately held companies. . . There is little doubt that more competition, not less, is being called for and that artificial devices to protect CPA firms of all sizes from the ravages of competition are not likely to be permitted. Few would deny that there are great pressures to expand the role and responsibilities of auditors as part of a broader demand for greater accountability by publicly traded corporations. . . .

The social forces that are confronting us are not to be denied, and clinging to the old traditions is not likely to result in maintaining the status quo.

The profession's . . . program is designed to bring about changes that will deal realistically with the facts which confront us and keep us in harmony with the trends in our society. . . .

. . . it is difficult to predict with precision the future effects of the developments that have evolved during the past 30 years, and that have converged at a rapidly accelerating pace into the present state of affairs. When viewed in perspective, however, it is possible to conclude that what is happening is the evolution toward greater professionalism, not its death.

In the past, we laid claim to being a profession on the grounds of having all the trappings traditionally identified with those of other professions. However, our preoccupations have been largely with matters within the profession. Our understanding of the true public interest nature of our role has not been as clear as it is now becoming. It has been all too easy to espouse in our literature our dedication to serving the public. Now, however, we are being pressed to make our actions correspond more fully with the ideas that we have articulated in the past.

There are many signs that our professionalism is becoming more substantive. By dropping our bans on advertising and solicitation, we are getting away from the notion that being professional depends in part on such restraints. Instead, we have come to recognize that high levels of skills and expertise are far more important. Greater emphasis is being placed on pre-entry education as well as continuing post-entry education. Independence, quality controls and compliance with standards are being given much greater attention to assure that the highest possible levels of performance are attained.

The impact of liability suits has made it clear that auditors cannot afford to view their role as being primarily responsible to corporate management. The acceptance of a role that is more closely akin to that of a public servant is reflected in the accounting and auditing standards being adopted. Responsibilities to do more than find a way for clients to conform to generally accepted accounting principles are being more widely recognized. The implications of rule 203 of the rules of conduct, which requires the exercise of a judgment about whether financial statements are misleading on an overall basis, are being more fully recognized.

The need for a means to regulate CPA firms in addition to individuals has now gained acceptance and is bringing the profession's disciplinary machinery more squarely in line with the realities of modern practice.

Openly addressing the practical differences in practice between large and small firms and between serving publicly traded companies as compared to small, privately held companies has caused CPAs in public practice to have a growing appreciation of the need for a satisfactory way to deal with these differences. We are trying to do this by working together to establish appropriate practice sections under the umbrella of the AICPA so that we can remain a unified profession on a national basis.

These are all indications that our profession is coming of age. We are tackling the hard problems that have been accumulating since the late 1940s. We are becoming more professional in the sense that we are addressing our public obligations in a more substantive way than ever before. We are developing skills and expertise that far transcend those of earlier times and that give us a more legitimate claim to being professionals.

There is little doubt that much remains to be accomplished and that some of our present initiatives may prove to be wrong in the light of hindsight. But one thing seems certain when viewed in the perspective of events of the past 30 years: our professionalism is far from dead or in danger of becoming extinct. To the contrary, we are moving rapidly in the opposite direction toward making our claim to professional status more soundly based than it has ever been. If we keep this firmly in mind during this difficult period of transition, we will steer a safe course into the future.[16]

QUESTIONS

1–1 What are the essential elements of a profession? Discuss each in relation to accounting. Does accounting measure up?

1–2 Are accountants practicing in industry, government, or with a not-for-profit organization, members of the profession? What is the meaning of CPA, CMA, or CIA after an individual's name?

1–3 Have any formal codes of professional ethics been adopted within the profession? Who has adopted them? How are technical standards established within the profession?

[16]Wallace E. Olson, "Is Professionalism Dead?" *The Journal of Accountancy,* July 1978, pp. 78–82.

1-4 Discuss the role of continuing education in a profession. What requirements are there for continuing education in the accounting profession?

1-5 Name seven professional associations in the area of accounting. What group of professionals does each serve?

1-6 What authority does the Securities and Exchange Commission have with regard to accounting principles? How does it exercise it? What other authority does the SEC have over those practicing accounting?

1-7 Discuss the role which the Congress of the United States has played and is playing in the establishment of accounting principles and auditing standards.

1-8 What are some of the issues considered by the Commission on Auditor's Responsibilities (Cohen Commission)? The Treadway Commission? The Anderson Committee?

1-9 What are the ten Statements of Policy on Education Requirements for Entry into the Accounting Profession approved by the governing council of the AICPA? How many semester hours of collegiate education are recommended?

1-10 What types of standards were recommended by the Board on Standards for Programs and Schools of Professional Accounting? Has any other group performed a similar study?

1-11 What steps have been taken by the AICPA to respond to criticisms and recommendations of the Commission on Auditors' Responsibilities (Cohen Commission), congressional subcommittees, the Justice Department, and the SEC?

2

INDEPENDENCE, INTEGRITY, AND OBJECTIVITY

INTRODUCTION

Webster's Dictionary defines the adjective "independent" as "not subject to control by others; self-governing." This comes very close to its use in accounting, where independence refers to freedom from relationships which impair or appear to impair the ability of the accountant to exercise objectivity. The appearance of impairment is as important as impairment in fact.

Objectivity is a state of mind and imposes upon an individual the obligation to be impartial, intellectually honest, and free of conflicts of interest.[1] It also implies that the individual will not subordinate his or her judgment to others.[2]

Integrity is an element of character and is essential to the maintenance of public trust. As stated in the Code of Professional Conduct of the American Institute of Certified Public Accountants:

> It is . . . the benchmark against which a member must ultimately test all decisions. Integrity requires a member to be, among other things, honest and candid within the constraints of client confidentiality. Service and public trust should not be subor-

[1]"Objectivity and Independence," *AICPA Professional Standards,* vol. 2, ET Section 55.01.
[2]"Integrity and Objectivity," *AICPA Professional Standards,* vol. 2, ET Section 102.01.

> dinated to personal gain and advantage. Integrity can accommodate the inadvertent error and the honest difference of opinion; it cannot accommodate deceit or subordination of principle.
>
> Integrity is measured in terms of what is right and just.[3]

Independence, the state of being free from relationships which impair or appear to impair objectivity, is of primary concern in public accounting where an individual is providing auditing or other attestation services. In addition to requiring independence of auditors who are expressing an opinion on the fairness of financial statements, it is required by professional standards when performing other types of attestation services. Standards issued by the Accounting and Review Services Committee of the AICPA, for example, call for independence on the part of a CPA conducting a "review" of unaudited financial statements of a nonpublic entity. Reports on attest engagements under Statements on Standards for Attestation Engagements, and engagements under several of the Statements on Auditing Standards also require independence.

In the nonpublic accounting area, internal auditors are concerned with independence. Although they obviously cannot be separate from the company by which they are employed, they can have organizational independence within the company. The head of the internal auditing function, for example, should be responsible to an officer whose authority is sufficient to assure both a broad range of audit coverage and the adequate consideration of and effective action on the audit findings and recommendations.[4] Internal auditors should not be responsible to those whom they are auditing.

The definition of independence given here is the one adopted by the American Institute of Certified Public Accountants. It is a narrower definition than the one used prior to 1988, however, and has not been uniformly adopted by all organizations and writers. When referring to independence, some do not restrict it to the concept of "freedom from relationships" which impair or appear to impair the ability to exercise objectivity, but refer to it in a broad sense as the possession of objectivity itself. Thus "independence" might mean mental independence or objectivity, which could be present whether or not there was a "freedom from relationships."

STANDARDS OF INDEPENDENCE, INTEGRITY, AND OBJECTIVITY

Principles, rules, standards, statements of responsibility, and codes of ethics have been developed by accountants practicing in various segments of the profession. In addition, the Securities and Exchange Commission, the Internal Revenue Service,

[3] "Integrity," *AICPA Professional Standards,* vol. 2, ET Section 54. Copyright © 1988 by the American Institute of Certified Public Accountants, Inc.

[4] *Statement of Responsibilities of Internal Auditing,* Institute of Internal Auditors, Appendix 7.

the Comptroller General of the United States, private companies, CPA firms, State Boards of Accountancy and CPA Societies in the various states have their own rules. All of these address issues of integrity and objectivity, and where appropriate, independence. Included in the appendixes are promulgations dealing with auditing, tax practice, management advisory services, management accounting, governmental accounting, and internal auditing.

The American Institute of Certified Public Accountants has a Code of Professional Conduct consisting of two parts: Principles and Rules. The Principles section contains goal-oriented, positively stated principles that provide the framework for technical standards and ethics rules, and that prescribe the ethical responsibilities members should strive to achieve. They are not enforced in their own terms, but through underlying rules. Included among the Principles are the following articles on Integrity and on Objectivity and Independence:

> **ARTICLE III. INTEGRITY**
>
> To maintain and broaden public confidence, members should perform all professional responsibilities with the highest sense of integrity.[5]
>
> **ARTICLE IV. OBJECTIVITY AND INDEPENDENCE**
>
> A member should maintain objectivity and be free of conflicts of interest in discharging professional responsibilities. A member in public practice should be independent in fact and appearance when providing auditing and other attestation services.[6]

Included among the Rules of the AICPA Code are ones on independence, and on integrity and objectivity. They are as follows:

> **RULE 101. INDEPENDENCE**
>
> A member in public practice shall be independent in the performance of professional services as required by standards promulgated by bodies designated by Council.[7]
>
> **RULE 102. INTEGRITY AND OBJECTIVITY**
>
> In the peformance of any professional service, a member shall maintain objectivity and integrity, shall be free of conflicts of interest, and shall not knowingly misrepresent facts or subordinate his or her judgment to others.[8]

Supporting these Rules are a series of Interpretations and Rulings. The interpretations set forth the many details needed to make the Rules operational, and the rulings address specific questions raised by members or others. In the independence area, for example, an interpretation prohibits the expression of an opinion on finan-

[5] *AICPA Professional Standardds,* vol. 2, ET Section 54. Copyright © 1988 by the American Institute of Certified Public Accountants, Inc.

[6] Ibid., ET Section 55.

[7] Ibid., ET Section 101.

[8] Ibid., ET Section 102.

cial statements when certain financial relationships with clients exist, or when relationships exist in which the CPA is virtually a part of management or an employee under management's control. As detailed in Appendix 1, they deal specifically with such issues as directorships, accounting services, family relationships, financial interests, and loans.

Although the CPA is bound to abide by specified rules, there are also other forces and restraints that cause honest, objective, and independent behavior. The Securities and Exchange Commission, for example, has set forth certain guidelines relating to the independence of accountants who audit and report on financial statements filed with the commission. Violation of these rules can result in loss of the right to practice before the Commission. The possibility of legal action is, of course, present if the accountant acts improperly. In addition, improper conduct may cause a loss of the license to practice as a CPA, with the subsequent loss of income and reputation in the community. Perhaps most importantly, the sense of responsibility and pride which goes with being a member of a respected profession acts as an invisible barrier to improper behavior.

Whether or not a particular act or relationship would impair an accountant's independence is often not clear. Intepretations of the rules are constantly being issued by the AICPA to cover new situations that arise in practice. When in doubt, it is a good rule of thumb for the professional accountant to assume that the proposed relationship or act *would* be in violation of ethical conduct. In this way, any possible embarrassment or censure will be avoided, and there will be no possibility of even the appearance of a lack of independence or objectivity.

THE AUDITOR

The concept of independence has long been vital to a successful audit practice. When expressing an opinion on the financial statements of a client, the judgment of the certified public accountant must not only be impartial and unbiased, but it must also appear to be so to any outside observer. Great importance is attached to the presence of this state of independence because of the reliance placed upon the work of the auditor by third parties and the general public. Those who rely on the financial statements of business enterprises as a fair presentation of financial position and of the results of operations must be assured that those statements have been examined and reported upon by someone who is completely objective.

Independence may be impaired because of a financial relationship. For example, assume that as a partner in a large regional public accounting firm, you have been asked by a close friend of yours, who is the chief executive officer of a local bank, whether your firm would be interessted in becoming the bank's auditors. Assume that your own home mortgage and that of several of your partners are with this bank, and that the firm has a line of credit with the bank to provide working capital at certain times of the year. Assume also that you have a personal loan from the bank to finance the purchase of some land you are considering developing. Do these facts destroy independence and prevent your accepting the engagement?

An interpretation of Rule 101 (101–1) specifically exempts home mortgages from the general rule that independence will be considered to be impaired if "during the period of a professional engagement, or at the time of expressing an opinion," the member or his firm has "any loan to or from the enterprise" being audited, or from "any officer, director, or principal stockholder" thereof. The mortgage must, however, be "made under normal lending procedures, terms and requirements." A similar exception applies to loans obtained by a member or his firm which are "not material in relation to the net worth" of the borrower, and to "other secured loans, except loans guaranteed by a member's firm which are otherwise unsecured."[9] Thus, independence would probably not be impaired in this case by the line of credit with the bank or by the personal loan.

What if one of the partners had just completed service as executor of an estate that had a direct material financial interest in the bank? The key fact here is that the partner's service as executor has been completed. Independence is not therefore impaired. However, if the service takes place during the period of the engagement or at the time of expressing an opinion, independence would be impaired.[10]

Auditors must also possess the highest integrity. This demand often conflicts with the desire to succeed in one's career. For example, assume that a new senior accountant has been working particularly hard to meet the time budget agreed upon at the start of an audit. It becomes apparent to him that he is not going to make it. While driving home at midnight for the second straight day, it occurs to him that one way of meeting the deadline and still getting the job done would be to work straight through the upcoming long holiday weekend but not record the time on his report.

Would following the contemplated course of action be a violation of the AICPA Code of Professional Conduct? Would it matter if he discussed it with his superior, an audit manager, who tacitly gave his consent? What if he knew that he had not been working at top speed early in the audit and thus had taken longer than normal to complete the earlier phases? Would such action be justified if this were an audit of the United Fund or the Red Cross? While there is no easy answer to this question, the importance of maintaining the very highest standard of integrity leads to the conclusion that the contemplated action should not be taken under any of the described circumstances.

The receipt of gifts by auditors from clients also raises issues of independence and integrity. Friendships develop in the normal course of events, and social contacts are inevitable. These contacts frequently lead to situations involving ethical problems. For example, assume that an accountant has had a long and friendly relationship with the controller of one of his clients. When the accountant first joined the CPA firm in which he is now a partner, the controller was in a lower level posi-

[9] "Independence," *AICPA Professional Standards,* vol. 2, ET Section 101.02.
[10] Ibid.

tion with his company. The accountant has served over the years as junior, senior, and now partner on the audit of the company. Having moved up together, the two are now good friends. The controller invites the accountant to join him and several other officers of the company on a weekend fishing trip. The accountant offers to pay his share of the expenses, but his friend refuses on the grounds that the company owes it to him for his good service.

Would the accountant be acting in an unethical way if he accepted the offer? If acceptance would not be unethical in this case, what if the offer was for a free trip to Europe? Is the value of the gift significant? Anything "more than a token gift" would at least raise a question as to the appearance of independence, and it might well impair independence itself.[11] The accountant in this case would be wise to insist upon paying his share of the expenses.

Problems such as the foregoing might be avoided or reduced somewhat by rotation of the audit staff on individual engagements. Rotation may not affect the independence of the staff, but it certainly will increase the appearance of independence. The latter is just as important as the former.

Family relationships also create difficult issues for auditors. For example, assume that for many years a partner in a firm maintained a close relationship with his sister and her husband. The two families have frequently gone on vacation together, and often talked long distance over the phone. The sister is an astute businesswoman and has recently been promoted to an executive position with a client of the firm. Since she is located in a distant city, the partner has nothing to do with the audit. Is the independence of the firm impaired? Is the appearance of independence impaired?

An interpretation of the AICPA rule on independence (101–9) states that even though a nondependent close relative can exercise significant influence over operating, financial, or accounting policies of a client, independence would not be impaired unless the partner either participated in the engagement or was in an office participating in a significant portion of the engagement. The following caveat is given, however, which might cause a different conclusion:

> In situations involving assessment of the association of any relative or dependent person with a client, members must consider whether the strength of personal business relationships between the member and the relative or dependent person, considered in conjunction with the specified association with the client, would lead a reasonable person aware of all the facts and taking into consideration normal strength of character and normal behavior under the circumstances to conclude that the situation poses an unacceptable threat to the member's objectivity and appearance of independence.[12]

Tables 1 and 2 set forth some of the definitions, relationships, and conclusions contained in Interpretation 101–9, "The meaning of certain independence

[11]"Ethics Rulings on Independence, Integrity, and Objectivity," *AICPA Professional Standards,* vol. 2, ET Section 191.002.

[12]"Independence," *AICPA Professional Standards,* vol. 2, ET Section 101.11.

Table 1

"A MEMBER OR A MEMBER'S FIRM" AS DEFINED BY INTERPRETATION 101-9

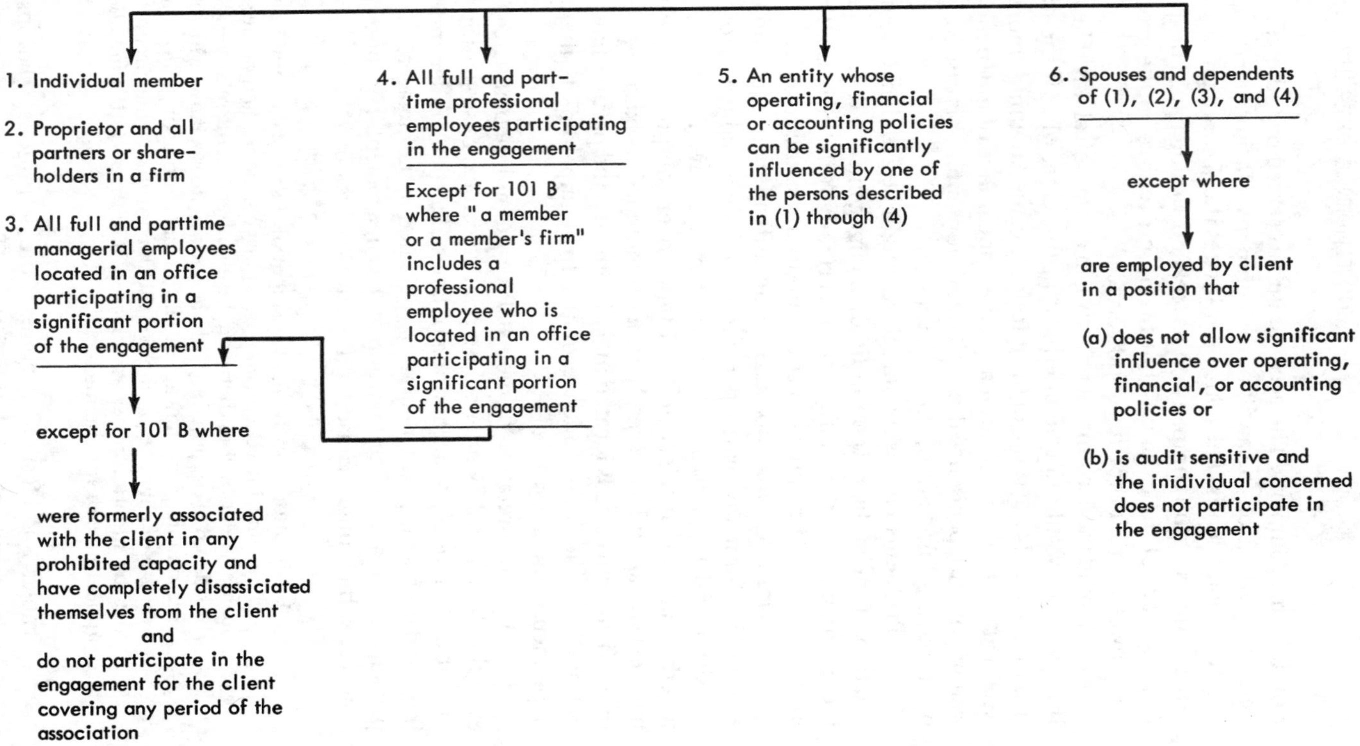

1. Individual member

2. Proprietor and all partners or share-holders in a firm

3. All full and parttime managerial employees located in an office participating in a significant portion of the engagement

except for 101 B where

were formerly associated with the client in any prohibited capacity and have completely disassiciated themselves from the client

and

do not participate in the engagement for the client covering any period of the association

4. All full and part-time professional employees participating in the engagement

Except for 101 B where "a member or a member's firm" includes a professional employee who is located in an office participating in a significant portion of the engagement

5. An entity whose operating, financial or accounting policies can be significantly influenced by one of the persons described in (1) through (4)

6. Spouses and dependents of (1), (2), (3), and (4)

except where

are employed by client in a position that

(a) does not allow significant influence over operating, financial, or accounting policies or

(b) is audit sensitive and the inidividual concerned does not participate in the engagement

Table 2

FINANCIAL RELATIONSHIPS AND BUSINESS RELATIONSHIPS OF NONDEPENDENT CLOSE RELATIVES DESCRIBED IN INTERPRETATION 101-9

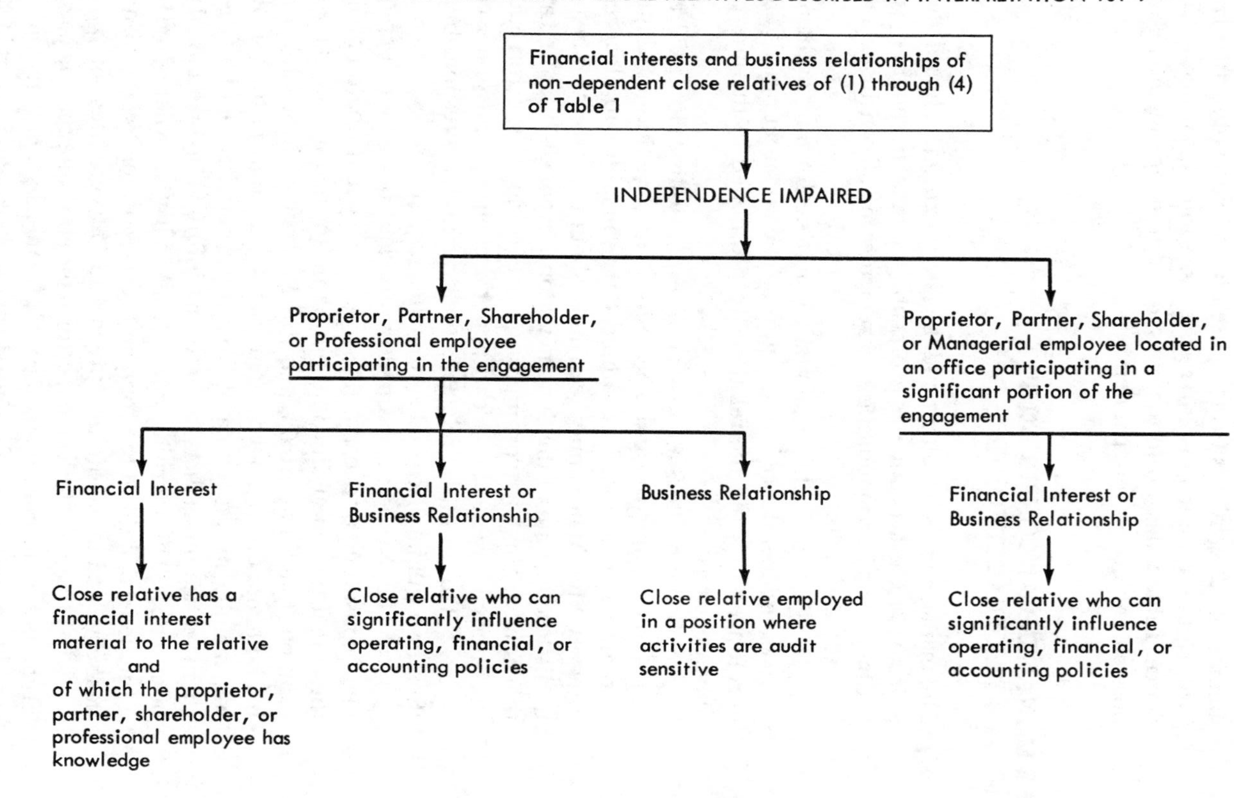

terminology and the effect of family relationships on indepencence." Table 1 deals with the question of which individuals and entities are included in the phrase "a member or a member's firm" as used in Interpretaiton 101–1, which in turn sets forth certain transactions, interests or relationships which would impair independence. Table 2 deals with the question of nondependent close relatives and their possible impact on independence.

THE MANAGEMENT CONSULTANT AND THE TAX PRACTITIONER

The management consultant and the tax practitioner should always maintain their objectivity. The accountant's professional judgment should never be subordinated to others even in nonauditing engagements, and all conclusions should be expressed honestly and objectively.

When a public accountant is not performing audit or other attestation services, independence is not required. The nonaudit practitioner is, nevertheless, encouraged to avoid the relationship prohibited in the interpretation of the independence rules.

Some of the Statements on Responsibilities in Tax Practice deal with the practitioner's integrity and objectivity. A tax practitioner's knowledge of an error in return preparation, for example, or of the failure to file a return challenges his integrity. Should he simply keep quiet about the error or is he under an obligation to disclose it? One of the Statements on Responsibilities in Tax Practice requires that he advise his client promptly upon learning of the error, but he may not inform the Internal Revenue Service without the client's permission except where required by law.[13] This issue also relates to the practitioner's responsibility to his client and therefore will be discussed further in Chapter 4.

The question is frequently raised as to whether the rendering of management consulting or accounting services to a client would impair independence to the extent that an audit could not be performed for the same client. Assume, for example, that for approximately three years your local CPA firm has been preparing both monthly financial statements and tax returns for a small, but rapidly growing, manufacturing company. One of your staff accountants goes regularly to the client's office and gathers the necessary information maintained there by a part-time bookkeeper. This morning you were asked by the owner of the business to perform a full-fledged audit of the company. You were told by the owner that a local bank has requested the audit, as a precondition to granting an expansion loan.

Is it ethical for you to perform the audit after having been regularly involved in the preparation of the company's financial statements and tax returns? Would it make any difference if you had kept the books and records in your office and done all of the bookkeeping for the company? Generally, the performance of accounting

[13] "Statements on Responsibilities in Tax Practice," *AICPA Professional Standards,* vol. 2, TX Section 162.03 (See Appendix 3 for all the statements).

services for an audit client will not impair the auditor's independence. Nevertheless, an accountant "performing accounting services for an audit client must meet the following requirements to retain the appearance that he is not virtually an employee, and therefore lacking in independence in the eyes of a reasonable observer."

1. The CPA must not have any relationship or combination of relationships with the client or any conflict of interest which would impair his integrity and objectivity.
2. The client must accept the responsibility for the financial statements as his own. A small client may not have anyone in his employ to maintain accounting records and may rely on the CPA for this purpose. Nevertheless, the client must be sufficiently knowledgeable of the enterprise's activities and financial condition and the applicable accounting principles so that he can reasonably accept such responsibility, including, specifically, fairness of valuation and presentation and adequacy of disclosure. When necessary, the CPA must discuss accounting matters with the client to be sure that the client has the required degree of understanding.
3. The CPA must not assume the role of employee or of management conducting the operations of an enterprise. For example, the CPA shall not consummate transactions, have custody of assets or exercise authority on behalf of the client. The client must prepare the source of documents on all transactions in sufficient detail to identify clearly the nature and amount of such transactions and maintain an accounting control over data processed by the CPA such as control totals and document counts. The CPA should not make changes in such basic data without the concurrence of the client.
4. The CPA, in making an examination of financial statements prepared from books and records which he has maintained completely or in part, must conform to generally accepted auditing standards. The fact that he has processed or maintained certain records does not eliminate the need to make sufficient audit tests.[14]

"When a client's securities become subject to regulation by the Securities and Exchange Commission or some other federal or state regulatory body, responsibility for maintenance of the accounting records, including accounting classification decisions, must be assumed by accounting personnel employed by the client. The assumption of this responsibility must commence with the first fiscal year after which the client's securities qualify for such regulation."[15]

What if it has been the practice of your client to regularly discuss with you the business problems he is facing and to get your advice as to the course of action he should take? What if he usually follows your advice? Again, this type of service normally would not impair independence, whether or not the advice given is followed. The four requirements stated previously for accounting services would still have to be met, however.[16]

Another independence question involving a management advisory service engagement arises when the accountant designs an accounting system for a client

[14] "Independence," *AICPA Professional Standards*, vol. 2, ET Section 101.05. Copyright © 1988 by the American Institute of Certified Public Accountants, Inc.

[15] Ibid.

[16] "Ethics Rulings on Independence, Integrity, and Objectivity," *AICPA Professional Standards*, vol. 2, ET Section 191.015-.016.

and then is asked to audit that client. Assume, for example, that you are a partner in the Management Advisory Services Division of a large international CPA firm. You and other members of your firm have just completed an engagement in which you designed a management information system for a medium-sized manufacturing company. As part of this job, you assisted your client in the installation of new data-processing equipment and helped train the client's personnel in its use and in the operation of the new information system. In fact, some of your staff are still at the client's offices until the client's personnel feel competent to operate on their own. The firm also has this company as an audit client. In fact, the systems job arose out of a recommendation from the audit staff.

Was the independence of your firm compromised by the acceptance of this MAS engagement? How can your firm serve as auditor for the system you have designed and installed? What about the presence of your firm's own staff in the client's office? Independence "would not be considered to be impaired under these circumstances provided the client makes all significant management decisions related to the hiring of new personnel and the implementation of the system." The member's firm must also "take reasonable precautions to restrict its supervisory activities to initial instruction and training of personnel," and it "should avoid direct supervision of the actual operation of the system or any related activities that would constitute undue involvement in or identification with management functions."[17]

THE INTERNAL PROFESSIONAL

Internal professional accountants practicing in the private or the public sector must also abide by a high standard of integrity and objectivity. These certified public accountants, certified management accountants, and certified internal auditors cannot, of course, be independent of the company, governmental unit, or association for which they work. They can, however, always perform their duties with honesty and objectivity.

The internal professional who is responsible for the preparation of his company's financial statements would, for example, be obligated to insure that they are not misleading or inaccurate and that no material items are omitted. It should be remembered that external financial statements are representations of the company and not of the auditor who has examined and perhaps approved them. It is extremely important that professional accountants, whether they work as auditors, management consultants, tax practitioners, or internal accountants, be regarded by the public and all those who rely upon their work as persons of integrity and objectivity.

One type of internal professional who is faced with an independence question is the internal auditor. Assume that you are an internal auditor, a member of the Institute of Internal Auditors, and that you subscribe wholeheartedly to the Institute's Code of Ethics, its Statement of Responsibilities of Internal Auditing, and

[17]Ibid., ET Section 191.110.

its Standards for the Professional Practice of Internal Auditing.[18] You are considering a job change and are concerned about the organizational arrangement in the company you are thinking of joining. In that company, the internal audit staff reports to the company controller, who in turn reports to the vice president-finance.

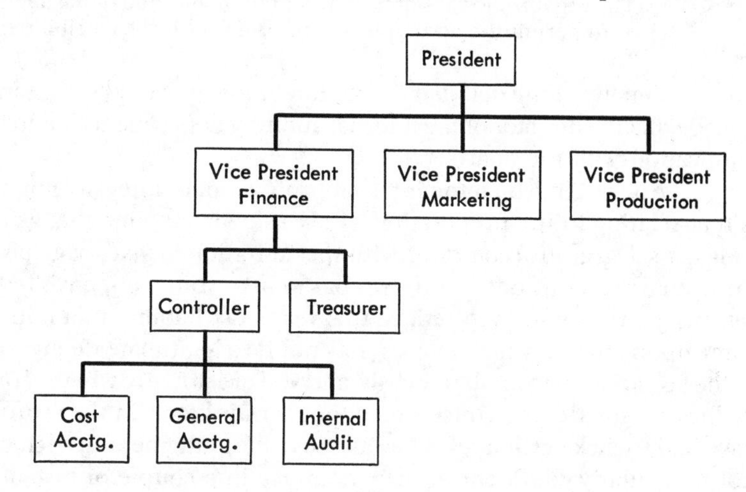

You find it hard to understand how the internal audit staff can maintain its independence under this arrangement. You are not sure that you will be able to effectively audit the work of the controller if you report directly to him. You are also concerned about your relationship on the organization chart to the treasury operations, which you will also be auditing.

Will the performance of your job under the organizational setup outlined cause you to violate any ethical code? Yes, this arrangement would very likely be in violation of both the Statement of Responsibilities of Internal Auditing and the Standards for the Professional Practice of Internal Auditing. The former states:

> Internal auditors should be independent of the activities they audit. Internal auditors are independent when they can carry out their work freely and objectively. Independence permits internal auditors to render the impartial and unbiased judgments essential to the proper conduct of audits. It is achieved through organizational status and objectivity.
>
> Organizational status should be sufficient to assure a broad range of audit coverage, and adequate consideration of and effective action on audit findings and recommendations.[19]

One of the general standards set forth for the professional practice of internal auditing reinforces the above statements:

[18]See Appendix 6 for the Code of Ethics, Appendix 7 for the Statement of Responsibilities, and Appendix 8 for the Standards.

[19]*Statement of Responsibilities of Internal Auditing* (Altamonte Springs, Florida: The Institute of Internal Auditors, Inc., 1981). Copyright © 1981 by the Institute of Internal Auditors, Inc., 249 Maitland Avenue, Altamonte Springs, Florida 32701 U.S.A. Reprinted with permission.

> Internal Auditors should be independent of the activity they audit.[20]

One of the specific standards supporting the general standard is:

> The organizational status of the internal auditing department should be sufficient to permit the accomplishment of its audit responsibilities.

Finally, in the detailed discussion of the above specific standard, the point is made that the director of the internal auditing department should have direct communication with the board.[21]

An area in which the internal professional's integrity might be questioned is that relating to the preparation of tax returns. Assume that as the possessor of a Master's degree in accounting, with specialization in taxes, you have been assigned the primary responsibilty for the preparation of your company's federal income tax returns. In your efforts to reduce this year's tax liability to a minimum, you have come upon an item which may or may not be a legitimate deduction. The wording of the tax law is not completely clear, and you are not sure whether or not you should deduct it. You are also concerned about certain items in the return for which you have had to make estimates. They are your best judgment in each case, but you are not particularly confident of their accuracy in a couple of instances.

Are there any ethical considerations in your handling of the doubtful deductions? Can you in good conscience take a deduction that is questionable? Is it acceptable for you to use estimates in your preparation of the return? If so, how accurate do they need to be?

As long as there is reasonable support for the position you are taking, there is no reason why you cannot resolve a doubtful question in favor of your company. This would not, by itself, be deemed an impairment of integrity or objectivity. One of the statements on Responsibilities in Tax Practice does set forth the following limitation, however:

> "A CPA should not recommend to a client that a position be taken with respect to the tax treatment of any item on the return unless the CPA has a good faith belief that the position has a realistic possibility of being sustained administratively or judicially on its merits if challenged."[22]

With regard to the use of estimates, another one of the Statements on Responsibilities in Tax Practice takes the following position. These statements are written for the CPA in tax practice but apply equally well to an internal professional:

[20] *Standards for the Professional Practice of Internal Auditing* (Altamonte Springs, Florida: The Institute of Internal Auditors, Inc., 1978). Copyright © 1978 by the Institute of Internal Auditors, Inc., 249 Maitland Avenue, Altamonte Springs, Florida 32701 U.S.A. Reprinted with permission.

[21] Ibid.

[22] "Statements on Responsibilities in Tax Practice," *AICPA Professional Standards,* vol. 1, TX Section 112.02.

"A certified public accountant may prepare tax returns involving the use of the taxpayer's estimates if it is impractical to obtain exact data, and the estimated amounts are reasonable under the facts and circumstances known to the CPA. When the taxpayer's estimates are used, they should be presented in such a manner as to avoid the implication of greater accuracy than exists."[23]

REPORTING A LACK OF INDEPENDENCE: GENERAL STANDARDS

In those instances where a certified public accountant is not independent but is still "associated" with the financial statements of a public entity or with a nonpublic entity's financial statements that he has been engaged to examine in accordance with generally accepted auditing standards, he must disclaim an opinion with regard to those statements and state specifically that he is not independent. Association may occur either when the CPA has "consented to the use of his name in a report, document, or written communication containing the statements," or when he has submitted "to his client or others financial statements that he has prepared or assisted in preparing."[24]

Because independence is lacking, *any* procedures performed by the CPA would not be in accordance with generally accepted auditing standards, thus precluding the expression of an opinion. In order to avoid confusing the reader about the importance of the impairment of independence, the reasons for a lack of independence should not be given. The CPA is either independent or he is not. Furthermore, the procedures performed should not be described. Such a description might add unwarranted credibility to the statements. An example of a report setting forth a lack of independence is as follows:

> We are not independent with respect to XYZ Company, and the accompanying balance sheet as of December 31, 19XX, and the related statements of income, retained earnings, and cash flows for the year then ended, were not audited by us and, accordingly, we do not express an opinion on them.
>
> (Signature and date)[25]

This report may accompany the financial statements or be placed directly on them. In addition, each page of the statements should be "clearly and conspicuously marked as unaudited."[26]

[23]Ibid., TX Section 142.02.
[24]"Association with Financial Statements," *AICPA Professional Standards,* Vol. 1, AU Section 504.03.
[25]Ibid., AU Section 504.10.
[26]Ibid., AU Section 504.05.

INTERPRETATION OF REPORTING STANDARDS

Many questions of interpretation have arisen with regard to the disclosure of a lack of independence. D. R. Carmichael, formerly of the AICPA staff, and J. V. Bencivenga responded to some of them in the following article, which appeared in the *Journal of Accountancy*. Problems associated with the CPA not in public practice were among the several questions discussed.

> A greater degree of confidence is given to reports prepared by independent CPAs than to those prepared by CPAs serving as employees of a business concern. Unavoidably, the implication of "audit" attaches itself to CPAs because they are generally known as a profession of auditors. Therefore, an accountant who is serving as an employee rather than an independent contractor, and in so doing is associated with financial statements, must take care not to identify himself in a manner that may lead others to believe he is an independent public accountant. . . .

CPAs NOT IN PUBLIC PRACTICE

> Many CPAs are employed by, or otherwise connected with, organizations other than public accounting firms, such as business enterprises and government agencies. When a CPA so engaged allows his name to be associated with financial statements and adds the designation "certified public accountant" or similar title, a reader may erroneously conclude that he is engaged in public practice. Consequently, a CPA not in public practice should avoid that implication by including a narrative which does not resemble the report of an independent CPA. If the CPA is a treasurer, for example, he should preferably sign as "treasurer." As the following inquiry and response illustrate, a simple narrative could be included if a statement of responsibility is desired. This would not be the expression of a professional opinion, but rather a declaration by a member of management since financial statements are the direct responsibility of management. Note that a scope paragraph would not be appropriate. However, a full-time company officer who is incidentally a CPA and is merely listed along with other company officers in a report released to the public would not be deemed to be "associated" with the accompanying financial statements. . . . The following inquiry highlights the problem of CPAs not in public practice.
>
> *Inquiry.* Recently I assumed the responsibility for the financial audit section of X Company's internal audit division. This section of the audit division has, from time to time, been asked to examine the financial statements and the underlying books and records of small companies related to X Company and to render an opinion as to the fairness of presentation of these statements. These examinations are generally quite thorough and include what would be considered normal auditing procedures. I recognize that an internal auditor, by the very nature of his position, cannot adhere to the generally accepted auditing standards, particularly the second standard on independence, and that phrase would not be included in any scope paragraph. I would like to know, however, if it would be permissible for me (a CPA) to sign an opinion on the financial statements in my capacity as an internal auditor.
>
> *Response.* . . . if CPAs in public practice are prohibited from adding unwarranted credibility to financial statements when they lack independence, certainly CPAs in private practice should be similarly restricted.

It is not too unusual for a corporate officer to sign a report taking responsibility for financial statements issued by the company, but in doing so he must make clear that he is acting as an officer of the company and not as an independent accountant. Such a statement might read as follows:

Controller's Report

In my opinion, as an officer of the XYZ Company, the accompanying balance sheet and related statements of income and retained earnings present fairly the financial position of the XYZ Company. . . .

By: John Doe, Controller

For a company treasurer, controller or internal auditor, any representations made on behalf of the company should be in the designated capacity of officer or employee.

A CPA cannot serve two masters: he cannot hold himself out to the public in a manner resembling a traditional auditor-client relationship and at the same time serve that client as a controller, treasurer or internal auditor.

RATIONALE AND TERMINOLOGY OF DISCLAIMER

Inquiry. We believe that the recommended disclaimer of opinion may raise more questions than it settles. . . . We present the following reasons for our thinking:

If it is thought that the lack of independence must be spelled out, then it would appear to us that the reason for the lack of independence should be set forth. Failure to do so would seem to violate one of our other standards—that of full disclosure. We do not believe that any more credence will be given to the financial statements simply because we explain why we are not independent, but we think it would help the reader if he were told why we were not independent. We feel quite sure that the vast majority of the readers of financial statements do not understand our Code of Professional Ethics and would only be confused by the statement. . .

We do not believe that the lack of independence is significantly more important than the failure to comply with the other generally accepted auditing standards. It seems to us that if financial statements have not been examined in accordance with generally accepted auditing standards, then they are simply unaudited. We see no particular reason to spell out any one particular item that does not comply with generally accepted auditing standards.

Response. . . . the basic concept of independence is more important than is the reason why independence is lacking. . . . explaining the reason for lack of independence would tend to confuse the reader and cause misleading inferences as to its significance. There are no varying degrees of lack of independence; the auditor is either independent or he is not independent. . . .

You question why the independence standard was deemed to be more important than any of the other standards. . . . the general standards—all three of them—are of such a pervasive nature that when one, or more, of them is not met the remaining seven standards are not really relevant. If inadequately trained people are used in the examination, due professional care is not exercised or independence is lacking, consideration of the field work and reporting standards from a compliance viewpoint has little meaning. To use an incompetent person to evaluate internal control or make decisions requiring professional judgment is not logical. . . . if a CPA lacks independence, there should not be a recitation of procedures performed in order to add credibility to financial statements used by a third party.

PUBLIC UNDERSTANDING OF "INDEPENDENCE"

Several inquiries focused on the public's understanding of independence. The following exchange is representative.

Inquiry. The disclaimer of opinion starts with the phrase, "We are not independent with respect to XYZ Company." I believe the general public is not familiar with the concept of independence which was developed by the profession. Therefore the phrase quoted above would, in my opinion, create confusion or misunderstanding on the part of most of the readers of such a disclaimer. I believe that it would be sufficient if the disclaimer merely stated that the financial statements presented were unaudited and, accordingly, no opinion is expressed on them. I do not feel that a reference to independence is essential and if it is likely not to be understood, it might as well be omitted.

Response. Your premise that the general public is not familiar with the concept of independence is questionable. On the contrary, independence is a rather simple, well-understood concept from the layman's standpoint. An ordinary dictionary definition conveys the meaning quite adequately. On the other hand, specific reasons for lack of independence probably would be difficult for the layman to comprehend and evaluate if he were required to make a judgment as to the importance of a particular reason set forth in a CPA's report.

SERVING AS OFFICER

Several inquiries related to the appropriate wording of a disclaimer when an accountant in public practice serves part-time as an officer of a company as a service to a client. . . .

Inquiry. . . . Here's an example of a disclaimer released by this office. "The accompanying balance sheet of X Company as of November 30, 19XX and the related statement of income and retained earnings for the six-month period then ended were prepared by me in the capacity of an officer of the corporation. Accordingly, I cannot express an opinion concerning them in the manner that would be expected had I not served as an officer and had an examination in accordance with generally accepted auditing standards been conducted. (Signed as Treasurer.)" Do you mean to tell me that a disclaimer such as this is more confusing to the stockholders than your recommended disclaimer? . . .

Response. . . . phrases of the sort used in your disclaimer are more confusing because they do not state that an examination was not performed; also the phrase you suggest contains an implication that the only reason for not being able to express an opinion is the fact that as treasurer you are not independent. A reader could infer that you did perform an examination but are barred from stating that you did, or from expressing an opinion, solely because of your "technical" lack of independence. In other words, there is an implication that since you are a member of a CPA firm there is no need for an independent audit because you prepared the statements.

DESCRIPTION OF PROCEDURES

Several inquiries were received concerning the prohibition against describing the procedures the auditor has performed or giving some indication that an examination was performed even though the examination was not in accordance with generally accepted auditing standards because the auditor was not independent.

Inquiry. Why... prohibit the CPA from describing the procedures he performed in his report? Why can we not state the facts simply because we are not independent?

Response. The essential reason for requiring the auditor to state in his report that the statements are unaudited, regardless of the extent of procedures performed, was to prevent the association of the CPA's name with financial statements from adding credibility to those statements.

If a client wishes a CPA to perform auditing procedures even though the CPA is not independent, the CPA may furnish this service. In this case, the CPA may function as an internal auditor and provide the client with a service which the client would not otherwise be in a position to obtain. The nature and extent of the procedures may be described in full in an engagement letter. However, the CPA is precluded from including any description of those procedures in his report on the financial statements. If the client's only objective is to have the procedures performed, this objective should be adequately fulfilled by the engagement letter. However, if the client's objective is to add credibility to financial statements for the use of third parties, this is a service which a CPA who is not independent cannot and should not seek to perform. In this case, describing the procedures or otherwise indicating that some type of examination was performed could give a third party reason to believe that the auditor had formed some conclusion on the fair presentation of the statements. The third party would be justified in this belief even though the auditor stated in his report that he was precluded from expressing an opinion because he was not independent. . . .[27]

QUESTIONS AND CASES

2–1 What is the meaning of "independence" in accounting? Is it of significance to the management consultant, the tax practitioner, and the internal professional, as well as to the auditor?

2–2 What are the various avenues for insuring the presence of independence, integrity, and objectivity?

2–3 Assume that a particular Savings and Loan Association holds the house mortgage

[27]D. R. Carmichael and J. B. Bencivenga, "Lack of Indepencence—Some Reporting Problems," *The Journal of Accountancy*, August 1972, pp. 79–81. Copyright © 1972 by the American Institute of Certified Public Accountants, Inc.

for several members of your firm. Could you ethically serve as its auditor? What is the general rule with regard to loans to or from an enterprise being audited?

2–4 Will the performance of accounting services for a client impair independence? What are the four requirements that must be met to retain independence and the appearance of independence? Does the Securities and Exchange Commission ageee with this position?

2–5 If you were the management consultant for the design and installation of a company's accounting system, can you ethically serve as that company's auditor? What ground rules must be observed in order to insure independence?

2–6 What subgroup of internal professional accountants has its own statement of responsibilities and set of standards? What do they have to say about independence?

2–7 Is it ethical for a tax practitioner to resolve doubts in favor of his client? What if the tax return in question is being prepared by an internal professional rather than a public accountant?

2–8 What is the distinction between Principles and Rules in the AICPA Code of Professional Conduct? What Principles are there in the area of independence, integrity, and objectivity?

2–9 Assume that you are not independent with respect to a particular audit client, but have consented to the use of your name in a written communication containing the client's financial statements. What are your reporting requirements? Should you set forth your lack of independence and the reasons for it?

2–10 If you are working in private industry and your name is associated with your company's financial statements, can you ethically add the designation "certified public accountant" after your name? Would it be appropriate for you to be listed as a CPA in a public report which identifies the officers of the company?

2–11 If your examination of the financial statements of a particular company was not in accordance with generally accepted auditing standards, can you describe in your report the procedures you did apply? Discuss the reasons for and against such disclosure.

2–12 Larry Backus, a heavy senior with the public accounting firm of Porter and Company, has been given the responsibility for negotiating and collecting fees for engagements and for marketing the firm's services. His brother-in-law, John Wilkes, is a purchasing agent for a client of the firm. The audit of the client is done out of the Atlanta office of Porter and Company, where Larry is located, but Larry does not participate in the audit.

Is the firm's independence impaired? Why or why not? Give all the steps in your reasoning process.

2–13 Bill Blass joined the firm of May & Company as an audit partner on October 5, 19XX. Previously he had been employed by the Sexton Manufacturing Company as its controller. He has completely disassociated himself from the company. The Sexton Manufacturing Company is an audit client of May and Company and is audited out of the firm's Denver office, where Bill is located. Bill did not participate in the audit. Is the independence of May and Company impaired for the 19XX calendar year audit? Why or why not? Give all the steps in your reasoning process.

2–14 Bill Slack is a partner in the regional CPA firm of Slack, Tight and Company. His son, Marty, has just graduated from Iowa Technical University with an engineering degree and has accepted a position with a client of Slack, Tight and Company. Marty's position would not be considered to be "audit sensitive." Bill is the partner in charge of the audit of the client. Is the firm's independence impaired? Why or why not?

2–15 Asceneth Black works part-time for the local CPA firm of Winken, Blinken and Nodd. She participated in the audit of the Stroper Corporation, a locally owned manufacturing company. Her husband, Jake (Hunk) Black, a local attorney, is a trustee of the profit-sharing trust of Stroper. Is Winken, Blinken, and Nodd independent with regard to the Stroper Corporation? Why or why not?

2–16 Barton Holter is a partner in Arthur Peat and Company. His wife, Sally, is employed by a client as a cashier. In what circumstances, if any, would the firm's independence be impaired? Why?

2–17 (*Pamela Lang*)
In 19XX, PKL & Co., an accounting firm, was hired by the Green Co. to establish a system of internal control. No system of internal control had ever been established. PKL & Co. performed an operational audit to determine if there was adequate separation of duties and if proper accounting procedures were being used. They then made recommendations for implementation of certain controls and procedures. The Board of Directors approved these and asked PKL & Co. to assist in the implementation. PKL & Co. worked very closely with the employees in the accounting department during the initial period of implementation. They also observed the transition process to determine that recommended procedures were being correctly interpreted and followed. One year after the internal control system was instituted, Green Co. asked PKL & Co. to audit their financial records. The Green Co. wants a large loan from a bank that requests audited financial statements. Should PKL & Co. accept the engagement?

2–18 After passing the CPA exam, Mike Allison accepted a position with Peterson and Company, CPAs. Peterson and Company does an annual audit for Goddard, Incorporated and has issued an unqualified opinion for the last four years. Mike Allison was assigned to the audit team of Goddard, Incorporated and began work on the audit for 19XX. In his research of the management of Goddard, Incorporated he discovered that his Uncle Berrymore Allison is a director of Goddard, Incorporated. The annual audit was two thirds complete at the time.

Assume no close relationship between Mike and his Uncle Berrymore. Would the independence of Peterson and Company be considered impaired with respect to Goddard, Incorporated?

2–19 (*Chandler Russell*)

REGIONAL CPA FIRM, PEAT ANDERSON:

Richard Professional	–Partner, CPA
Kathy Misguided	–Supervisor, CPA (married)
Joe Academic	–New Staff

CLIENT, "OUT OF TOWN SPECIALISTS, INC.":

Fred Intimidator	–President and Chairman
Leroy Shifty	–Controller (single)
Mary Gorgeous	–Accounts Receivable Bookkeeper (former Miss Georgia)

Out of Town Specialists is Peat Anderson's biggest client, with annual billings in excess of $5,000,000. Many accounting adjustment issues have arisen in the past, as well as two significant suits that are unsettled, but have been disclosed. Past adjustments have arisen primarily due to audit findings of unusual entries passed through shell subsidiaries.

The 19X0 audit has gone unusually well—so well, in fact, that the controller has invited Kathy, Joe, and Mary to a little party at his midtown bachelor pad. The final workpapers have all been reviewed by Kathy but the "adjustment" meeting has not yet taken place. Richard is in Atlanta and unable to attend, but he is aware of the party and he tells us Fred has dropped hints that he will "test the water" for possible new auditors in 19X1. This has been common practice for years.

The party goes well and many client personnel are present. Unfortunately, Kathy, Joe, and Mary are the last to leave. Joe has been asked by Mary to escort her home but since Joe had performed work on the sales and accounts receivable, he thought that would be inappropriate. As Joe and Mary are leaving, Leroy informs them that he will drive Kathy back to the hotel. As Joe and Mary leave, at 2 A.M., Kathy and Leroy are waving at the door.

Should Joe take any action as a result of what he has seen?

2–20 Willie Weakley, CPA, CMA, is the controller of the Athens Division of the Northwest Corporation. He reports directly to the Division Manager, Sam Gump. Willie is responsible for the preparation of quarterly financial statements for the division which are forwarded to corporate headquarters in Seattle, Washington.

As he was preparing the statements for the quarter ending March 31, Sam suggested that he delay booking a large sale that had taken place on March 31. Sam's reasoning was that the division had already made its budget for the quarter and this sale would give them a head start on meeting the budget for next quarter.

What should Willie do?

2–21 (*Peter Wertheim*)

Assume that you are a partner in a local CPA firm that has been providing management consulting services and preparing the financial statements and tax returns for a client for the past ten years. This company has grown phenomenally during these years; from $100,000 a year in sales to $15 million. The president and chief stockholder has decided to go public and sell stock in the company. If your firm performs the audit, will SEC filing requirements be met?

2–22 (*Pamela Lang*)
Speigel Company is a manufacturing concern. It employs 500 people who make plastic parts for automotive companies. The company also employs three internal auditors who report and are responsible only to the president. All three auditors have moved up through the ranks of the company and consequently have a personal relationship with some of the people they audit. The president believes this relationship enables the auditors to get to the root of the problem efficiently. Occasionally the auditors replace persons on vacation from the Accounting Department. During these times, the auditors found problems which needed correction. They discussed the problems with the president, who almost always approved corrective action.

Can the independent auditors rely on the work performed by internal auditors in performing the year-end audit? Explain.

2–23 (*Mike Winchester*)
Assume that a CPA tax practitioner is preparing a wealthy individual's tax return for the first time. In the process of reviewing the client's previous returns, he discovers an error in the last year's return that, due to an accidental omission of income, materially understates the correct tax liabilty for that year. In accordance with one of the Statements on Responsibilities in Tax Practice, he promptly informs the client of the error and advises her that an amended return should be filed to take into account this error. The client does not agree to file an amended return, nor does she give the CPA permission to inform the IRS of the error. Assume that the previous error will not affect the current year's tax and that the CPA has calculated this year's tax liability correctly.

Should the CPA continue to complete the current return or should he withdraw from the engagement? Should any other steps be taken?

2–24 (*Daryl Burkhard*)
Mr. Baker is a CPA and practicing tax accountant in Kalamazoo, Michigan. Last year he prepared a tax return for Mr. Jones. On the return, Mr. Baker took an aggressive stand in several areas in order to reduce Mr. Jones' tax liability. This year, the IRS audited Mr. Jones' tax return and challenged five issues. Of the areas challenged, two appeared to be favorable toward Mr. Baker's position, whereas the remaining three were probably incorrectly treated by Mr. Baker. Due to the expense of litigation on both sides, regardless of who would win, the Revenue agent and Mr. Baker resorted to "horse-trading," in which Mr. Baker conceded to the government on the last three areas, and the government conceded to Mr. Baker on the first two areas.

Although it is acceptable for a tax accountant to be the advocate of the client, has the tax practitioner violated his sense of integrity and objectivity in the above case?

3

GENERAL AND TECHNICAL STANDARDS

INTRODUCTION

All professional accountants, whether they are in the public practice as auditors, management consultants, or tax practitioners or are internal to some organization, must abide by rigorous general standards.[1] First, each professional must undertake only those tasks or engagements which can be completed with *professional competence.* Second, those tasks which are undertaken must be accomplished with *due professional care.* Third, each engagement or task must have adequate *planning and supervision.* Fourth, *sufficient relevant data* must be obtained to afford a reasonable basis for conclusions or recommendations.

In addition to these four general standards, the professional accountant must adhere to certain technical standards. In the area of accounting principles, statements of the Financial Accounting Standards Board are considered authoritative. In addition, any Accounting Research Bulletins issued by the AICPA Committee on Accounting Research (1939–1959) and any opinions issued by the Accounting Principles Board (1959–1973) should be considered authoritative unless and until they are

[1] "General Standards," *AICPA Professional Standards,* vol. 2, ET Section 201. Copyright © 1988 by the American Institute of Certified Public Accountants, Inc.

expressly superseded by the FASB. Also in the area of accounting principles, the standards promulgated by the Cost Accounting Standards Board must be adhered to by defense contractors under federal contracts. The Governmental Accounting Standards Board establishes financial accounting principles for state and local governmental entities.

In the area of auditing, the professional accountant must follow generally accepted auditing standards. These standards have been approved and adopted by the membership of the American Institute of Certified Public Accountants and are continually being interpreted by the Auditing Standards Board in their Statements on Auditing Standards. The Comptroller General has also issued a set of standards for audits of government organizations, programs, activities, and functions, and of government funds received by contractors, nonprofit organizations, and other nongovernment organizations. The standards are to be followed by auditors and audit organizations when required by law, regulation, agreement or contract, or policy.[2]

THE AUDITOR

The independent external auditor, in addition to adhering to the general standards relating to professional competence, due professional care, planning and supervision, and sufficient relevant data, must abide by the technical standards relating to accounting principles, and auditing standards. In the area of accounting principles, he may not "(1) express an opinion or state affirmatively that the financial statements or other financial data of any entity are presented in conformity with generally accepted accounting principles, or (2) state that he or she is not aware of any material modifications that should be made to such statements or data in order for them to be in conformity with generally accepted accounting prinicples, if such statements or data contain any departure from any accounting principle promulgated by bodies designated by Council to establish such principles that has a material effect on the statements or data taken as a whole. If, however, the statements or data contain such a departure and the member can demonstrate that due to unusual circumstances the financial statements or data would otherwise have been misleading, the member can comply with the rule by describing the departure, its approximate effects, if practicable, and the reasons why compliance with the principle would result in a misleading statement."[3]

The following generally accepted auditing standards must be adhered to by the practicing certified public accountant. Although some of them are similar to the general standards outlined earlier, they have special application to the auditor.

GENERAL STANDARDS

1. The audit is to be performed by a person or persons having adequate technical training and proficiency as an auditor.

[2]Comptroller General of the United States, *Government Auditing Standards* (United States General Accounting Office, 1988), p. 1.

[3]"Accounting Principles," *AICPA Professional Standards,* vol. 2, ET Section 203.

2. In all matters relating to the assignment, an independence in mental attitude is to be maintained by the auditor or auditors.
3. Due professional care is to be exercised in the performance of the examination and the preparation of the report.

STANDARDS OF FIELD WORK

1. The work is to be adequately planned and assistants, if any, are to be properly supervised.
2. A sufficient understanding of the internal control structure is to be obtained to plan the audit and to determine the nature, timing, and extent of tests to be performed.
3. Sufficient competent evidential matter is to be obtained through inspection, observation, inquiries, and confirmations to afford a reasonable basis for an opinion regarding the financial statements under examination.

STANDARDS OF REPORTING

1. The report shall state whether the financial statements are presented in accordance with generally accepted accounting principles.
2. The report shall identify those circumstances in which such principles have not been consistently observed in the current period in relation to the preceding period.
3. Informative disclosures in the financial statements are to be regarded as reasonably adequate unless otherwise stated in the report.
4. The report shall either contain an expression of opinion regarding the financial statements, taken as a whole, or an assertion to the effect that an opinion cannot be expressed. When an overall opinion cannot be expressed, the reason therefore should be stated. In all cases where an auditor's name is associated with financial statements, the report should contain a clear-cut indication of the character of the auditor's examination if any, and the degree of responsibility the auditor is taking.[4]

To illustrate the application of the general and technical standards, consider the following situations:

1. Your local CPA firm has been in existence for only three years. After working on the audit staff of a large international firm for six years, you and a former college classmate decided to form a partnership and practice in the small city where you both grew up. You have just finished talking with the city manager of the town, a forward-looking administrator who feels strongly that the city should be audited by an independent CPA. You would very much like to have the engagement but have never before been involved with a government audit. Furthermore, because of scheduling problems in school, you were unable to take a governmental accounting course. Are you prohibited from seeking this engagement because of a lack of professional competence? Do the qualifications of your partner or your staff, if any, have any bearing on the question?

The fact that you have never had a governmental accounting course and

[4]"Generally Accepted Auditing Standards," *AICPA Professional Standards,* vol. 1, AU Section 150. Copyright © 1988 by the American Institute of Certified Public Accountants, Inc.

have never before been involved with a government audit would not necessarily prohibit you or your firm from seeking the engagement. The question to be asked is whether you or your firm can reasonably expect to complete the engagement with professional competence.[5] If your partner already has the necessary knowledge and skill, even though you do not, the engagement can be undertaken. Furthermore, you and your staff may be able to acquire the necessary competence through additional research or consultation with others, which would not ordinarily represent a lack of competence. Rather, it would be regarded as "a normal part of the professional conduct of the engagement."[6]

2. Financial accounting standards require that all research and development costs are to be charged as expenses when incurred. Assume that you generally agree with this position but feel strongly that an exception should be made in the case of the enterprise you are now auditing. The research and development costs incurred by this company during the past year are so material in relation to the company's earnings that you feel expensing them would render the financial statements misleading. Can your firm render an opinion that the financial statements of this enterprise are presented in conformity with generally accepted accounting principles if the research and development costs are capitalized rather than expensed? Isn't it permissible to depart from generally accepted accounting principles if following those principles would cause the financial statements to be misleading?

Rule 203 of the AICPA Code of Professional Conduct does indeed provide that financial statements can contain a departure from an accounting principle promulgated by the FASB if it can be demonstrated that "due to unusual circumstances the statements. . . would otherwise have been misleading."[7] The key question, however, is what constitutes an "unusual" circumstance. The answer is a matter of professional judgment and involves the ability to support the position that adherence to a promulgated principle would be generally regarded by reasonable men as producing a misleading result. An interpretation of Rule 203 specifically states, however, that an unusual degree of materiality, as in this case, "would not ordinarily be regarded as unusual."[8] Therefore, you would probably have to qualify your opinion.

3. Assume that as the partner in charge of the audit of a large department store chain, you are in the process of reviewing the working papers. Included therein is a memo from the senior auditor on the job to the manager entitled "On the Possibility of Fictitious Receivables." In the memo, the senior discusses the reasons for his concern and the logic which led him to conclude that his fears were unjustified. There is a notation by the manager at the bottom of the memo indicating his concurrence with the conclusions of the senior and noting that the amount involved is immaterial. You are inclined to agree with the logic of the senior and the manager but have a nagging doubt that further audit procedures should perhaps be employed to be "absolutely certain" that no fraud exists. After discussing the situation with

[5]"General Standards," *AICPA Professional Standards*, vol. 2, ET Section 201.01.
[6]Ibid., ET Section 201.02.
[7]"Accounting Principles," ET Section 203.01.
[8]Ibid., ET Section 203.02.

several of your partners, however, you finally conclude that nothing further needs to be done. Should you raise this issue with the company's management? the Board of Directors? the local sheriff?

If it is concluded in this case that the possible irregularity could not be so significant as to materially affect the financial statements under examination, the auditor should refer the matter "to an appropriate level of management that is at least one level above those involved." Also, he should "be satisfied that, in view of the organizational position of the likely perpetrator, the irregularity has no implications for other aspects of the audit or that those implications have been properly considered."[9] Because of the importance of the subject of errors and irregularities, it will be discussed in greater detail later in this chapter.

THE MANAGEMENT CONSULTANT AND THE TAX PRACTITIONER

All of the general standards requiring professional competence, due professional care, adequate planning, and supervision, and sufficient relevant data in connection with engagements apply to the management consultant and the tax practitioner, as well as to the auditor. Guidance to the management consultant and to the tax practitioner in complying with the general standards are provided in Statements on Standards for Management Advisory Services (see Appendix 2) and Statements on Responsibilities in Tax Practice (see Appendix 3). These statements also set forth other standards deemed appropriate for their respective areas.

The Statements on Standards for Management Advisory Services are issued by the Management Advisory Services Executive Committee and are enforceable under the AICPA Code of Professional Conduct. Assume that a small manufacturing company has just retained your firm to study the feasibility of purchasing some new data processing equipment. In discussing the engagement with the president of the company, you mention that your first step will be to document the details of their operation and of their present system as a prelude to determining the need for a more sophisticated system. He informs you that another consultant installed the accounting system just a year ago and that all of the information you need is contained in his report. To what extent can you rely upon the information contained in the previous consultant's report? In general, what kind of documentation is needed to support the conclusions and recommendations of a management consulting engagement?

The information contained in the previous consultant's work should probably not be relied upon without validation. The MAS practitioner is obligated to obtain sufficient relevant data to complete the engagement and must exercise professional judgment in determining the nature and quantity of information required to develop conclusions or recommendations that fulfill the objectives of the engage-

[9] "The Auditor's Responsibility to Detect and Report Errors and Irregularities," *AICPA Professional Standards,* vol. 1, AU Section 316.24, (Statement on Auditing Standards No. 53).

ment.[10] This data "may be obtained by interview, observation, review of client documents, research, computation and analysis."[11]

Several of the Statements on Responsibilties in Tax Practice also have a relationship to the general standards. These statements have been approved by the AICPA's Federal Taxation Executive Committee, but are not enforceable under its Code of Professional Conduct. Assume, for example, that a tax client supplies you with all the information you need to prepare a return but does not provide you with any documentation or other evidence to support the information. Can you complete the engagement?

Although you should encourage your client to provide you with the supporting data, you are not required to examine or review documents or other evidence in order to sign the preparer's declaration. A CPA may ordinarily rely on information provided by his client. If the information appears to be incorrect or incomplete, however, he or she cannot ignore the implications of information known by him and, accordingly, must make reasonable inquiries.[12]

THE INTERNAL PROFESSIONAL

As indicated in the introduction to this chapter, every professional accountant, no matter where employed, must abide by rigorous general and technical standards. The internal professional, even if he is not a CPA, must set personal standards that are at least as demanding as those set forth in the AICPA Code of Professional Conduct.

As discussed earlier, several organizations representing internal professionals have their own code of ethics and one, The Institute of Internal Auditors, has a separate set of professional standards and a Statement of Professional Responsibilities. The codes of the National Association of Accountants, the Financial Executives Institute, the Association of Government Accountants, and the IIA all set standards of practice for their members, (see Appendixes). Several of the Standards of Conduct in the IIA Code, for example, address the general standards.

> Standard VI. Members and CIAs shall undertake only those services which they can reasonably expect to complete with professional competence.
>
> Standard X. Members and CIAs shall continually strive for improvement in their proficiency, and in the effectiveness and quality of their service.
>
> Standard XI. Members and CIAs. . . shall be ever mindful of their obligation to maintain the high standards of competence, morality, and dignity promulgated by *The Institute.*

[10] "MAS Engagements," *AICPA Professional Standards,* Vol. 2, MS Section 21.14.

[11] Ibid., MS Section 21.13.

[12] "Certain Procedural Aspects of Preparing Return," *AICPA Professional Standards,* TX Section 132.

Included among the separate set of Standards for the Professional Practice of Internal Auditing are the following:

- The internal auditing department should provide assurance that the technical proficiency and educational background of internal auditors are appropriate for the audits to be performed.
- The internal auditing department should possess or should obtain the knowledge, skills, and disciplines needed to carry out its audit responsibilities.
- The internal auditing department should provide assurance that internal audits are properly supervised.
- Internal auditors should possess the knowledge, skills, and disciplines essential to the performance of internal audits.
- Internal auditors should maintain their technical competence through continuing education.
- Internal auditors should exercise due professional care in performing internal audits.
- Internal auditors should plan each audit.
- The director of internal auditing should establish plans to carry out the responsibilities of the internal auditing department.
- The director of internal auditing should provide written policies and procedures to guide the audit staff.[13]

What are some of the issues facing the internal professional in the area of general and technical standards? Assume that you are the controller for a company that manufacturers and markets fruitcakes throughout the southern part of the country. Having graduated from a prominent school of accounting in Georgia, you are very conscious of your ethical responsibility as an accounting professional. One of your responsibilities as controller is to put together a budget for the next year, as well as a projection for the ensuing two years. Much of your data is gathered from company personnel in production and sales, but you are the one charged with the final preparation. In fact, your name is the one that will be associated with it, as it is printed and reproduced for all appropriate company personnel. You have some problem with this because you are a CPA, and vaguely remember a statement issued by the Auditing Standards Board dealing with forecasts. Does the statement apply to you now that you are an internal professional? What if you are a CMA? What if you hold no professional certification?

"Financial Forcasts and Projections," a *Statement on Standards for Accountants' Services on Prospective Financial Information* [AICPA Professional Standards, vol. 1, AT

[13]*Standards for the Professional Practice of Internal Auditing* (Altamonte Springs, Florida: The Institute of Internal Auditors, Inc., 1978), pp. 3–4. Copyright © 1978 by the Institute of Internal Auditors, Inc., 242 Maitland Avenue, Altamonte Springs, Florida 32701 U.S.A. Reprinted with permission.

Section 200.] issued by the Auditing Standards Board, does not apply when the accountant's services are restricted to internal use. The guidelines in the statement, however, are still worthy of review by the internal professional as a minimum standard of conduct, whether he or she is a CPA, CMA or holds no professional certification. The statement includes, for example, suggested compilation procedures, and makes reference to presentation guidelines contained in the AICPA *Guide for Prospective Financial Statements.*

Assume that immediately upon graduating from college you went to work for a local CPA in a medium-sized city near your school. During your four years with the firm, you gained valuable experience and passed the CPA examination. Three years ago, a prominent local business asked you to join them as assistant controller. The financial offer was very attractive and you were promised a promotion to controller as soon as the current controller retired. Just this year you received the promised promotion.

As controller, you now have responsibility for the preparation of the company's financial statements, copies of which are regularly forwarded to the local bank pursuant to a loan agreement. Upon preparing these statements for the first time and after reviewing the statements for the past several months, you note that the earnings picture of the company is rapidly deteriorating. Although you had no trouble putting the statement together, you were surprised to find that the president personally kept the receivables ledger and furnished you with the current balance. When you asked him about it, he pointed out that he handled most of the sales for the company so it was easier for him to maintain it. Are you under any obligation as a professional to verify further the receivables balance and amount of sales before including them on the statement and forwarding the statement to the bank? What obligation do you have as an accounting professional to be alert to the possibility of management misrepresentation or fraud? What action would you take if you strongly suspect that the financial statements are being intentionally distorted?

As an internal professional, you have an obligation to verify further the figure given to you for inclusion on the statements. The banker receiving them has a right to expect that you exercised due professional care in their preparation. As a professional, you also have an obligation to be alert to the possibility of fraud. Should you strongly suspect that the financial statements are being intentionally distorted, you should discuss the matter with an appropriate level of management, at least one level above those involved. It may be appropriate to bring the matter to the attention of the Board of Directors or its audit committee. You may even wish to consult legal counsel. Certainly, you should do no less than would be required of an auditor in similar circumstances.[14] The auditor's obligation will be fully discussed in the next section.

[14] "The Auditor's Responsibility to Detect and Report Errors and Irregularities," *AICPA Professional Standards,* vol. 1, AU Section 316.24 and 316.25, (Statement on Auditing Standards No. 53). Copyright © 1989 by the American Institute of Certified Public Accountants, Inc.

DETECTION OF FRAUD: THE STANDARD

It is a common misconception that audits are performed primarily for the detection of fraud. This is not the case. The independent auditor's objective in examining financial statements is to form an opinion on whether the financial statements present fairly, in all material respects, the financial position of a company, and the results of its operations and its cash flows in conformity with generally accepted accounting principles. In order to form such an opinion, however, "the auditors should assess the risk that errors and irregularities may cause the financial statements to contain a material misstatement. Based on that assessment, the auditor should design the audit to provide reasonable assurance of detecting errors and irregularities that are material to the financial statements."[15]

"The term *errors* refers to unintentional misstatements or omissions of amounts or disclosures in financial statements,"[16] while "the term *irregularities* refers to intentional misstatements or omissions. Irregularities include fraudulent financial reporting undertaken to render financial statements misleading, sometimes called *management fraud,* and misappropriation of assets, sometimes called *defalcations.*"[17]

"Because of the characteristics of irregularities, particularly those involving forgery and collusions, a properly designed and executed audit may not detect a material irregularity."[18] "Since the auditors opinion on the financial statements is based on the concept of reasonable assurance, the auditor is not an insurer and his report does not constitute a guarantee. Therefore, the subsequent discovery that a material misstatement exists in the financial statements does not, in and of itself, evidence inadequate planning, performance, or judgment on the part of the auditor."[19]

"An audit of financial statements in conformance with generally accepted auditing standards should be planned and performed with an attitude of professional skepticism. The auditor neither assumes that management is dishonest nor assumes unquestioned honesty. Rather, the auditor recognizes that conditions observed and evidential matter obtained, including information from prior audits, need to be objectively evaluated to determine whether the financial statements are free of material misstatement."[20]

Because of the importance of this subject to the professional auditor, the following standard should be studied in its entirety.

1. This Statement provides guidance on the independent auditor's responsibility for the detection of errors and irregularities in an audit of financial statements in accordance with generally accepted auditing standards. It describes factors that influence the auditor's ability to detect errors and irregularities and explains how the exercise of due care should give appropriate consideration to the possibility

[15]Ibid., AU Section 316.05.
[16]Ibid., AU Section 316.02.
[17]Ibid., AU Section 316.03.
[18]Ibid., AU Section 316.07.
[19]Ibid., AU Section 316.08.
[20]Ibid., AU Section 316.16.

of errors or irregularities. It also provides guidance on the auditor's responsibility to communicate detected matters both within and outside the entity whose financial statements are under audit.

DEFINITION OF ERRORS AND IRREGULARITIES

2. The term *errors* refers to *unintentional* misstatements or omissions of amounts or disclosures in financial statements. Errors may involve:

- Mistakes in gathering or processing accounting data from which financial statements are prepared.
- Incorrect accounting estimates arising from oversight or misinterpretation of facts.
- Mistakes in the application of accounting principles relating to amount, classification, manner of presentation, or disclosure.*

3. The term *irregularities* refers to *intentional* misstatements or omissions of amounts or disclosures in financial statements. Irregularities include fraudulent financial reporting undertaken to render financial statements misleading, sometimes called *management fraud,* and misappropriation of assets, sometimes called *defalcations.* Irregularities may involve acts such as the following:

- Manipulation, falsification, or alteration of accounting records or supporting documents from which financial statements are prepared.
- Misrepresentation or intentional omission of events, transactions, or other significant information.
- Intentional misapplication of accounting principles relating to amounts, classification, manner of presentation, or disclosure.

4. The primary factor that distinguishes errors from irregularities is whether the underlying cause of a misstatement in financial statements is intentional or unintentional. Intent, however, is often difficult to determine, particularly in matters involving accounting estimates or the application of accounting principles. For example, an unreasonable accounting estimate may result from unintentional bias or may be an intentional attempt to misstate the financial statements.

THE AUDITOR'S RESPONSIBILITY TO DETECT ERRORS AND IRREGULARITIES

5. The auditor should assess the risk that errors and irregularities may cause the financial statements to contain a material misstatement. Based on that assessment, the auditor should design the audit to provide reasonable assurance of detecting errors and irregularities that are material to the financial statements.†‡

*Errors do not include the effect of accounting processes employed for convenience, such as maintaining accounting records on the cash basis or the tax basis and periodically adjusting those records to prepare financial statements in conformity with generally accepted accounting principles.

†The concept of reasonable assurance is recognized in the third standard of field work, "Sufficient competent evidential matter is to be obtained through inspection, observation, inquiries and confirmation to afford a reasonable basis for an opinion regarding the financial statements under examination" and is discussed in Statement on Auditing Standards No. 31, *Evidential Matter* (*AICPA Professional Standards,* vol. 1, AU sec. 326) and SAS No. 39, *Audit Sampling* (*AICPA Professional Standards,* vol. 1, AU Sec. 350).

‡The auditor's responsibility for detecting misstatements resulting from illegal acts, as defined in SAS No. 54, *Illegal Acts by Clients,* having a direct and material effect on the determination of financial statement amounts is the same as that for other errors and irregularities.

6. The auditor's assessment of the risk of material misstatement of the financial statements requires the auditor to understand the characteristics of errors and irregularities that are discussed in the Appendix and the complex interaction of those characteristics. Based on that understanding, the auditor designs and performs appropriate audit procedures and evaluates the results.

7. Because of the characteristics of irregularities, particularly those involving forgery and collusion, a properly designed and executed audit may not detect a material irregularity. For example, generally accepted auditing standards do not require that an auditor authenticate documents, nor is the auditor trained to do so. Also, audit procedures that are effective for detecting a misstatement that is unintentional may be ineffective for a misstatement that is intentional and is concealed through collusion between client personnel and third parties or among management or employees of the client.

8. The auditor should exercise (a) due care in planning, performing, and evaluating the results of audit procedures, and (b) the proper degree of professional skepticism to achieve reasonable assurance that material errors or irregularities will be detected. Since the auditor's opinion on the financial statements is based on the concept of reasonable assurance, the auditor is not an insurer and his report does not constitute a guarantee. Therefore, the subsequent discovery that a material misstatement exists in the financial statements does not, in and of itself, evidence inadequate planning, performance, or judgment on the part of the auditor.

CONSIDERATION OF THE POSSIBILITY OF MATERIAL MISSTATEMENTS IN AUDIT PLANNING

9. In developing an audit plan, the auditor should consider factors influencing audit risk that relate to several or all account balances and obtain an understanding of the internal control structure.* These matters often have effects pervasive to the financial statements taken as a whole and also influence the auditor's consideration of risk at the account balance or class-of-transactions level.

Consideration of Audit Risk at the Financial Statement Level

10. An assessment of the risk of material misstatements should be made during planning. The auditor's understanding of the internal control structure should either heighten or mitigate the auditor's concern about the risk of material misstatements. The factors considered in assessing risk should be considered in combination to make an overall judgment; the presence of some factors in isolation would not necessarily indicate increased risk. Factors such as those listed below may be considered.

MANAGEMENT CHARACTERISTICS

- Management operating and financing decisions are dominated by a single person.
- Management's attitude toward financial reporting is unduly aggressive.
- Management (particularly senior accounting personnel) turnover is high.
- Management places undue emphasis on meeting earnings projections.
- Management's reputation in the business community is poor.

*See SAS No. 55, *Consideration of the Internal Control Structure in a Financial Statement Audit.*

OPERATING AND INDUSTRY CHARACTERISTICS

- Profitability of entity relative to its industry is inadequate or inconsistent.
- Sensitivity of operating results to economic factors (inflation, interest rates, unemployment, etc.) is high.
- Rate of change in entity's industry is rapid.
- Direction of change in entity's industry is declining with many business failures.
- Organization is decentralized without adequate monitoring.
- Internal or external matters that raise substantial doubt about the entity's ability to continue as a going concern are present. (See SAS No. 59, *The Auditor's Consideration of an Entity's Ability to Continue as a Going Concern.*)

ENGAGEMENT CHARACTERISTICS

- Many contentious or difficult accounting issues are present.
- Significant difficult-to-audit transactions or balances are present.
- Significant and unusual related party transactions not in the ordinary course of business are present.
- Nature, cause (if known), or the amount of known and likely misstatements detected in the audit of prior period's financial statements is significant.
- It is a new client with no prior audit history or sufficient information is not available from the predecessor auditor.

11. The size, complexity, and ownership characteristics of the entity have a significant influence on the risk factors considered to be important. For example, for a large entity, the auditor would ordinarily give consideration to factors that constrain improper conduct by senior management, such as the effectiveness of the board of directors, the audit committee or others with equivalent authority and responsibility,* and the internal audit function. Consideration would also be given to the measures taken to enforce a formal code of conduct and the effectiveness of the budgeting or responsibility reporting system. For a small entity some of these matters might be considered inapplicable or unimportant, particularly if the auditor's past experience with the entity has been that effective owner-manager or trustee involvement creates a good control environment.

12. The auditor should assess the risk of management misrepresentation by reviewing information obtained about risk factors and the internal control structure. Matters such as the following may be considered:

- Are there known circumstances that may indicate a management predisposition to distort financial statements, such as frequent disputes about aggressive application of accounting principles that increase earnings, evasive responses to audit inquiries, or excessive emphasis on meeting quantified targets that must be achieved to receive a substantial portion of management compensation?
- Are there indications that management has failed to establish policies and procedures that provide reasonable assurance of reliable accounting estimates, such as personnel who develop estimates appearing to lack necessary knowledge and experience, supervisors of these personnel appearing careless or inexperienced, or there is a history of unreliable or unreasonable estimates?

*For entities that do not have audit committees, the phrase "others with equivalent authority and responsibility" may include the board of directors, the board of trustees, or the owner in owner-managed entities.

- Are there conditions that indicate lack of control of activities, such as constant crisis conditions in operating or accounting areas, disorganized work areas, frequent or excessive back orders, shortages, delays, or lack of documentation for major transactions?
- Are there indications of a lack of control over computer processing, such as a lack of controls over access to applications that initiate or control the movement of assets (for example, a demand deposit application in a bank), high levels of processing errors, or unusual delays in providing processing results and reports?
- Are there indications that management has not developed or communicated adequate policies and procedures for security of data or assets, such as not investigating employees in key positions before hiring, or allowing unauthorized personnel to have ready access to data or assets?

13. The auditor should consider the effect of the matters described in paragraphs 10 to 12 on the overall audit strategy and the expected conduct and scope of the audit.

The Auditor's Response to Risk at the Financial Statement Level

14. The auditor's overall judgment about the level of risk in an engagement may affect engagement staffing, extent of supervision, overall strategy for expected conduct and scope of audit, and degree of professional skepticism applied. Thus, the auditor's assessment of risk may affect audit planning in one or more of the following ways. The experience and training of personnel assigned significant engagement responsibilities should be commensurate with the auditor's assessment of the level of risk for the engagement. Ordinarily, higher risk requires more experienced personnel or more extensive supervision by the auditor with final responsibility for the engagement during both the planning and the conduct of the engagement. Higher risk may cause the auditor to expand the extent of procedures applied, apply procedures closer to or as of the balance sheet date, particularly in critical audit areas, or modify the nature of procedures to obtain more persuasive evidence. Higher risk will also ordinarily cause the auditor to exercise a heightened degree of professional skepticism in conducting the audit (see paragraphs 16 to 21).

The Auditor's Consideration of Audit Risk at the Balance or Class Level

15. The following matters are examples of factors that may influence the auditor's consideration of risk of material misstatement related to particular assertions at the balance or class level:*

- Effect of risk factors identified at the financial statement or engagement level on the particular account balance or transaction class.
- Complexity and contentiousness of accounting issues affecting balance or class.
- Frequency or significance of difficult-to-audit transactions affecting balance or class.
- Nature, cause, and amount of known and likely misstatements detected in the balance or class in the prior audit.
- Susceptibility of related assets to misappropriation.

*Additional factors relating to risk assessment are found in SAS No. 47, *Audit Risk and Materiality in Conducting an Audit* (*AICPA Professional Standards,* vol. 1, AU sec. 312).

- Competence and experience of personnel assigned to processing data that affect the balance or class.
- Extent of judgment involved in determining the total balance or class.
- Size and volume of individual items constituting the balance or class.
- Complexity of calculations affecting the balance or class.

PROFESSIONAL SKEPTICISM

16. An audit of financial statements in accordance with generally accepted auditing standards should be planned and performed with an attitude of professional skepticism. The auditor neither assumes that management is dishonest nor assumes unquestioned honesty. Rather, the auditor recognizes that conditions observed and evidential matter obtained, including information from prior audits, need to be objectively evaluated to determine whether the financial statements are free of material misstatement.

17. Management integrity is important because management can direct subordinates to record transactions or conceal information in a manner that can materially misstate financial statements. When approaching difficult-to-substantiate assertions, the auditor should recognize the increased importance of his consideration of factors that bear on management integrity. A presumption of management dishonesty, however, would be contrary to the accumulated experience of auditors. Moreover, if dishonesty were presumed, the auditor would potentially need to question the genuineness of all records and documents obtained from the client and would require conclusive rather than persuasive evidence to corroborate all management representations. An audit conducted on these terms would be unreasonably costly and impractical.

Professional Skepticism in Audit Planning

18. Whenever the auditor has reached a conclusion that there is significant risk of material misstatement of the financial statements, the auditor reacts in one or more ways. The auditor should consider this assessment in determining the nature, timing, or extent of procedures, assigning staff, or requiring appropriate levels of supervision. The auditor may identify specific transactions involving senior management and confirm the details with appropriate external parties and review in detail all material accounting entries prepared or approved by senior management.

19. The auditor should consider whether accounting policies are acceptable in the circumstances. However, when the auditor has reached a conclusion that there is significant risk of intentional distortion of financial statements, the auditor should recognize that management's selection and application of significant accounting policies, particularly those related to revenue recognition, asset valuation, and capitalization versus expensing, may be misused. Increased risk of intentional distortion of the financial statements should cause greater concern about whether accounting principles that are otherwise generally accepted are being used in inappropriate circumstances to create a distortion of earnings. For example, management might use the percentage of completion method in circumstances that do not justify its use to misstate operating results.

20. When evaluation at the financial statement level indicates significant risk, the auditor requires more or different evidence to support material transactions than would be the case in the absence of such risk. For example, the auditor may

perform additional procedures to determine that sales are properly recorded, giving consideration to the possibility that the buyer has a right to return the product. Transactions that are both large and unusual, particularly at year-end, should be selected for testing.

Professional Skepticism in Performance of the Audit

21. In performing procedures and gathering evidential matter, the auditor continually maintains an attitude of professional skepticism. The performance of auditing procedures during the audit may result in the detection of conditions or circumstances that should cause the auditor to consider whether material misstatements exist. If a condition or circumstance differs adversely from the auditor's expectation, the auditor needs to consider the reason for such a difference. Examples of such conditions or circumstances are as follows:

- Analytical procedures disclose significant differences from expectations.
- Significant unreconciled differences between reconciliations of a control account and subsidiary records or between a physical count and a related account are not appropriately investigated and corrected on a timely basis.
- Confirmation requests disclose significant differences or yield fewer responses than expected.
- Transactions selected for testing are not supported by proper documentation or are not appropriately authorized.
- Supporting records or files that should be readily available are not promptly produced when requested.
- Audit tests detect errors that apparently were known to client personnel, but were not voluntarily disclosed to the auditor.

When such conditions or circumstances exist, the planned scope of audit procedures should be reconsidered. As the number of differences from expectations or the frequency with which the auditor is unable to obtain satisfactory explanations increases, the auditor should consider whether the assessment of the risk of material misstatement of the financial statements made in the planning stage of the engagement is still appropriate.

EVALUATION OF AUDIT TEST RESULTS

22. The auditor should evalute the significance of differences between the accounting records and the underlying facts and circumstances detected by the application of auditing procedures. The auditor should consider both the quantitative and qualitative aspects of these matters and whether they are indicative of an error or an irregularity. Often a particular matter considered in isolation cannot be identified as an error or irregularity; nevertheless, this evaluation is important. Because irregularities are intentional, they have implications beyond their direct monetary effect and the auditor needs to consider the implications for other aspects of the audit.

23. The auditor's objective is to reach a conclusion on whether the financial statements, taken as a whole, are materially misstated. The auditor should accumulate potential audit adjustments during the audit and summarize and evaluate the combined effect. In this regard, the auditor may designate an amount below which poten-

tial audit adjustments need not be accumulated. This amount would be set so that any such adjustments, either individually or when aggregated with other adjustments, would not be material to the financial statements.

24. If the auditor has determined that an audit adjustment is, or may be, an irregularity, but has also determined that the effect on the financial statements could not be material, the auditor should—

a. Refer the matter to an appropriate level of management that is at least one level above those involved.

b. Be satisfied that, in view of the organizational position of the likely perpetrator, the irregularity has no implications for other aspects of the audit or that those implications have been adequately considered.

For example, irregularities involving misappropriation of cash from a small imprest fund would normally be of little significance because both the manner of operating the fund and its size would tend to establish a limit on the amount of loss and the custodianship of such a fund is normally entrusted to a relatively low-level employee.

25. If the auditor has determined that an audit adjustment is, or may be, an irregularity and has either determined that the effect could be material or has been unable to evaluate potential materiality, the auditor should—

a. Consider the implications for other aspects of the audit.

b. Discuss the matter and the approach to further investigation with an appropriate level of management that is at least one level above those involved.

c. Attempt to obtain sufficient competent evidential matter to determine whether, in fact, material irregularities exist and, if so, their effect.

d. If appropriate, suggest that the client consult with legal counsel on matters concerning questions of law.

THE EFFECT OF IRREGULARITIES ON THE AUDIT REPORT

26. If the auditor has concluded that the financial statements are materially affected by an irregularity, the auditor should insist that the financial statements be revised and, if they are not, express a qualified or an adverse opinion on the financial statements, disclosing all substantive reasons for his opinion.

27. If the auditor is precluded from applying necessary procedures, or if, after the application of extended procedures, the auditor is unable to conclude whether possible irregularities may materially affect the financial statements, the auditor should—

a. Disclaim or qualify an opinion on the financial statements.

b. Communicate his findings to the audit committee or the board of directors.

If the client refuses to accept the auditor's report as modified for the circumstances described above, the auditor should withdraw from the engagement and communicate the reasons for withdrawal to the audit committee or board of directors. Whether the auditor concludes that withdrawal from the engagement is appropriate in other circumstances depends on the diligence and cooperation of senior management and the board of directors in investigating the circumstances and taking appropriate remedial action. For example, if the auditor is precluded by the client from obtaining reasonably available evidential matter, withdrawal ordinarily would be appropriate. However, because of the variety of circumstances that may arise, it is not possible to describe all those circumstances when withdrawal would be appropriate.

COMMUNIATIONS CONCERNING ERRORS OR IRREGULARITIES

28. For the audit committee* to make the informed judgments necessary to fulfill its responsibility for the oversight of financial reporting, the auditor should assure himself that the audit committee is adequately informed about any irregularities of which the auditor becomes aware during the audit unless those irregularities are clearly inconsequential.† For example, a minor defalcation by an employee at a low level in the organization might be considered inconsequential. However, irregularities involving senior management of which the auditor becomes aware should be reported directly to the audit committee. Irregularities that are individually immaterial may be reported to the audit committee on an aggregate basis, and the auditor may reach an undrestanding with the audit committee on the nature and amount of reportable irregularities.

29. Disclosure of irregularities to parties other than the client's senior management and its audit committee or board of directors is not ordinarily part of the auditor's responsibility, and would be precluded by the auditor's ethical or legal obligation of confidentiality unless the matter affects his opinion on the financial statements. The auditor should recognize, however, that in the following circumstances a duty to disclose outside the client may exist:

a. When the entity reports an auditor change under the appropriate securities law on Form 8-K.‡

b. To a successor when the successor makes inquiries in accordance with SAS No. 7, *Communications Between Predecessor and Successor Auditors* (AICPA, *Professional Standards,* vol. 1, AU sec. 315).§

c. In response to a subpoena.

d. To a funding agency or other specified agency in accordance with requirements for the audits of entities that receive financial assistance from a government agency.

Because potential conflicts with the auditor's ethical and legal obligations for confidentiality may be complex, the auditor may wish to consult with legal counsel before discussing irregularities with parties outside the client.

RESPONSIBILITIES IN OTHER CIRCUMSTANCES

30. This Statement describes the auditor's responsibilities to detect and report errors and irregularities in an audit of a complete set of financial statements made in accordance with generally accepted auditing standards. In other engagements, the auditor's responsibilities may be more extensive or more restricted, depending on the terms of the engagement.

31. The auditor may accept an engagement that necessitates a more extensive responsibility to detect or report irregularities. For example, in an audit in

*See note on page 59.

†The auditor's responsibility to communicate errors within certain entities whose financial statements are under audit is described in SAS No. 61, *Communication With Audit Committees.*

‡Disclosure to the Securities and Exchange Commission may be necessary if, among other matters, the auditor withdraws because the board of directors has not taken appropriate remedial action. Such failure may be a reportable disagreement on Form 8-K.

§In accordance with SAS No. 7, communications between predecessor and successor auditors require the specific permission of the client.

accordance with *Standards for Audit of Governmental Organizations, Programs, Activities, and Functions, 1981 Revision,* issued by the U.S. General Accounting Office, the auditor should be aware that such standards go beyond generally accepted auditing standards as they relate to notification when the audit indicates that irregularities may exist. These standards require the auditor not only to promptly report instances of irregularities to the audited entity's management, but also to report the matter to the funding agency or other specified agency.

32. When an examination does not encompass a complete set of financial statements or a complete individual financial statement, or when the scope is less extensive than an audit in accordance with generally accepted auditing standards, the auditor's ability to detect material misstatements may be considerably reduced. For example, in an engagement to report on specified elements, accounts, or items of financial statements, the auditor's procedures focus on the specific element, account, or item and the special purpose of the engagement. In these circumstances, the auditor's assessment of risk at the financial statement level and other aspects of the examination that relate to the entity and its financial statements taken as a whole is necessarily more restricted.

APPENDIX

Characteristics of Errors and Irregularities

1. Characteristics of errors and irregularities that are relevant because of their potential influence on the auditor's ability to detect such matters are materiality of the effect on financial statements, level of management or employees involved, extent and skillfulness of any concealment, relationship to established specific control procedures, and the specific financial statements affected.

Materiality

2. SAS No. 47, *Audit Risk and Materiality in Conducting an Audit* (AICPA, *Professional Standards,* vol. 1, AU sec. 312.04), states that "financial statements are materially misstated when they contain errors or irregularities whose effect, individually or in the aggregate, is important enough to cause them not be presented fairly in conformity with generally accepted accounting principles." SAS No. 47, paragraph 13, also states: "The auditor generally plans the audit primarily to detect errors that he believes could be large enough, individually or in the aggregate, to be quantitatively material to the financial statements." As used in SAS No. 47, the term *errors* refers to both errors and irregularities.

3. In planning the audit, the auditor is concerned with matters that could be material to the financial statements. An audit in accordance with generally accepted auditing standards may detect errors or irregularities that are not material to the financial statements, but such an audit can provide no assurance of detecting immaterial errors or irregularities. In this regard, there is no important distinction between errors and irregularities. There is a distinction, however, in the auditor's response to detected matters. Generally, an isolated, immaterial error in processing accounting data or applying accounting principles is not significant to the audit. In contrast, detection of an irregularity requires consideration of the implications for the integrity of management or employees and the possible effect on other aspects of the audit.

Level of Involvement

4. An irregularity may be caused by an employee or by management and, if by management, by a relatively high or low level of management. The experience of auditors indicates that the level of involvement often combines with other characteristics in ways that have an influence on the auditor's ability to detect.

5. Defalcations by employees are often immaterial in amount and concealed in a manner that does not misstate net assets or net income. This type of irregularity can be more efficiently and effectively dealt with by an effective internal control structure and fidelity bonding of employees.

6. Material irregularities perpetrated by senior levels of management, including an owner-manager of a small business, are infrequent, but when they do occur they often engender widespread attention. These irrgularities may not be susceptible to prevention or detection by specific control procedures because senior management is above the controls that deter employees or may override these controls with relative ease. Culture, custom, and the corporate governance system inhibit irregularities by senior management, but are not infallible deterrents. For this reason, an audit in accordance with generally accepted auditing standards necessarily gives due consideration to factors that bear on management integrity and the control environment.

Concealment

7. Concealment is any attempt by the perpetrator of an irregularity to reduce the likelihood of detection. Concealment usually involves manipulation of accounting records or supporting documents to disguise the fact that the accounting records are not in agreement with the underlying facts and circumstances. Concealment can be skillful and elaborate or clumsy and limited. The auditor's ability to detect a concealed irregularity depends on the skillfulness of the perpetrator, the frequency and extent of manipulation, and the relative size of individual amounts manipulated.

8. Forgery may be used to create false signatures, other signs of authenticity, or entire documents. Collusion may result in falsified confirmations or other evidence of validity. Also, unrecorded transactions are normally more difficult to detect than concealment achieved by manipulation of recorded transactions. However, the effect of concealment on the ability to detect an irregularity is dependent on the particular circumstances. For example, an attempt to mislead users of financial statements by recording large, fictitious revenue transactions late in the period without supporting documentaiton would be more readily detected than fictitous revenue transactions spread throughout the period, individually immaterial in amount, and supported by legitimate-appearing invoices and shipping documents. Moreover, both of these irregularities might be extremely difficult, if not impossible, to detect if collusion of customers is added to the concealment scheme.

Internal Control Structure

9. A lack of control procedures could permit an error or irregularity to occur repeatedly and the repeated occurrence could accumulate to a material amount. However, the auditor may not detect an error or irregularity that results from a nonrecurring breakdown of a specific control procedure because a rate item permitted by temporary conditions may not come to light in the performance of analytical or other procedures.

10. Irregularities may also be perpetrated or concealed by circumvention of specific control procedures or may be perpetrated by a level of management above

specific control procedures. These types of irregularities are generally more difficult for an auditor to detect. However, the auditor should consider whether there are circumstances or factors that indicate a higher risk of these types of irregularities and modify auditing procedures accordingly.

Financial Statement Effect

11. Other matters remaining equal, errors or irregularities that involve overstatement will generally be more readily detected than those that involve understatement because the audit evidence available is more reliable for detecting such errors or irregularities. Also, misstatements that are charged to the income statement are less likely to be detected than those that are concealed in the balance sheet, because the process of comparing recorded accountability with the existing assets should detect significant errors concealed in the balance sheet.

Summary

12. The foregoing discussion considers characteristics of errors and irregularities individually and explains the effect an individual characteristic tends to have on the auditor's detection ability. However, these characteristics may interact in particular circumstances in ways that also affect the auditor's ability to detect a specific error or irregularity.[21]

ILLEGAL ACTS BY CLIENTS: THE STANDARD

The auditor's responsibility for detecting misstatements resulting from illegal acts having a direct and material effect on the determination of financial statement amounts is the same as that for other errors and irregularities. Although an examination made in accordance with generally accepted auditing standards cannot be expected to provide assurance that illegal acts will be detected, the auditor should be aware of the possibility that illegal acts may have occurred that may have a material effect on the financial statements. Procedures that are performed for the purpose of expressing an opinion on the financial statements may bring possible illegal acts to the auditor's attention.[22]

"When the auditor becomes aware of information concerning a possible illegal act, the auditor should obtain an understanding of the nature of the act, the circumstances in which it occurred, and sufficient other information to evaluate the effect on the financial statements. In doing so, the auditor should inquire of management at a level above those involved, if possible."[23]

[21]"The Auditor's Responsibility to Detect and Report Errors and Irregularities," *AICPA Professional Standards,* vol. 1, AU Section 316 (Statement on Auditing Standards No. 53). Copyright © 1989 by the American Institute of Certified Public Accountants, Inc.

[22]"Illegal Acts by Clients," *AICPA Professional Standards,* vol. 1, AU Section 317.08 (Statement on Auditing Standards No. 54). Copyright © 1988 by the American Institute of Certified Public Accountants, Inc.

[23]Ibid., AU Section 317.10.

"When the auditor concludes, based on information obtained and, if necessary, consultation with legal counsel, that an illegal act has or is likely to have occurred, the auditor should consider the effect on the financial statements as well as the implications for other aspects of the audit."[24]

"The auditor should assure himself that the audit committee, or others with equivalent authority and responsibility, is adequately informed with respect to illegal acts that come to the auditor's attention. The auditor need not communicate matters that are clearly inconsequential and may reach agreement in advance with the audit committee on the nature of such matters to be communicated."[25]

"Disclosure of an illegal act to parties other than the client's senior management and its audit committee or board of directors is not ordinarily part of the auditor's responsibility, and such disclosure would be precluded by the auditor's ethical or legal obligation of confidentiality, unless the matter affects his opinion on the financial statements. The auditor should recognize, however, that in the following circumstances a duty to notify parties outside the client may exist:

a. When the entity reports an auditor change under the appropriate securities law on Form 8-K.
b. To a successor auditor when the successor makes inquiries in accordance with SAS No. 7, *Communications Between Predecessor and Successor Auditors* (AICPA, *Professional Standards,* vol. 1, AU sec. 315).
c. In response to a subpoena.
d. To a funding agency or other specified agency in accordance with requirements for the audits of entities that receive financial assistance from a government agency.

Because potential conflicts with the auditor's ethical and legal obligations for confidentiality may be complex, the auditor may wish to consult with legal counsel before discussing illegal acts with parties outside the client."[26] These same rules apply for the disclosure of irregularities referred to in Statement on Auditing Standards No. 53, *The Auditor's Responsibility to Detect and Report Errors and Irregularities* (AU Section 316).

There are a variety of circumstances associated with the discovery of illegal acts on the part of the client when the auditor will need to consider qualifying his opinion, disclaiming an opinion, expressing an adverse opinion, or withdrawing from the engagement.[27] The following standard discusses the problem of illegal acts and details those situations in which the auditors' report may be affected:

> 1. This Statement prescribes the nature and extent of the consideration an independent auditor should give to the possibility of illegal acts by a client in an audit of financial statements in accordance with generally accepted auditing standards.

[24]Ibid., AU Section 317.12.
[25]Ibid., AU Section 317.17.
[26]Ibid., AU Section 317.23.
[27]Ibid., AU Section 317.18–317.22.

The Statement also provides guidance on the auditor's responsibilities when a possible illegal act is detected.

DEFINITION OF ILLEGAL ACTS

2. The term *illegal acts,* for purposes of this Statement, refers to violations of laws or governmental regulations. Illegal acts by clients are acts attributable to the entity whose financial statements are under audit or acts by management or employees acting on behalf of the entity. Illegal acts by clients do not include personal misconduct by the entity's personnel unrelated to their business activities.

Dependence on Legal Judgment

3. Whether an act is, in fact, illegal is a determination that is normally beyond the auditor's professional competence. An auditor, in reporting on financial statements, presents himself as one who is proficient in accounting and auditing. The auditor's training experience, and understanding of the client and its industry may provide a basis for recognition that some client acts coming to his attention may be illegal. However, the determination as to whether a particular act is illegal would generally be based on the advice of an informed expert qualified to practice law or may have to await final determination by a court of law.

Relation to Financial Statements

4. Illegal acts vary considerably in their relation to the financial statements. Generally, the further removed an illegal act is from the events and transactions ordinarily reflected in financial statements, the less likely the auditor is to become aware of the act or to recognize its possible illegality.

5. The auditor considers laws and regulations that are generally recognized by auditors to have a direct and material effect on the determination of financial statement amounts. For example, tax laws affect accruals and the amount recognized as expense in the accounting period; applicable laws and regulations may affect the amount of revenue accrued under government contracts. However, the auditor considers such laws or regulations from the perspective of their known relation to audit objectives derived from financial statement assertions rather than from the perspective of legality *per se.* The auditor's responsibility to detect and report misstatements resulting from illegal acts having a direct and material effect on the determination of financial statement amounts is the same as that for errors and irregularities as described in SAS No. 53, *The Auditor's Responsibility to Detect and Report Errors and Irregularities.*

6. Entities may be affected by many other laws or regulations, including those related to securities trading, occupational safety and health, food and drug administration, environmental protection, equal employment, and price-fixing or other antitrust violations. Generally, these laws and regulations relate more to an entity's operating aspects than to its financial and accounting aspects, and their financial statement effect is indirect. An auditor ordinarily does not have sufficient basis for recognizing possible violations of such laws and regulations. Their indirect effect is normally the result of the need to disclose a contingent liability because of the allegation or determination of illegality. For example, securities may be purchased or sold based on inside information. While the direct effects of the purchase or sale may be recorded appropriately, their indirect effect, the possible contingent liability for violating securities laws, may not be appropriately disclosed.

Even when violations of such laws and regulations can have consequences material to the financial statements, the auditor may not become aware of the existence of the illegal act unless he is informed by the client, or there is evidence of a governmental agency investigation or enforcement proceeding in the records, documents, or other information normally inspected in an audit of financial statements.

THE AUDITOR'S CONSIDERATION OF THE POSSIBILITY OF ILLEGAL ACTS

7. As explained in paragraph 5, certain illegal acts have a direct and material effect on the determination of financial statement amounts. Other illegal acts, such as those described in paragraph 6, may, in particular circumstances, be regarded as having material but indirect effects on financial statements. The auditor's responsibility with respect to detecting, considering the financial statement effects of, and reporting these other illegal acts is described in this Statement. These other illegal acts are hereinafter referred to simply as *illegal acts*. The auditor should be aware of the possibility that such illegal acts may have occurred. If specific information comes to the auditor's attention that provides evidence concerning the existence of possible illegal acts that could have a material indirect effect on the financial statements, the auditor should apply audit procedures specifically directed to ascertaining whether an illegal act has occurred. However, because of the characteristics of illegal acts explained above, an audit made in accordance with generally accepted auditing standards provides no assurance that illegal acts will be detected or that any contingent liabilties that may result will be disclosed.

Audit Procedures in the Absence of Evidence Concerning Possible Illegal Acts

8. Normally, an audit in accordance with generally accepted auditing standards does not include audit procedures specifically designed to detect illegal acts. However, procedures applied for the purpose of forming an opinion on the financial statements may bring possible illegal acts to the auditor's attention. For example, such procedures include reading minutes; inquiring of the client's management and legal counsel concerning litigation, claims, and assessments; performing substantive tests of details of transactions or balances. The auditor should make inquiries of management concerning the client's compliance with laws and regulations. Where applicable, the auditor should also inquire of management concerning—

- The client's policies relative to the prevention of illegal acts.
- The use of directives issued by the client and periodic representations obtained by the client from management at appropriate levels of authority concerning compliance with laws and regulations.

The auditor also ordinarily obtains written representations from management concerning the absence of violations or possible violations of laws or regulations whose effects should be considered for disclosuure in the financial statements or as a basis for recording a loss contingency. (See SAS No. 19, *Client Representations* [AICPA, *Professional Standards,* vol. 1, AU sec. 333].) The auditor need perform no further procedures in this area absent specific information concerning possible illegal acts.

Specific Information Concerning Possible Illegal Acts

9. In applying audit procedures and evaluating the results of those procedures, the auditor may encounter specific information that may raise a question concerning possible illegal acts, such as the following:

- Unauthorized transactions, improperly recorded transactions, or transactions not recorded in a complete or timely manner in order to maintain accountability for assets.
- Investigation by a governmental agency, an enforcement proceeding, or payment of unusual fines or penalties.
- Violations of laws or regulations cited in reports of examinations by regulatory agencies that have been made available to the auditor.
- Large payments for unspecified services to consultants, affiliates, or employees.
- Sales commissions or agents fees that appear excessive in relation to those normally paid by the client or to the services actually received.
- Unusually large payments in cash, purchases of bank cashiers' checks in large amounts payable to bearer, transfers to numbered bank accounts, or similar transactions.
- Unexplaiined payments made to government officials or employees.
- Failure to file tax returns or pay government duties or similar fees that are common to the entity's industry or the nature of its business.

Audit Procedures in Response to Possible Illegal Acts

10. When the auditor becomes aware of information concerning a possible illegal act, the auditor should obtain an understanding of the nature of the act, the circumstances in which it occurred, and sufficient other information to evaluate the effect on the financial statements. In doing so, the auditor should inquire of management at a level above those involved, if possible. If management does not provide satisfactory information that there has been no illegal act, the auditor should—

a. Consult with the client's legal counsel or other specialists about the application of relevant laws and regulations to the circumstances and the possible effects on the financial statements. Arrangements for such consultation with client's legal counsel should be made by the client.
b. Apply additional procedures, if necessary, to obtain further understanding of the nature of the acts.

11. The additional audit procedures considered necessary, if any, might include procedures such as the following:

a. Examine supporting documents, such as invoices, canceled checks, and agreements and compare with accounting records.
b. Confirm significant information concerning the matter with the other party to the transaction or with intermediaries, such as banks or lawyers.
c. Determine whether the transaction has been properly authorized.
d. Consider whether other similar transactions or events may have occurred, and apply procedures to identify them.

THE AUDITOR'S RESPONSE TO DETECTED ILLEGAL ACTS

12. When the auditor concludes, based on information obtained and, if necessary, consultation with legal counsel, that an illegal act has or is likely to have occurred, the auditor should consider the effect on the financial statements as well as the implications for other aspects of the audit.

The Auditor's Consideration of Financial Statement Effect

13. In evaluating the materiality of an illegal act that comes to his attention, the auditor should consider both the quantitative and qualitative materiality of the act. For example, SAS No. 47, *Audit Risk and Materiality in Conducting an Audit* (AICPA, *Professional Standards,* vol. 1, AU sec. 312.07) states that "an illegal payment of an otherwise immaterial amount could be material if there is a reasonable possibility that it could lead to a material contingent liability or a material loss of revenue."

14. The auditor should consider the effect of an illegal act on the amounts presented in financial statements including contingent monetary effects, such as fines, penalties and damages. Loss contingencies resulting from illegal acts that may be required to be disclosed should be evaluated in the same manner as other loss contingencies. Examples of loss contingencies that may arise from an illegal act are: threat of expropriation of assets, enforced discontinuance of operations in another country, and litigation.

15. The auditor should evaluate the adequacy of disclosure in the financial statements of the potential effects of an illegal act on the entity's operations. If material revenue or earnings are derived from transactions involving illegal acts, or if illegal acts create significant unusual risks associated with material revenue or earnings, such as loss of a significant business relationship, that information should be considered for disclosure.

Implications for Audit

16. The auditor should consider the implications of an illegal act in relation to other aspects of the audit, particularly the reliability of representations of management. The implications of particular illegal acts will depend on the relationship of the perpetration and concealment, if any, of the illegal act to specific control procedures and the level of management or employees involved.

Communication With the Audit Committee

17. The auditor should assure himself that the audit committee or others with equivalent authority and responsibility, is adequately informed with respect to illegal acts that come to the auditor's attention.* The auditor need not communicate matters that are clearly inconsequential and may reach agreement in advance with the audit committee on the nature of such matters to be communicated. The communication should describe the act, the circumstances of its occurrence, and the effect on the financial statements. Senior management may wish to have its remedial actions communicated to the audit committee simultaneously. Possible remedial actions

*For entities that do not have audit committees, the phrase "others with equivalent authority and responsibility" may include the board of directors, the board of trustees, or the owner in owner-managed entities.

include disciplinary action against involved personnel, seeking restitution, adoption of preventive or corrective company policies, and modifications of specific control procedures. If senior management is involved in an illegal act, the auditor should communicate directly with the audit committee. The communication may be oral or written. If the communication is oral, the auditor should document it.

Effect on the Auditor's Report

18. If the auditor concludes that an illegal act has a material effect on the financial statements, and the act has not been properly accounted for or disclosed, the auditor should express a qualified opinion or an adverse opinion on the financial statements taken as a whole, depending on the materiality of the effect on the financial statements.

19. If the auditor is precluded by the client from obtaining sufficient competent evidential matter to evaluate whether an illegal act that could be material to the financial statements has, or is likely to have, occurred, the auditor generally should disclaim an opinion on the financial statements.

20. If the client refuses to accept the auditor's report as modified for the circumstances described in paragraphs 18 and 19, the auditor should withdraw from the engagement and indicate the reasons for withdrawal in writing to the audit committee or board of directors.

21. The auditor may be unable to determine whether an act is illegal because of limitations imposed by the circumstances rather than by the client or because of uncertainty associated with interpretation of applicable laws or regulations or surrounding facts. In these circumstances, the auditor should consider the effect on his report.*

OTHER CONSIDERATIONS IN AN AUDIT IN ACCORDANCE WITH GENERALLY ACCEPTED AUDITING STANDARDS

22. In addition to the need to withdraw from the engagement, as described in paragraph 20, the auditor may conclude that withdrawal is necessary when the client does not take the remedial action that the auditor considers necessary in the circumstances even when the illegal act is not material to the financial statements. Factors that should affect the auditor's conclusion include the implications of the failure to take remedial action, which may affect the auditor's ability to rely on management representations, and the effects of continuing association with the client. In reaching a conclusion on such matters, the auditor may wish to consult with his own legal counsel.

23. Disclosure of an illegal act to parties other than the client's senior management and its audit committee or board of directors is not ordinarily part of the auditor's responsibility, and such disclosure would be precluded by the auditor's ethical or legal obligation of confidentiality, unless the matter affects his opinion on the financial statements. The auditor should recognize, howver, that in the following circumstances a duty to notify parties outside the client may exist:

a. When the entity reports an auditor change under the appropriate securities law on Form 8-k.**

*See SAS No. 58, *Reports on Audited Financial Statements.*

**Disclosure to the Securities and Exchange Commission may be necessary if, among other matters, the auditor withdraws because the board of directors has not taken appropriate remedial action. Such failure may be a reportable disagreement on Form 8-K.

b. To a successor auditor when the successor makes inquiries in accordance with SAS No. 7, *Communications Between Predecessor and Successor Auditors* (AICPA, *Professional Standards,* vol. 1, AU sec. 315).*
c. In response to a subpoena.
d. To a funding agency or other specified agency in accordance with requirements for the audits of entities that receive financial assistance from a government agency.

Because potential conflicts with the auditor's ethical and legal obligations for confidentiality may be complex, the auditor may wish to consult with legal counsel before discussing illegal acts with parties outside the client.

RESPONSIBILITIES IN OTHER CIRCUMSTANCES

24. An auditor may accept an engagement that entails a greater responsibility for detecting illegal acts than that specified in this Statement. For example, a governmental unit may engage an independent auditor to perform an audit in accordance with the Single Audit Act of 1984. In such an engagement, the independent auditor is responsible for testing and reporting on the governmental unit's compliance with certain laws and regulations applicable to Federal financial assistance programs. Also, an independent auditor may undertake a variety of other special engagements. For example, a corporation's board of directors or its audit committee may engage an auditor to apply agreed-upon procedures and report on compliance with the corporation's code of conduct under the attestation standards.[28]

LETTER FROM LEGAL COUNSEL

One particularly difficult standard faced by the auditor concerns loss contingencies. A loss contingency is defined as "an existing condition, situation, or set of circumstances involving uncertainty" as to the possible loss to an enterprise that "will ultimately be resolved when one or more future events occur or fail to occur."[29]

"An estimated loss from a loss contingency" shall be accrued by a charge to income if *both* of the following conditions are met:

a. Information available prior to issuance of the financial statements indicates that it is probable that an asset had been impaired or a liability had been incurred at the date of the financial statements. It is implicit in this condition that it must be probable that one or more future events will occur confirming the fact of the loss.

*In accordance with SAS No. 7, communications between predecessor and successor auditors requires the specific permission of the client.

[28]"Illegal Acts by Clients," *AICPA Professional Standards,* vol. 1, AU Section 317 (Statement on Auditing Standards No. 54). Copyright 1988 by the American Institute of Certified Public Accountants, Inc.

[29]"Contingencies," *Accounting Standards Current Text* (Norwalk, Conn.: Financial Accounting Standards Board, 1988), Section C59.101. Copyright © 1988 by Financial Accounting Standards Board, 401 Merritt 7, P.O. Box 5116, Norwalk, Connecticut, 06856–5116. U.S.A. Reprinted with permission. Copies of the complete document are available from the FASB.

b. The amount of the loss can be reasonably estimated.[30]

If no accrual is made for a loss contingency because one or both of the above conditions are not met, or if an exposure to loss exists in excess of the amount accrued pursuant to the provisions above, "disclosure of the contingency shall be made when there is at least a reasonable possibility that a loss or an additional loss may have been incurred.[31] Disclosure may also be necessary with regard to losses or loss contingencies coming to the auditor's attention after the date of an enterprise's financial statements, but before those statements are issued.[32]

A major problem arises in connection with pending or threatened litigation and actual or possible claims and assessments. How does the auditor assure himself that losses or contingent losses therefrom have been properly accrued or disclosed?

He must look in this regard to management and to the client's lawyer. The following standard discusses this problem.

> 1. This section provides guidance on the procedures an independent auditor should consider for identifying litigation, claims, and assessments and for satisfying himself as to the financial accounting and reporting for such matters when he is performing an examination in accordance with generally accepted auditing standards.

ACCOUNTING CONSIDERATIONS

> 2. Management is responsible for adopting policies and procedures to identify, evaluate, and account for litigation, claims, and assessments as a basis for the preparation of financial statements in conformity with generally accepted accounting principles.
>
> 3. The standards of financial accounting and reporting for loss contingencies, including those arising from litigation, claims, and assessments, are set forth in Statement of Financial Accounting Standards No. 5., "Accounting for Contingencies."

AUDITING CONSIDERATIONS

> 4. With respect to litigation, claims, and assessments, the independent auditor should obtain evidential matter relevant to the following factors:
>
> a. The existence of a condition, situation, or set of circumstances indicating an uncertainty as to the possible loss to an entity arising from litigation, claims, and assessments.
> b. The period in which the underlying cause for legal action occurred.
> c. The degree of probability of an unfavorable outcome.
> d. The amount or range of potential loss.

[30]Ibid., Section C59.105.
[31]Ibid., Section C59.109.
[32]Ibid., Section C59.112.

Audit Procedures

5. Since the events or conditions that should be considered in the financial accounting for and reporting of litigation, claims, and assessments are matters within the direct knowledge and, often, control of management of an entity, management is the primary source of information about such matters. Accordingly, the independent auditor's procedures with respect to litigation, claims, and assessments should include the following:

a. Inquire of and discuss with management the policies and procedures adopted for identifying, evaluating, and accounting for litigation, claims, and assessments.
b. Obtain from management a description and evaluation of litigation, claims, and assessments that existed at the date of the balance sheet being reported on, and during the period from the balance sheet date to the date the information is furnished, including an identification of those matters referred to legal counsel, and obtain assurances from management, ordinarily in writing, that they have disclosed all such matters required to be disclosed by Statement of Financial Accounting Standards No. 5.
c. Examine documents in the client's possession concerning litigation, claims, and assessments, including correspondence and invoices from lawyers.
d. Obtain assurance from management, ordinarily in writing, that it has disclosed all unasserted claims that the lawyer has advised them are probable of assertion and must be disclosed in accordance with Statement of Financial Accounting Standards No. 5. Also the auditor, with the client's permission, should inform the lawyer that the client has given the auditor this assurance. This client representation may be communicated by the client in the inquiry letter or by the auditor in a separate letter.*

6. An auditor ordinarily does not possess legal skills and, therefore, cannot make legal judgments concerning information coming to his attention. Accordingly, the auditor should request the client's management to send a letter of inquiry to those lawyers with whom management consulted concerning litigation, claims, and assessments.

7. The independent auditor's examination normally includes certain other procedures undertaken for different purposes that might also disclose litigation, claims, and assessments. Example of such procedures are as follows:

a. Reading minutes of meetings of stockholders, directors, and appropriate committees held during and subsequent to the period being examined.
b. Reading contracts, loan agreements, leases, and correspondence from taxing or other governmental agencies, and similar documents.
c. Obtaining information concerning guarantees from bank confirmation forms.
d. Inspecting other documents for possible guarantees by the client.

*An example of a separate letter is as follows: We are writing to inform you that (name of company) has represented to us that (except as set forth below and excluding any such matters listed in the letter of audit inquiry) there are not unasserted possible claims that you have advised are probably of assertion and must be disclosed in accordance with *Statement of Financial Accounting Standards* No. 5 [AC Section 4311] in its financial statements of (balance sheet date) and for the (period) then ended. (List unasserted possible claims, if any.) Such a letter should be signed and sent by the auditor.

Inquiry of a Client's Lawyer

8. A letter of audit inquiry to the client's lawyer is the auditor's primary means of obtaining corroboration of the information furnished by management concerning litigation, claims, and assessments.* Evidential matter obtained from the client's inside general counsel or legal department may provide the auditor with the necessary corroboration. However, evidential matter obtained from inside counsel is not a substitute for information outside counsel refuses to furnish.

9. The matters that should be covered in a letter of audit inquiry include, but are not limited to, the following:

a. Identification of the company, including subsidiaries, and the date of examination.
b. A list prepared by management (or a request by management that the lawyer prepare a list) that describes and evaluates pending or threatened litigation, claims, and assessments with respect to which the lawyer has been engaged and to which he has devoted substantive attention on behalf of the company in the form of legal consultation or representation.
c. A list prepared by management that describes and evaluates unasserted claims and assessments that management considers to be probable of assertion, and that, if asserted, would have at least a reasonable possibility of an unfavorable outcome, with respect to which the lawyer has been engaged and to which he has devoted substantive attention on behalf of the company in the form of legal consultation or representation.
d. As to each matter listed in item b, a request that the lawyer either furnish the following information or comment on these matters as to which his views may differ from those stated by management, as appropriate:
   (1) A description of the nature of the matter, the progress of the case to date, and the action of the company intends to take (for example, to contest the matter vigorously or to seek an out-of-court settlement).
   (2) An evaluation of the likelihood of an unfavorable outcome and an estimate, if one can be made, of the amount or range of potential loss.
   (3) With respect to a list prepared by management, an identification of the omission of any pending or threatened litigation, claims, and assessments or a statement that the list of such matters is complete.
e. As to each matter listed in item c, a request that the lawyer comment on those matters as to which his views concerning the description or evaluation of the matter may differ from those stated by management.
f. A statement by the client that the client understands that whenever, in the course of performing legal services for the client with respect to a matter recognized to involve an unasserted possible claim or assessment that may call for financial statement disclosure, the lawyer has formed a professional conclusion that the client should disclose or consider disclosure concerning such possible claim or assessment, the lawyer, as a matter of professional responsibility to the client, will so advise the client and will consult with the client concerning the questions of such disclosure and the applicable requirements of Statement of Financial Accounting Standards No. 5.

*It is not intended that the lawyer be requested to undertake a reconsideration of all matters upon which he was consulted during the period under examination for the purpose of determining whether he can form a conclusion regarding the probability of assertion of any possible claim inherent in any of the matters so considered.

g. A request that the lawyer confirm whether the understanding described in item f is correct.

h. A request that the lawyer specifically identify the nature of and reasons for any limitation on his response.

Inquiry need not be made concerning matters that are not considered material, provided the client and the auditor have reached an understanding on the limits of materiality for this purpose.

10. In special circumstances, the auditor may obtain a response concerning matters covered by the audit inquiry letter in a conference, which offers an opportunity for a more detailed discussion and explanation than a written reply. A conference may be appropriate when the evaluation of the need for accounting for or disclosure of litigation, claims, and assessments involves such matters as the evaluation of the effect of legal advice concerning unsettled points of law, the effect of uncorroborated information, or other complex judgments. The auditor should appropriately document conclusions reached concerning the need for accounting for or disclosure of litigation, claims, and assessments.

11. In some circumstances, a lawyer may be required by his Code of Professional Responsibility to resign his engagement if his advice concerning financial accounting and reporting for litigation, claims, and assessments is disregarded by the client. When the auditor is aware that a client has changed lawyers or that a lawyer engaged by the client has resigned, the auditor should consider the need for inquiries concerning the reasons the lawyer is no longer associated with the client.

Limitations on the Scope of a Lawyer's Response*

12. A lawyer may appropriately limit his response to matters in which he has given substantive attention in the form of legal consultation or representation. Also, a lawyer's response may be limited to matters that are considered individually or collectively material to the financial statements, provided the lawyer and auditor have reached an understanding on the limits of materiality for this purpose. Such limitations are not limitations on the scope of the auditor's examination.

13. A lawyer's refusal to furnish the information requested in an inquiry letter either in writing or orally (see paragraphs 9 and 10) would be a limitation on the scope of the auditor's examination sufficient to preclude an unqualified opinion (see Section 509.10–11).** A lawyer's response to such an inquiry and the procedures set forth in paragraph 5 provide the auditor with sufficient evidential matter to satisfy himself concerning the accounting for and reporting of pending and threatened litigation, claims and assessments. The auditor obtains sufficient evidential matter to satisfy himself concerning reporting for those unasserted claims and assessments required to be disclosed in financial statements from the foregoing procedures and the lawyer's specific acknowledgment of his responsibility to his

*The American Bar Association has approved a "Statement of Policy Regarding Lawyer's Response to Auditor's Requests for Information," which explains the concerns of lawyers and the nature of the limitations an auditor is likely to encounter. (See Appendix 11.)

**A refusal to respond should be distinguished from an inability to form a conclusion with respect to certain matters of judgment (see paragraph 14). Also, lawyers outside the United States sometimes follow practices at variance with those contemplated by this section to the extent that different procedures from those outlined herein may be necessary. In such circumstances, the auditor should exercise judgment in determining whether alternative procedures are adequate to comply with the requirement of this section.

client in respect of disclosure obligations (see paragraph 9g). This approach with respect to unasserted claims and assessments is necessitated by the public interest in protecting the confidentiality of lawyer-client communications.

Other Limitations on a Lawyer's Response

14. A lawyer may be unable to respond concerning the likelihood of an unfavorable outcome of litigation, claims, and assessment or the amount or range of potential loss, because of inherent uncertainties. Factors influencing the likelihood of an unfavorable outcome may sometimes not be within a lawywer's competence to judge; historical experience of the entity in similar litigation or the experience of other entities may not be relevant or available; and the amount of the possible loss frequently may vary widely at different stages of litigation. Consequently, a lawyer may not be able to form a conclusion with respect to such matters. In such circumstances, the auditor ordinarily will conclude that the financial statements are affected by an uncertainty concerning the outcome of a future event which is not susceptible of reasonable estimation. If the effect of the matter on the financial statements could be material, the auditor ordinarily will conclude that he is unable to express an unqualified opinion (see Section 509.21–26).[33]

QUESTIONS AND CASES

3–1 What are the four general standards which all professional accountants must follow?

3–2 What should be your authority in the area of accounting principles? Your own good judgment? Are opinions issued by the Accounting Principles Board still valid? What about the Cost Accounting Standards Board?

3–3 As an auditor expressing an opinion on the financial statements of a client, is it ever ethical for you to sanction a departure from "generally accepted accounting principles?" What reporting responsibilities do you have if such a departure takes place?

3–4 What are the ten generally accepted auditing standards? Where did these standards originate and who interprets them?

3–5 Are any general or technical standards addressed in the Statements on Standards for Management Advisory Services? The Statements on Responsibilities in Tax Practice? What are they?

3–6 What general and technical standards are addressed in the Code of Ethics of the Institute of Internal Auditors? In the Standards for the Professional Practice of Internal Auditing?

3–7 As an audit partner with a large CPA firm, you have assumed a major role in practice development. In a discussion with the Audit Committee of a prospective client, it becomes apparent to you that the committee regards the detection of fraud as one

[33]"Inquiry of a Client's Lawyer Concerning Litigation, Claims, and Assessments," *AICPA Professional Standards,* vol. 1, AU Section 337 (Statement on Auditing Standards No. 12). Copyright 1989 by the American Institute of Certified Public Accountants, Inc.

of an auditor's main responsibilities. How would you respond to them? What are the auditor's responsibilities in this area according to the written standards of the profession?

3–8 To what extent can an auditor rely upon the representations of management? Is it reasonable for him to assume that no material misrepresentations have been made and that control procedures have not been overridden?

3–9 What is the auditor's obligation when his examination causes him to believe that material errors or irregularities may exist? With whom should he discuss the matter? Should he extend his audit procedures? Under what circumstances should he consider withdrawing from the engagement?

3–10 How does an auditor assure himself that losses or contingent losses from pending or threatened litigation have been properly accrued or disclosed? What audit procedures are needed? What is the role of a letter of inquiry to the client's lawyer? Are there any limitations on the scope of a lawyer's response?

3–11 (*Joann Gidday*)

Assume that in conducting an audit, you review minutes of the Board of Directors' meetings as well as correspondence and invoices from lawyers, and you hold discussions with management concerning contingencies which may need to be disclosed. You request and receive from management a written description of litigation, claims, and assessments as of the balance sheet date and also for the period from the balance sheet date to the date the information is published. Management also states in writing that it has disclosed all matters required by Statement of Financial Accounting Standards No. 5.

What additional assurances do you, as an auditor, require?

3–12 (*Mark Farner*)

John Doe, CPA, was asked to audit the books and financial statements of a pharmaceutical division of Jones Chemical Company, which manufactures many prescription drugs. This is the first audit of Jones that Mr. Doe has performed. When Mr. Doe inquired of management as to why they had changed auditors, he was told that due to an increase in clients, the former auditor believed he could not spend the time necessary to do a thorough audit and that it would be in the company's best interests to seek another auditor. Communication between Mr. Doe and the former auditor confirmed this.

Mr. Doe obtained an understanding of the company's internal control structure, assessed the control risk, and used this understanding to determine the nature, timing, and extent of substantive tests. Mr. Doe then proceeded to conduct the audit, and, as a result of preliminary work, reduced the number of transactions to be tested by using a statistical sampling technique. He followed generally accepted auditing procedures and found no irregularities and only a few material errors, which were promptly corrected by the management and related departments. Based on his audit findings, he issued an unqualified report on the financial statements.

Two years later, two Jones Chemical Company employees and one bank officer were charged with misappropriation of assets. Suits were filed by the company against the employees and the bank officer, and a suit was threatened against the auditor.

Has the auditor, John Doe, violated the AICPA Code of Professional Conduct in his conduct of the audit? Should he have detected the fraud?

3–13 (*Mark Farner*)

You are one of the staff of CPAs assigned to audit the financial statements of an automobile manufacturer. The company has been doing fairly well despite a soft market industry-wide. During the past few years, however, the company has experienced safety problems with one of their better selling models, which has been associated with the deaths of several drivers and occupants of the car. The government ordered the manufacturer to recall the car model and correct the situation. Lawsuits have been filed against the company by survivors of the accident victims. These are multi-million dollar suits and may have an impact on the financial statements that the company intends to issue.

Legal counsel for the company indicates an inability to predict any outcomes. To date, there are no case precedents which could indicate whether the ruling would be in favor of the plaintiff or defendent.

How should this situation be reflected in the manufacturer's financial statements? Can the auditor give an unqualified opinion?

3–14 (*Ann Sapp*)

As part of their audit procedures, Fast and Goode, CPA's, requested a cutoff statement from their client's bank. Fast and Goode found that the checks that cleared the cutoff statement and the remaining outstanding checks did not tie to the bookkeeper's reconciliation. The senior on the job asked the bookkeeper about the discrepancies and after working on the problem for an hour or so, she explained the differences. However, the senior found that in recent months the bookkeeper had been separating the bank statements and the canceled checks, and had been filing all canceled checks in numerical order. An exception occurred for one month's statement, which happened to arrive on a day when she was at home ill. That day a part-time assistant filed the checks.

The senior consulted with the audit manager, who spoke with the company's president about their suspicion that the bookkeeper was misappropriating funds.

After securing duplicate copies of certain missing canceled checks from the bank, the auditors determined that the bookkeeper had written almost $2,500 in extra payroll checks to herself over the last 14 months. (This amount is not material to the client.) She had used various methods to conceal the thefts, one of which was the use of a signature plate used to sign payroll checks.

The investigation revealed that the bookkeeper had already taken two extra checks at the time of the previous year's audit. These were not discovered last year even though the audit was conducted in accordance with generally accepted auditing standards.

Should Fast and Goode be held responsible for not uncovering the fraud in the previous year? Should their opinion on the current year's financial statements be qualified?

3–15 (*Michael Schuh*)

At mid-year the entire management team changed at a large hotel audited by your firm. In September, the new management fired the former night auditor and the bookkeeper. Previously, the hotel had good control procedures, but preliminary observations this year indicate a lowering of standards. Additionally, analytical review of the account balances reveals several "red flag" areas.

Should the audit program be modified to detect possible errors and irregularities?

3–16 (*Charles Belote*)

After two years of experience as a sole practitioner, a CPA is asked to perform an audit of a small electronic parts manufacturing firm. The procedures used by the manufacturer are specialized and many of its contracts are with the Federal government, which requires the use of separate cost accounting systems. The CPA has had no previous experience with the electronics industry or with governmental accounting.

Is the CPA prohibited from accepting the engagement because of lack of professional competence?

3–17 (*Joyce Christian*)

The firm of Smith and Warner has done the audit of Lifo Health Insurance Company for the past two years. The hierarchy of control at Lifo Health Insurance Company is as follows:

Associates
•
Field Representatives
•
Office Manager
•
Assistant Office Manager

During the customary inquiry of Lifo's assistant office manager, the audit senior of Smith and Warner was told of a number of irregularities in various expense accounts which were originated by one of the field representatives, who charged many of his personal expenses (including groceries, traffic tickets, mileage on personal trips, and veterinary bills) to the business. Additionally, legitimate business expense accounts were adjusted downward at year-end when necessary to ensure a desirable net income figure.

The strategy used to implement these irregularities was for the field representative to require the assistant office manager to record the personal transactions throughout the year. At year end, adjusting entries were made to insure an "appropriate" year-end balance in the different accounts. The assistant office manager was told that if she did not make these entries, she would lose her job. As a divorced high school dropout and mother of three, she believed she had no choice but to comply with these demands. Recently, however, she has become unhappy with her job since she did not receive a promised increase in weekly income. Her dissatisfaction brought about these confessions.

What course of action should the audit senior take at this point in time? How do materiality considerations affect the appropriate course of action? What impact might uncertainty concerning the irregularities have on the reporting responsibilities in this case?

3–18 (*Victor Goetz*)
You are a young CPA whose major client requests advice about a tax matter. Your advice is to take an aggressive stand on the matter, which lowers the tax liability by $50,000. Shortly thereafter, you notice in a tax publication that a law relevant to the matter has been changed, which may render your advice incorrect: a Tax Court case upon which you relied has been overruled by the Sixth Circuit Court of Appeals. You are in the Fifth Circuit.

Do you have to inform your client of this change in the law?

Assume that you do so inform her. Can you still prepare the return using your first position if she requests that you do?

Would it make any difference in the preceding questions if the U.S. Supreme Court had been the overruling court?

3–19 Elliott Blake, a CPA who practices in Lansing, Michigan, is in the process of completing the design and implementation of a new accounting system for one of his clients. As he is walking out the door one day, the controller asks him a question relative to the possible purchase of some new equipment. Are there any professional standards relating to this situation? Can Elliott respond orally to the controller's question?

3–20 Jim Dandy, after ten years with an international public accounting firm, accepted an offer to join a smaller firm in his home town. The smaller firm had only five partners, and he was now the sixth and youngest. In addition to an extensive tax practice, the firm has a number of audit clients.

In a conversation with one of his senior partners, Jim is surprised to learn that no attempt is made in any of the audits to detect fraud. Oscar Oldhead patiently explained to Jim that the purpose of an audit was to form an opinion on whether the financial statements present fairly the financial position, results of operations, and cash flows in conformity with generally accepted accounting principles consistently applied. "Didn't they teach you that in school, young fellow," said Oscar.

How should Jim reply to Oscar?

4

RESPONSIBILITIES TO CLIENTS, MANAGEMENT, AND OWNERS

INTRODUCTION

Every professional accountant has certain responsibilities to the party or parties he serves. If in public accounting, that party is a client. If practicing internally, it may be top management, a board of directors, and owners. One of the Principles of the Code of Professional Conduct of the American Institute of Certified Public Accountants, although written for CPAs, applies equally to all internal professionals.

> In carrying out their responsibilities as professionals, members should exercise sensitive professional and moral judgments in all their activities.[1]

The elaboration of the Principle reads as follows:

> As professionals, certified public accountants perform an essential role in society. Consistent with that role, members of the American Institute of Certified Public Accountants have responsibilities to all those who use their professional services. Members also have a continuing responsibility to cooperate with each other to

[1]"Responsibilities," *AICPA Professional Standards*, vol. 2, ET Section 52. Copyright © 1988 by the American Institute of Certified Public Accountants, Inc.

improve the art of accounting, maintain the public's confidence, and carry out the profession's special responsibilities for self-governance. The collective efforts of all members are required to maintain and enhance the traditions of the profession.[2]

THE AUDITOR

One of an auditor's first responsibilities to a client deals with confidential information obtained in the course of a professional engagement. Generally, such information cannot be disclosed without the specific consent of the client. This rule, however, has several exceptions. For example, the auditor is required to comply with generally accepted auditing standards and to describe departures from these standards. He is also required to describe departures from generally accepted accounting principles.

It would not be a violation of responsibility to a client, for example, if an auditor qualified his opinion and disclosed the fact that a client had dividend arrearages or liens on some of his assets.[3] It would also not be a violation of the auditor's responsibility to a client if it were disclosed that a client capitalized research and development costs, for example, rather than expensing them as required by generally accepted accounting principles.[4]

The rule requiring auditors not to disclose confidential information is not used (a) "to affect in any way the member's obligation to comply with a validly issued and enforceable subpoena or summons," (b) "to prohibit review of a member's professional practice under AICPA or state CPA society authorization," or (c) "to preclude a member from initiating a complaint with or responding to any inquiry made by a recognized investigative or disciplinary body."[5]

Suppose that you are the managing partner of a major CPA firm, and that you have two audit clients, one of which sold some natural resource properties to the other. Suppose further that you know the assets are being overvalued by the selling company. Do you have an obligation to tell the buying company about it or is that information confidential?

In a real life case similar to this, the auditor concluded that such information is confidential and did not tell the second client. Unfortunately, the buying company subsequently went bankrupt and its stockholders sued the auditor for not disclosing the information to them. In a jury trial, the auditors were found guilty and ordered to pay a substantial sum to the injured party (*Arthur Andersen & Co.* v. *Fund of Funds, Ltd.*).

In a parallel case, another major public accounting firm learned that the liabilities of one of its clients exceeded its assets by a substantial amount. The firm

[2]Ibid., ET Section 52.01.

[3]"Adequacy of Disclosure in Financial Statements," *AICPA Professional Standards*, vol. 1, AU Section 431.03.

[4]"Research and Development," *Accounting Standards Current Text* (Norwalk, Conn.: Financial Accounting Standards Board, 1989) Section R50, and "Adherence to Generally Accepted Accounting Principles," *AICPA Professional Standards*, vol. 1, AU Section 410.

[5]"Confidential Client Information," *AICPA Professional Standards*, vol. 2, ET Section 301.01.

advised several of its other clients to stop sending money to the ailing client, a bookkeeping and payroll company. The ailing company subsequently went into receivership, and sued the accounting firm, charging that the disclosures had put it out of business. In another jury trial, the firm was found guilty of negligence and breach of contract for breaking an obligation of confidentiality (*Alexander Grant & Co.* v. *Consolidata Services, Inc.*).

Thus, two separate juries came to opposite conclusions on the issue of confidential information. One firm was found guilty of not disclosing information and another was found guilty of disclosing it. The best advice still, however, is to follow the AICPA Code of Professional Conduct (ET Section 301), and not disclose any confidential client information without the specific consent of the client.

The auditor also has definite responsibilities arising out of the consideration of an entity's internal control structure made in connection with an audit. Such a consideration is required under generally accepted auditing standards.[6] Any significant deficiencies in the design or operation of the internal control structure which could adversely affect the organization's ability to record, process, summarize, and report financial data consistent with the assertions of management in the financial statements (referred to as reportable conditions) must be communicated to the audit committee.[7] The question of internal control and the auditor's duties will be more thoroughly discussed in a later section of this chapter.

THE MANAGEMENT CONSULTANT

Statements on Standards for Management Advisory Services have a direct relation to the accountant's responsibility to the client. "Before beginning an MAS engagement," a practitioner should "obtain an understanding of the possible benefits, both tangible and intangible, that the client wishes to achieve." Furthermore, the practitioner should "communicate to the client reservations concerning the achievability of the anticipated benefits."[8] Assume, for example, that you have been asked by a small manufacturing company in your area to conduct a detailed study and evaluation of their cost accounting system. Having just completed an audit of the company less than six months ago, you are very familiar with the system and are convinced that it is a sound one. Should you accept the engagement?

Clearly, you would have an obligation in this case to communicate your reservations about the need for a review to the client. If the client still wants you to conduct the study, you may do so. Even though no direct financial benefit may come from the study, it may reassure the client that his system is a good one, and only he can decide whether that kind of benefit is worthwhile.

[6]"Generally Accepted Auditing Standards," *AICPA Professional Standards,* vol. 1, AU Section 150.02.

[7]"Communications of Internal Control Structure Related Matters Noted in an Audit," *AICPA Professional Standards,* vol. 1, AU Section 325.02 (Statement on Auditing Standards No. 60).

[8]"MAS Engagements," *AICPA Professional Standards,* vol. 2, MS Section 21.21 and 21.22. Copyright © 1982 by the American Institute of Certified Public Accountants, Inc.

Before undertaking an engagement, a practitioner should consider such matters as the following in reaching an appropriate understanding with the client:

1. Engagement objectives
2. Nature of the services to be performed
3. Engagement scope, including areas of client operations to be addressed and limitations or constraints, if any
4. Respective roles, responsibilities, and relationships of the MAS practitioner, the client, and other parties to the engagement
5. The anticipated engagement approaches, including major tasks or activities to be performed and, if appropriate, methods to be used
6. The manner in which engagement status and results are to be communicated
7. Work schedule
8. Fee arrangements[9]

MAS engagements normally include a documented understanding with the client, which may be in the form of an accepted proposal letter, a confirmation letter, an engagement arrangement letter, a contract, or a file memorandum documenting an oral understanding. When the engagement is completed, the principal findings, conclusions, recommendations, or other results, including the major facts and assumptions upon which results are based, should be communicated to the client, together with limitations, reservations, or other qualifications.[10]

When an engagement is completed, a final report should be given to the client. This report "may be written or oral, depending on such factors as:

1. The understanding with the client
2. The degree to which the engagement results are provided to the client as the engagement progresses
3. The intended use of engagement results
4. Sensitivity or significance of material covered
5. The need for a formal record of the engagement

When an MAS practitioner does not issue a written report to the client, a memorandum to the file should be considered, outlining matters such as results achieved and documentation provided to the client."[11]

What about a situation in which a management consultant attains expertise as a result of work for one client and is then engaged by another client with a similar problem? Assume, for example, that you have just completed an evaluation of the feasibility of purchasing a particular computer system. This study, which led you

[9]Ibid., MS Section 21.17.
[10]Ibid., MS Sections 21.18 and 21.24.
[11]Ibid., MS Sections 21.26 and 21.27.

to a negative conclusion as regards Client A, also suggests a negative conclusion with regard to Client B. Can you disclose to Client B the information and conclusions you reached with regard to Client A? Should you disclose the facts of your prior study without the conclusions?

Rule 301 of the AICPA Code of Professional Conduct provides that "a member in public practice shall not disclose any confidential client information without the specific consent of the client."[12] "Knowledge and expertise which results in a special competence in a particular field" can be provided to a client, however, without violating the confidence of another client. The reservations you have concerning the purchase of the computer system should be communicated to Client B, but the details of the other engagement should not be disclosed. If the circumstances are such that Client B would "clearly know the origin of the information" on which the advice is based and "such information is sensitive," the engagement should not be accepted without clearance from Client A.[13]

THE TAX PRACTITIONER

A tax practitioner, upon learning of an error in a client's previously filed tax return, or of the failure of a client to file a required return, is faced both with a problem of maintaining his objectivity and integrity and with fulfilling his responsibility to the client. The basic position taken in one of the Statements of Responsibilities in Tax Practice is that the client should be promptly advised of the error. The CPA is not obligated to inform the Internal Revenue Service, nor may he do so without his client's permission, except where required by law.[14]

Contingent Fees

Another area of concern to the tax practitioner deals with the setting of his fees. Would it be ethical, for example, to tie the amount of the fee to the amount of taxes saved? The profession has long regarded this as improper. Its position has been that a properly prepared tax return results in a proper tax liability, and that there is therefore no basis for computing a saving. The accountant's responsibility has been considered to be the determination of the correct tax liability, not the reduction of some already established amount. If the fees are based upon the results of judicial proceedings or the findings of governmental agencies, however, they have not been regarded as being contingent and thus have been allowed.

If the terms of a 1988 agreement with the Federal Trade Commission are finalized, these ground rules will change. Under the agreement, the AICPA could

[12]"Confidential Client Information," *AICPA Professional Standards,* vol. 2, ET Section 301.01.

[13]"Ethics Rulings on Responsibilities to Clients," *AICPA Professional Standards,* vol. 2, ET Section 391.030.

[14]"Knowledge of Error: Return Preparation," *AICPA Professional Standards,* vol. 1, TX Section 162.03.

prohibit contingent fees only in those instances where the CPA also performs one of the following attest services for the client:

1. Any audit.
2. Any review of a financial statement.
3. Any compilation of a financial statement when the CPA expects, or reasonably might expect, that a third party will use the compilation and the CPA does not disclose a lack of independence.
4. Any examination of prospective financial information.

In these situations, the AICPA could prohibit a contingent fee during the period of the attest engagement and the period covered by any historical financial statement involved in such attest services.

In this case, for example, the CPA would be able to calculate his fees on the basis of taxes saved, provided he did not also perform attest services for the client. How the calculation of taxes saved would be made is a matter of speculation!

THE INTERNAL PROFESSIONAL

The internal professional has a responsibility to be fair and candid with management, directors, and owners, and to serve them to the best of his ability, with professional concern for their best interests, consistent with his responsibilities to the public. It is important to note that an internal professional, even though not in the public practice, still has a responsibility to the public. Just as a lawyer working for a corporation or the government still has an ethical and moral responsibility to the public and to the courts, so does the accountant. External parties should be able to rely upon financial statements prepared internally because they were prepared by accounting professionals and, therefore, were prepared correctly and honestly.

One area where management and directors must place great reliance upon their internal professional accountants is in the establishment of an accounting system and a system of internal control. The Foreign Corrupt Practices Act of 1977 amended the Securities Exchange Act of 1934 to require that:

> Every issuer which has a class of securities registered pursuant to section 12 of this title and every issuer which is required to file reports pursuant to section 15(d) of this title shall—
> (A) make and keep books, records, and accounts, which, in reasonable detail, accurately and fairly reflect the transactions and dispositions of the assets of the issuer; and
> (B) devise and maintain a system of internal accounting controls sufficient to provide reasonable assurances that—
> (i) transactions are executed in accordance with management's general or specific authorization;
> (ii) transactions are recorded as necessary (1) to permit preparation of finan-

cial statements in conformity with generally accepted accounting principles or any other criteria applicable to such statements, and (2) to maintain accountability for assets;

(iii) access to assets is permitted only in accordance with management's general or specific authorization; and

(iv) the recorded accountability for assets is compared with the existing assets at reasonable intervals and appropriate action is taken with respect to any differences.

To knowingly fail to comply with these provisions subjects management and others to possible fines and imprisonment. It is very important, therefore, for the internal professional to fulfill his responsibility in this area.

What responsibility does the internal professional have with regard to internal reports? Assume, for example, that you are the accountant putting together the budget for your division. You become aware that some of the cost estimates submitted by department heads in the division are deliberately overstated. Should you simply include the figures without question and forward the budget to corporation headquarters? Clearly, to do so would be a violation of professional ethics. The internal professional must always act with integrity, and he would have a responsibility in this case to question the department heads and determine the correct figures to use.

INTERNAL CONTROL: RESPONSIBILITIES OF THE AUDITOR

As indicated earlier, the external auditor has definite responsibilities to his client with regard to internal control. The second auditing standard of field work is as follows:

> A sufficient understanding of the internal control structure is to be obtained to plan the audit and to determine the nature, timing, and extent of tests to be performed.[15]

"An entity's internal control structure consists of the policies and procedures established to provide reasonable assurance that specific entity objectives will be achieved."[16] The structure consists of three elements: the control environment, the accounting system, and control procedures. In all audits, the auditor should obtain a sufficient understanding of each of these elements to plan the audit. This understanding is acquired by performing procedures to (1) understand the design of policies and procedures relevant to audit planning, and (2) to determine whether they have been placed in operation.[17]

[15]"Generally Accepted Auditing Standards," *AICPA Professional Standards,* vol. 1, AU Section 150.02.

[16]"Consideration of the Internal Control Structure in a Financial Statement Audit," *AICPA Professional Standards,* vol. 1, AU Section 319.06, (Statement on Auditing Standards No. 55). Copyright © 1988 by the American Institute of Certified Public Accountants, Inc.

[17]Ibid., AU Section 319.02.

The three elements are defined and described as follows in the professional literature:

Control Environment

The control environment represents the collective effect of various factors on establishing, enhancing, or mitigating the effectiveness of specific policies and procedures. Such factors include the following:

- Management's philosophy and operating style.
- The entity's organizational structure.
- The functioning of the board of directors and its committees, particularly the audit committee.
- Methods of assigning authority and responsibility.
- Management's control methods for monitoring and following up on performance, including internal auditing.
- Personnel policies and practices.
- Various external influences that affect an entity's operations and practices, such as examinations by bank regulatory agencies.

The control environment reflects the overall attitude, awareness, and actions of the board of directors, management, owners, and others concerning the importance of control and its emphasis in the entity.[18]

Accounting System

The accounting system consists of the methods and records established to identify, assemble, analyze, classify, record, and report an entity's transactions and to maintain accountability for the related assets and liabilities. An effective accounting system gives appropriate consideration to establishing methods and records that will:

- Identify and record all valid transactions.
- Describe on a timely basis the transactions in sufficient detail to permit proper classification of transactions for financial reporting.
- Measure the value of transactions in a manner that permits recording their proper monetary value in the financial statements.
- Determine the time period in which transactions occurred to permit recording of transactions in the proper accounting period.
- Present properly the transactions and related disclosures in the financial statements.[19]

Control Procedures

Control procedures are those policies and procedures in addition to the control environment and accounting system that management has established to provide reasonable assurance that specific entity objectives will be achieved. Control

[18]Ibid., AU Section 319.09.
[19]Ibid., AU Section 319.10.

procedures have various objectives and are applied at various organizational and data processing levels. They may also be integrated into specific components of the control environment and the accounting system. Generally, they may be categorized as procedures that pertain to:

- Proper authorization of transactions and activities.
- Segregation of duties that reduce the opportunities to allow any person to be in a position to both perpetrate and conceal errors or irregularities in the normal course of his duties—assigning different people the responsibilities of authorizing transactions, recording transactions, and maintaining custody of assets.
- Design and use of adequate documents and records to help ensure the proper recording of transactions and events, such as monitoring the use of prenumbered shipping documents.
- Adequate safeguards over access to and use of assets and records, such as secured facilities and authorization for access to computer programs and data files.
- Independent checks on performance and proper valuation of recorded amounts, such as clerical checks, reconciliations, comparison of assets with recorded accountability, computer-programmed controls, management review and reports that summarize the detail of account balances (for example, an aged trial balance of accounts receivable), and user review of computer-generated reports.[20]

After obtaining an understanding of the three elements of the control structure,

the auditor assesses control risk for the assertions embodied in the account balance, transaction class, and disclosure components of the financial statements. The auditor may assess control risk at the maximum level (the greatest probability that a material misstatement that could occur in an assertion will not be prevented or detected on a timely basis by an entity's internal control structure) because he believes policies and procedures are unlikely to pertain to an assertion, are unlikely to be effective, or because evaluating their effectiveness would be inefficient. Alternatively, the auditor may obtain evidential matter about the effectiveness of both the design and operation of a policy or procedure that supports a lower assessed level of control risk. Such evidential matter may be obtained from tests of controls planned and performed concurrently with obtaining the understanding or from procedures performed to obtain the understanding that were not specifically planned as tests of controls.[21]

After obtaining the understanding and assessing control risk, the auditor may desire to seek a further reduction in the assessed level of control risk for certain assertions. In such cases, the auditor considers whether evidential matter sufficient to support a further reduction is likely to be available and whether performing additional tests of controls to obtain such evidential matter would be efficient.[22]

The auditor uses the knowledge provided by the understanding of the internal control structure and the assessed level of control risk in determining the nature, timing, and extent of substantive tests for financial statement assertions.[23]

When considering the internal control structure of an entity or during some other phase of an audit, the auditor may become aware of significant deficiencies

[20]Ibid., AU Section 319.11.
[21]Ibid., AU Section 319.03.
[22]Ibid., AU Section 319.04.
[23]Ibid., AU Section 319.05.

in the design or operation of the internal control structure which could adversely affect the organization's ability to record, process, summarize, and report financial data consistent with the assertions of management in the financial statements. These deficiencies are referred to as "reportable conditions" and must be reported, preferably in writing, to the audit committee of the entity, or to individuals with a level of authority and responsibility equivalent to an audit committee in organizations that do not have one, such as the board of directors, the board of trustees, an owner in an owner-managed enterprise, or others who may have engaged the auditor.[24]

> A reportable condition may be of such magnitude as to be considered a material weakness. A *material weakness* in the internal control structure is a reportable condition in which the design or operation of the specific internal control structure elements do not reduce to a relatively low level the risk that errors or irregularities in amounts that would be material in relation to the financial statements being audited may occur and not be detected within a timely period by employees in the normal course of performing their assigned functions.[25] Although he or she is not required to "separately identify and communicate material weaknesses," the auditor may choose or the client may request the auditor to separately identify and communiate as material weaknesses those reportable conditions that, in the auditor's judgment, are considered to be material weaknesses.[26]

INTERNAL CONTROL AND THE FINANCIAL EXECUTIVE

The role of the internal accounting professional as it relates to internal control is discussed in the following excerpts from an article by Harvey V. Guttry, Jr. and Jesse R. Foster of the Times Mirror Company. The authors also outline the approach being taken in their company to ensure compliance with the Foreign Corrupt Practices Act of 1977.

> Recent developments have necessitated a re-examination of the role of internal controls in the efficient and orderly conduct of today's corporations. This re-examination must be based on an understanding that internal control is the composite of a company's arrangements to attain its objectives including maximizing the return on owners' investment; protecting the company's assets; providing a safe and fulfilling work environment for its employees; reporting properly and adequately to owners, regulators, and taxing authorities; and acting as a good citizen.
>
> The internal control arrangements adopted by a company will vary according to its own complex mix of objectives as well as the nature and size of its business... internal control effectiveness is primarily dependent on the people involved. No matter how extensive a company's framework of policies and procedures are, that

[24]"Communication of Internal Control Structure Related Matters Noted in an Audit," *AICPA Professional Standards,* vol. 1, Au Section 325.01, 325.02, and 325.09, (Statement on Auditing Standards No. 60).

[25]Ibid., AU Section 325.15.

[26]Ibid.

framework can only be effective to the extent that there are competent people exercising good judgment in the implementation of policies and procedures. . . .

Internal control has taken on a new dimension with the signing of the "Foreign Corrupt Practices Act of 1977" . . . This . . . statute is a lasting outgrowth of the questionable payments campaign of the Securities and Exchange Commission.* As the name of the Act implies, it prohibits the bribing of foreign officials and establishes severe penalties for offending corporations and corporate personnel. Of potentially greater concern to corporations and their auditors are the additional provisions pertaining to internal accounting controls.

The internal control provisions of the new law seems innocuous enough. The provisions include four required objectives of internal accounting control that are borrowed from the AICPA's definition as expressed in the Institute's Statement on Auditing Standards No. 1. [Superceded by SAS No. 55, AU Section 319]

When the internal control provisions were proposed, the AICPA and FEI took the positive approach of supporting the proposals provided certain refinements in the language were made. The Congress was generally amicable to these suggestions. Further, as recommended by the AICPA and FEI, related provisions pertaining to deceiving the auditors were dropped completely as being inappropriate.[27]

The SEC staff is disappointed that the new law does not include specific language requiring internal controls to prevent bribery. However, such emphasis on corporate rules and procedures is misplaced. Not only does internal control, per se, have limitations as a means to assuring reliable financial statements and safeguarding assets, but there are serious defects in depending on internal control as the means of preventing questionable payments and questionable acts. There has been no evidence presented that the companies who reported questionable acts did not have satisfactory internal accounting controls in the view of the independent auditors. In fact, the evidence indicates that a large percentage of the questionable payments and acts were accomplished by simple override of the controls through executive authority.

While there are some serious definitional and implementational problems posed in the internal control provisions of the statute, the overall thrust of these provisions does not unduly infringe upon individual and institutional freedoms. Rather, the requirements, when supported by additional guidance generated in the private sector, should be effective in emphasizing management's responsibility for internal control. The legislation goes beyond the concept of appropriate internal accounting controls in the context of the auditor's work and places a definite, explicit duty on the publicly held corporation. . . . To achieve adequate surveillance of controls at a reasonable cost, large enterprises should utilize internal specialists in internal control just as internal expertise is already employed in the areas of taxation, financial reporting, and management services. . . .

Public reporting on internal controls is also being advocated by some financial analysts . . . a group of financial analysts indicated that they were not interested in a simple statement on the adequacy of internal control as is already being provided by a few major corporations in their annual reports. Rather, they would prefer a detailed report describing all material weaknesses in internal control. . . .

*At the end of the major phase of its questionable payments compaign, the SEC summarized its conclusions and recommendations in a report entitled "Report on Questionable and Illegal Corporate Payments and Practices." Since the report was prepared for Senator Proxmire's committee, it has become known as the "Proxmire Report." This report recommended anti-bribery legislation containing internal control requirements as well as penalties for deceiving the independent auditors.

[27]Subsequent to the passing of the Act, the SEC issued regulations making it illegal for an officer or director to make false or incomplete statements to an auditor.

The analysts believe that comprehensive information on internal controls can be significant to the investment decision-making process. Such information, it is felt, could give some indication of the reliability of information used for internal decision-making and of the reliability of interim and other unaudited information.

Furthermore, the Commission on Auditor's Responsibilities (the Cohen Commission) after studying the needs and expectations of those who rely on the auditor's work, is recommending voluntary public disclosures relative to internal controls. The Cohen Commission envisions management placing a "Report by Management" in the annual report to acknowledge management's responsibility for the financial statements and to describe the status of internal controls.

The Cohen Commission is also recommending an expanded auditor's report that will focus on the company's representations contained in the report by management. The Commission recognizes that before issuing this expanded auditor's request, the auditors whould have to expand their study and evaluation of internal control. . . .

MANAGEMENT'S RESPONSIBILITY

Management's concept of internal control should begin with explicit acknowledgement of its overall responsibilities. For example, in its "report by management" representation, management could summarize its objectives and corporate policies and other controls designed to achieve those objectives. Then management can speak to the adequacy of the company's internal accounting controls. . . .

It must be recognized that the largest determinant of the effectiveness of any system of internal control is the people who are responsible for the functioning of the controls. Therefore, in evaluating internal control, management must keep uppermost the competence of personnel. Evaluating personnel performance is, of course, difficult because of subjective aspects and the potential for rapid and significant change in human performance. Good management practices, however, have always included adequate attention to employee evaluation and any review of the adequacy of a systsem of controls to detect and prevent errors must include sufficient consideration of how personnel performance affects the performance of the system.

The importance of the human element is such that management cannot afford to leave its control and ethical objectives to undirected perceptions and interpretations throughout the company. To effectively accomplish its objectives, top management must continuously communicate its philosophy as explicitly and as often as is reasonable.

While society should be reasonably tolerant of occasional internal control malfunctioning, management should assure itself that it is doing enough within the perspective of cost versus benefit. The effort for internal control excellence can be most effective if senior management is fully committed to the goal, and if key operating officers are actively supporting the chief financial and accounting officers by conveying a high degree of concern for the quality of internal controls. Management's philosophy on internal controls and corporate ethics, as perceived throughout the corporation, sets the tempo for internal control performance on every level.

As a key part of this communication, but certainly not a substitute for periodic discussions, board of directors and senior management should adopt a policy statement on internal controls. This statement should be disseminated throughout the company. It should convey to employees that just as they are expected to follow certain standards of accountability to higher management, the directors and senior management are committed to a standard of accountability to the shareholders and to the public.

ONE COMPANY'S APPROACH

At Times Mirror, while planning our approach and generally striving to increase the effectiveness of our system of internal controls, we seek to follow the basic philosophy of our senior management toward the subsidiaries—i.e., the best performance is obtained when operating management is free to make its own business decisions. Also, there is a commitment to the concept of decentralized accounting records and accounting controls that fit the unique aspects of the individual operating units. Of course, the operating units must conform their practices to corporate policies and to sound accounting and reporting requirements as set forth by the company's chief accounting officer.

The company's accounting management continuously considers the adequacy of controls. In addition to the normal controls at the operating levels, significant controls include the following:

- Organizational structure and reporting lines designed to preclude any single member of management from overriding the system of internal controls.
- A qualified and informed audit committee of the board of directors.
- A clear and concise corporate policy manual.
- Annual planning and budgeting at all operating units with subsequent monitoring of actual performance against budget plans on a period-by-period basis. (This program also provides for capital expenditure control.)
- An accounting policy manual which describes significant accounting policies to be followed throughout the company.
- Segregation of functions within the controller's organization, which includes a "policy and control" function and the company's primary internal audit function.
- Quarterly letters of representation from chief operating and accounting officers of divisions and subsidiaries encompassing, in addition to comprehensive representations as to the financial statements, statements of compliance with company policy, and representations covering compliance with public law.
- Mandatory rotation of audit personnel in accordance with audit committee policy.
- Pre-audit/post-audit conferences attended by representatives of the corporate accounting staff, independent auditors, and the management of the operating units.
- A post-audit closing conference of the company's senior management and the independent auditors as well as a meeting of the auditors with the audit committee.
- A corporate audit staff which historically has reviewed internal accounting controls and compliance with company policy and performs annual EDP audits and reviews of EDP systems during their development.

Additional controls being considered are:

- Even greater coordination of internal and independent audit resources to maximize audit effectiveness.

- A log of all accounting practice changes to formally document acknowledgement by the company's management of all accounting changes.

Experimenting with Monitoring and Evaluation Techniques

Beyond these contemplated refinements, the most revolutionary innovation being considered is a process of monitoring internal controls that provides for the measurement of risk. It is still undecided as to how formal and detailed a monitoring mechanism needs to be. However, in any company, the importance of internal controls needs to be stressed to operating management beyond the emphasis that comes through from the audit process. Most probably, the discipline of a monitoring process can help corporate and subsidiary management assign and maintain the proper priorities in addressing internal control deficiencies.

The guidelines for this monitoring program were adapted from Statement on Auditing Standards No. 1 and the audit manuals of several CPA firms. This approach calls for identifying all significant types of transactions and considering the types of errors that could occur with each. Using detailed systems descriptions, all of the pertinent controls will be matched with the error types and weaknesses will then be identified. Compensating controls will be considered before a bona fide deficiency in controls will be considered to exist. Once a control deficiency is identified, the risk of not eliminating the deficiency or weakness will be quantified. Then the cost of the additional controls needed to eliminate the weakness will be estimated. Finally, management will consider the risk and cost relationship and make a decision on whether the additional controls should be implemented.

CONCLUSION

The purpose of Times Mirror's experiment is to search for a means for operating management to make a comprehensive assessment of internal controls. Since the effectiveness of controls. . . is management's responsibility, management should make the primary representation concerning the adequacy of the controls. . .

Operating management should be able to benefit from a requirement to monitor controls if a method that does not create an undue burden can be devised. Operating management and senior management should have reasonable assurance that controls designed to achieve the company's objectives are in place and working. Shareholders and other external users of the company's information are entitled to know that adequate attention is being given to internal controls.[28]

INTERIM FINANCIAL INFORMATION

In addition to examining annual financial statements in accordance with generally accepted auditing standards, accountants are frequently called upon to review interim financial statements or information. The objective of such reviews is to provide the

[28]Harvey V. Guttry, Jr. and Jesse R. Foster, "Internal Controls and the Financial Executive," *Financial Executive,* April 1978, pp. 42–48. Reprinted by permission from *Financial Executive,* April 1978, copyright © 1978 by Financial Executives Institute.

accountant with "a basis for reporting whether material modifications should be made for such information to conform with generally accepted accounting principles."[29] They do not provide the basis for an expression of opinion on the financial statements taken as a whole, but consist primarily of inquiries and analytical review procedures concerning significant accounting matters. The procedures ordinarily applied are:

a. Inquiry concerning (1) the accounting system, to obtain an understanding of the manner in which transactions are recorded, classified, and summarized in the preparation of interim financial information and (2) any significant changes in the system of internal accounting control, to ascertain their potential effect on the preparation of interim financial information.
b. Application of analytical review procedures to interim financial information to identify and provide a basis for inquiry about relationships and individual items that appear to be unusual. Analytical review procedures, for purposes of this section, consist of (1) comparison of the financial information with comparable information for the immediately preceding interim period and for corresponding previous period(s), (2) comparison of the financial information with anticipated results, and (3) study of the relationships of elements of financial information that would be expected to conform to a predictable pattern based on the entity's experience. In applying these procedures, the accountant should consider the types of matters that in the preceding year or quarters have required accounting adjustments.
c. Reading the minutes of meetings of stockholders, board of directors, and committees of the board of directors to identify actions that may affect the interim financial information.
d. Reading the interim financial information to consider, on the basis of information coming to the accountant's attention, whether the information to be reported conforms with generally accepted accounting principles.
e. Obtaining reports from other accountants, if any, who have been engaged to make a review of the interim financial information of significant components of the reporting entity, its subsidiaries, or other investees.
f. Inquiry of officers and other executives having responsibility for financial and accounting matters concerning (1) whether the interim financial information has been prepared in conformity with generally accepted accounting principles consistently applied, (2) changes in the entity's business activities or accounting practices, (3) matters as to which questions have arisen in the course of applying the foregoing procedures, and (4) events subsequent to the date of the interim financial information that would have a material effect on the presentation of such information.
g. Obtaining written representations from management concerning its responsibility for the financial information, completeness of minutes, subsequent events, and other matters for which the accountant believes written representations are appropriate in the circumstances.[30]

These procedures apply to reviews of interim financial information that is presented alone, and to reviews of interim financial information that accompanies,

[29]"Review of Interim Financial Information," *AICPA Professional Standards,* vol. 1, AU Section 722.03 (Statement on Auditing Standards No. 36). Copyright © 1989 by the American Institute of Certified Public Accountants, Inc.

[30]Ibid., AU Section 722.06.

or is included in a note to, audited financial statements of a public or non-public entity.[31]

The accountant's report accompanying interim financial information that he has reviewed, which is presented other than in a note to audited financial statements, should consist of the following:

1. a statement that the review of interim financial information was made in accordance with the standards for such reviews,
2. an identification of the interim financial information reviewed,
3. a description of the procedures for a review of interim financial information,
4. a statement that a review of interim financial information is substantially less in scope than an examination in accordance with generally accepted auditing standards, the objective of which is an expression of opinion regarding the financial statements taken as a whole, and accordingly, no such opinion is expressed, and
5. a statement about whether the accountant is aware of any material modifications that should be made to the accompanying financial information so that it conforms with generally accepted accounting principles.[32]

As indicated above, this kind of report gives limited assurance regarding the interim information, but disclaims an expression of opinion. The interim information is unaudited and each page should be so marked.

When interim financial information designated as unaudited is presented in a note to audited financial statements, the auditor need not modify his report on the audited financial statements to make reference to his review or to the selected interim information.[33]

UNAUDITED FINANCIAL STATEMENTS OF PUBLIC ENTITIES

A public accountant sometimes has a responsibility to assist a public entity[34] with the preparation of unaudited financial statements or perhaps to prepare them entirely. In fulfilling this responsibility he may become *associated* with the statements. As indicated in Chapter 2, this *association* occurs when "he has consented to the use of his name in a report, document, or written communication containing the statements" or has submitted "to his client or others financial statements that he prepared or assisted in preparing."[35]

[31]Ibid., AU Section 722.02.

[32]Ibid., AU Section 722.17.

[33]Ibid., AU Section 722.28.

[34]A public entity is defined as any entity (a) whose securities trade in a public market either on a stock exchange (domestic or foreign), or in the over-the-counter market, including securities quoted only locally or regionally, (b) that makes a filing with a regulatory agency in preparation for the sale of any class of its securities in a public market, or (c) a subsidiary, corporate joint venture, or other entity controlled by an entity covered in (a) or (b). See "Association With Financial Statements," *AICPA Professional Standards,* vol. 1, AU Section 504.02.

[35]"Association With Financial Statements," *AICPA Professional Standards,* vol. 1, AU Section 504.03.

The danger with association lies in the possible misinterpretation by third parties that the financial statements have been audited, and that the accountant is in some way vouching for their accuracy and correctness. Generally accepted auditing standards require that a disclaimer of opinion accompany unaudited financial statements with which the CPA is associated. As pointed out in the preceding section, this includes interim statements which have been "reviewed" in accordance with Statement on Auditing Standards No. 36 (AU Section 722).

The form of report to be issued when an accountant is associated with the annual financial statement of a public entity, but has not audited or reviewed[36] them, is as follows:

> The accompanying balance sheet of X Company as of December 31, 19X1, and the related statements of income, retained earnings, and cash flows for the year then ended were not audited by us and, accordingly, we do not express an opinion on them.
>
> (Signature and date)[37]

This report "may accompany the unaudited financial statements or it may be placed directly on them. In addition, each page of the financial statements should be clearly and conspicuously marked as unaudited."[38] When issuing this type of opinion, the accountant has no obligation to apply any procedures beyond reading the financial statements for obvious material misstatements, nor should he describe any procedures that have been applied. Such a description might cause the reader to believe the statements have been audited or reviewed.[39]

> If the accountant is aware that his name is to be included in a client-prepared written communication of a public entity containing financial statements that have not been audited or reviewed, he should request (a) that his name not be included in the communication, or (b) that the financial statements be marked as unaudited and that there be a notation that he does not express an opinion on them. If the client does not comply, the accountant should advise the client that he has not consented to the use of his name and should consider what other actions might be appropriate.[40]
>
> If the accountant concludes on the basis of facts known to him that the unaudited financial statements on which he is disclaiming an opinion are not in conformity with generally accepted accounting principles, which include adequate disclosure, he should suggest appropriate revision; failing that, he should describe the departure in his disclaimer of opinion. This description should refer specifically to the

[36]If an accountant is requested to "review" the interim or annual statements of a public entity that does not have its annual financial statements audited, he should look to Statements on Standards for Accounting and Review Services for the standards and procedures and form of report applicable to such an engagement. See "Compilation and Review of Financial Statements," *AICPA Professional Standards,* vol. 1, AR Section 100.

[37]"Association With Financial Statements," *AICPA Professional Standards,* vol. 1, AU Section 504.05. Copyright © 1989 by the American Institute of Certified Public Accountants, Inc.

[38]Ibid.

[39]Ibid.

[40]Ibid., AU Section 504.06.

nature of the departure and, if practicable, state the effects on the financial statements or include the necessary information for adequate disclosure.[41]

When a departure from generally accepted accounting principles involves inadequate disclosure, it may not be practicable for the accountant to include the omitted disclosures in his report. For example, when management has elected to omit substantially all of the disclosures, the accountant should clearly indicate that in his report, but the accountant would not be expected to include such disclosures in his report.[42]

If the client will not agree to revision of the financial statements or will not accept the accountant's disclaimer of opinion with the description of the departure from generally accepted accounting principles, the accountant should refuse to be associated with the statements and, if necessary, withdraw from the engagement.[43]

UNAUDITED FINANCIAL STATEMENTS OF NONPUBLIC ENTITIES

The Accounting and Review Services Committee is the senior technical committee of the American Institute of Certified Public Accountants designated to issue pronouncements in connection with unaudited financial statements or other unaudited financial information of a nonpublic entity. Statements on Auditing Standards still provide guidance to the accountant who performs services in connection with the unaudited statements of a public entity.

In its first official statement on Standards for Accounting and Review Services, the committee defined two types of engagements leading to reports: (1) compilation of financial statements, and (2) review of financial statements.[44] Specific standards were established for each type of engagement.

Compilation of financial statements is defined by the committee as "presenting in the form of financial statements information that is the representation of management (owners) without undertaking to express any assurance on the statements." *Review* of financial statements is defined as "performing inquiry and analytical procedures that provide the accountant with a reasonable basis for expressing limited assurance that there are no material modifications that should be made to the statements in order for them to be in conformity with generally accepted accounting principles or, if applicable, with another comprehensive basis of accounting."[45]

As indicated previously, the statement sets forth standards for the guidance of accountants in both compilation and review engagements. It requires the issuance of a report, including an appropriate disclaimer of opinion, whenever a compilation or review is completed in compliance with these standards, and prohibits a report

[41]Ibid., AU Section 504.11.

[42]Ibid., AU Section 504.12.

[43]Ibid., AU Section 504.13.

[44]"Compilation and Review of Financial Statements," *AICPA Professional Standards*, vol. 2, AR Section 100. Copyright © 1989 by the American Institute of Certified Public Accountants, Inc.

[45]Ibid., AR Section 100.04. See "Special Reports," AU Section 623.04, for the definition of "another comprehensive basis of accounting." One example is a basis "that the reporting entity uses or expects to use to file its income tax return for the period covered by the financial statements."

when they are not followed. The accountant, furthermore, is not allowed to submit unaudited statements to clients or to others unless the standards have been met. Merely typing or reproducing financial statements as a service to a nonpublic client is prohibited. Should the accountant "consent to the use of his name in a document or written communication containing unaudited financial statements of a nonpublic entity" for which he has issued no report, the financial statements must be "accompanied by an indication that the accountant has not compiled or reviewed the financial statements and that he assumes no responsibility for them."[46]

Following the standards and procedures set forth for compilations and reviews will enable the accountant to comply with the general standards of the profession set forth in AICPA Rule 201. A review, however, may not be performed if the accountant is not independent. A compilation may be performed even though independence is lacking, but this fact must be disclosed in the report.

The inquiry and analytical procedures set forth for a "review of financial statements" are similar to the "review" requirements found in Statement on Auditing Standards No. 36, Review of Interim Financial Information (AU Section 722). They are:

a. Inquiries concerning the entity's accounting principles and practices and the methods followed in applying them.
b. Inquiries concerning the entity's procedures for recording, classifying, and summarizing transactions, and accumulating information for disclosure in the financial statements.
c. Analytical procedures designed to identify relationships and individual items that appear to be unusual. For the purposes of this statement, analytical procedures consist of (1) comparison of the financial statements with statements for comparable prior period(s), (2) comparison of the financial statements with anticipated results if available (for example, budgets and forecasts), and (3) study of the relationships of the elements of the financial statements that would be expected to conform to a predictable pattern based on the entity's experience. In applying these procedures, the accountant should consider the types of matters that required accounting adjustments in preceding periods. Examples of relationships of elements in financial statements that would be expected to conform to a predictable pattern may be the relationships between changes in sales and changes in accounts receivable and expense accounts that ordinarily fluctuate with sales, and between changes in property, plant, and equipment and changes in depreciation expense and other accounts that may be affected, such as maintenance and repairs.
d. Inquiries concerning actions taken at meetings of stockholders, board of directors, committees of the board of directors, or comparable meetings that may affect the financial statements.
e. Reading the financial statements to consider, on the basis of information coming to the accountant's attention, whether the financial statements appear to conform with generally accepted accounting principles.
f. Obtaining reports from other accountants, if any, who have been engaged to audit or review the financial statements of significant components of the reporting entity, its subsidiaries, and other investees.

[46]Ibid., AR Section 100.06.

g. Inquiries of persons having responsibility for financial and accounting matters concerning (1) whether the financial statements have been prepared in conformity with generally accepted accounting principles consistently applied, (2) changes in the entity's business activities or accounting principles and practices, (3) matters as to which questions have arisen in the course of applying the foregoing procedures, and (4) events subsequent to the date of the financial statements that would have a material effect on the financial statements.[47]

The objective of these and other procedures is to provide the accountant with "a reasonable basis for expressing limited assurance that there are no material modifications that should be made to the financial statements."[48] This is quite different from the objective of a compilation, in which no expression of assurance is contemplated.

For a compilation, the accountant is not required to "make inquiries or perform other procedures to verify, corroborate or review information supplied by the entity."[49] However, he must possess or acquire a "level of knowledge of the accounting principles and practices of the industry in which the entity operates that will enable him to compile financial statements that are appropriate in form for an entity operating in that industry."[50]

In addition, the accountant must possess or acquire "a general understanding of the nature of the entity's business transactions, the form of its accounting records, the stated qualifications of its accounting personnel, the accounting basis on which the financial statements are to be presented, and the form and content of the financial statements.[51] Before issuing his report, the accountant should read the compiled financial statements and consider whether they appear to be "appropriate in form and free from obvious material errors."[52]

DIVISIONAL REPORTS AND THE INTERNAL PROFESSIONAL

The following article sets forth a problem which may be encountered by the internal professional. When preparing internal reports, what responsibility does the accountant have to his immediate supervisor, to the central office, to top management, to the owners, to himself?

A MORAL DILEMMA

A young accountant was . . . told by his superior that he would have to drop his moralistic notions about accounting reports if he hoped to be a success with the company. He was informed that it was normal practice to have some hidden book-

[47]Ibid., AR Section 100.27.
[48]Ibid., AR Section 100.04.
[49]Ibid., AR Section 100.12.
[50]Ibid., AR Section 100.10.
[51]Ibid., AR Section 100.11.
[52]Ibid., AR Section 100.13.

keeping dollars to adjust the reported figure for his division, and thus present it in a more favorable light to the central office. This was not wrong, he was told, because the dollars used were not fictitious, but only handled in a way that was timely and advantageous to the division.

This young man was unable to live with this kind of arrangement, and subsequently left the company. Who was right, he or his superior?

WHAT IS THE ACCOUNTANT'S ROLE?

At issue here are the basic objectives and purposes of accounting. Is the accountant primarily a manipulator of figures, an advocate of his particular division or segment of the company? Or is he a professional expert, interpreting the activities of the division in an unbiased manner to all concerned? Should he be an unwilling middle man, caught between his inherent desire to present the facts as clearly as he can perceive them, and the will of his immediate superior to present the division in a favorable, though perhaps inaccurate, light?

It is submitted here that the accountant should be regarded as a professional expert, and allowed to present the facts in as accurate and honest a manner as he is able.

THE SANCTION OF GENERAL ACCEPTANCE

There are, of course, a number of gray areas associated with the problem. It is well known that many different practices and procedures fall under the umbrella of "generally accepted accounting principles." Should the accountant be chastised for not using that generally accepted practice which presents his division most favorably? Maybe so. Perhaps the fact that the practice giving the more favorable result is generally accepted is sufficient grounds to insist on its use by the division accountant, even though he personally feels that an alternate practice presents the facts more accurately. Perhaps the general acceptability of the more favorable practice is prima facie evidence that the accountant's preference is merely a personal judgment and not binding.

It does appear clear, however, that figure juggling outside of the umbrella of generally accepted accounting principles should be loudly denounced by all accountants.

WHO IS TO BLAME?

At whose doorstep can this problem be laid? Is it the fault of the division superior who insists that his accountant compromise conscience for the good of the division? Is it the accountant himself for submitting to this pressure? Is it an excessive emphasis placed on divisional cost or profit reports by central office executives? Many of the control advantages claimed for these reports may be strictly paper advantages if figure manipulation is practiced. Surely, if the reports generated by the system are inaccurate, much of the control is fictitious. It is submitted that central office executives, division managers, and division accountants are all partly to blame

A SUGGESTION FOR IMPROVEMENT

What can be done to improve the situation? Basic to the problem is the necessity for a change of attitude on the part of all concerned. First, and perhaps most important, must come a change of approach by top-level management. These people set the tone for the entire business organization. If they are inflexible about budget and profit deviations, never giving any credence to the circumstances surrounding a particular period's report, their subordinates will adapt their reporting procedures to fit this attitude. If explainable deviations are met with the same critical attitudes that would face unjustified deviations, every effort will be made to conceal deviations, whatever their nature.

An attitude of cooperation and professionalism needs to be engendered throughout the organization. Divisions should not be made to feel they are separate from the parent organization, but rather that they are an integral part of the whole. Although it is frequently useful to compute profit by division, this end figure should not be the sole criterion of success for a division. Nor should it become the single basis of reward to a division manager. Such a policy is short-sighted and can create unhealthy attitudes throughout the company.

Let's hire back the young man with the high standards and let the kind of thinking he embodies permeate the entire company.[53]

QUESTIONS AND CASES

4–1 Are there any limits to an auditor's obligation not to disclose confidential information obtained in the course of a professional engagement? If so, what are they? Give specific examples of situations where the obligation does not apply.

4–2 Statements on Standards for Management Advisory Services state that before undertaking an engagement, a practitioner should consider various matters in reaching an understanding with the client. What are some examples of these "matters?"

4–3 What is the ethical responsibility of a tax practitioner upon learning of an error in a client's previously filed tax return or of the failure of a client to file a required return?

4–4 Is it proper for a tax practitioner to accept an engagement under an arrangement whereby his fee will be related to the amount of tax he saves the client? Explain the rationale underlying your answer.

4–5 Does the Foreign Corrupt Practices Act of 1977 have any relevance to the internal accounting professional? If so, what provisions are pertinent and why?

4–6 Distinguish between control environment and control procedures. What three elements are included in an entity's internal control structure?

4–7 What are the responsibilities of the external auditor with regard to the internal control structure of a client? What reporting obligations does he have?

[53]Floyd W. Windal, "A Problem of Integrity," *Managerial Planning,* May/June 1969, pp. 26–27.

4–8 What is the purpose of the "disclaimer of opinion" which must accompany unaudited financial statements? What if the accountant has come to the conclusion as a result of his work that the statements are not in conformity with generally accepted accounting principles?

4–9 What is meant by a "review" of interim financial information? What is its purpose? What should be included in the auditor's report following such an examination?

4–10 What is meant by the "compilation of financial statements?"

4–11 Who is responsible for the issuance of pronouncements in connection with unaudited financial statements of a nonpublic entity? What is meant by a "review" of such statements? What standards have been established for a review?

4–12 Does the internal professional have any ethical responsibility for the correctness of the financial information he provides for management's use?

4–13 *(Pamela Lang)*
ABC is a fairly large oil company with significant research and development expenditures. An international accounting firm, LT & Co., was hired to review ABC's interim financial statements. LT & Co. did review them and found that research and development costs were improperly capitalized rather than expensed. They brought this to the attention of management but management did nothing to correct the situation. In the report accompanying the interim financial statements, the auditors stated that research and development costs should be expensed in conformity with GAAP.

At year end, ABC asked LT & Co. to audit their annual financial statements. Since ABC chose not to change their treatment of R&D expenses, should LT & Co. accept this engagement, and if so, what effect would the interim review have on their audit and the audit report?

4–14 *(Ann Sapp)*
Murphy Mixner and Blake Zerosky were partners in a small local CPA firm. Zerosky, the firm's tax partner, and his wife left on a long-awaited trip to Europe during the summer when the firm's business slowed down. In the usual course of events, Mixner handled most of the audit and accounting work and Zerosky handled the tax end of the business.

After Zerosky had been gone for a week of his three week vacation, Roseanna Danner, a client, called with a somewhat complicated tax question. As a partner of the firm, Mixner felt obligated to provide an answer before Zerosky returned in two weeks. However, he was rusty in tax matters. So he spent about 15 minutes perusing some tax service volumes and found a couple of similar cases on which to base a recommendation.

In light of his recent experience in tax matters, did Mixner fulfill his responsibility to Ms. Danner with respect to professional competence and technical proficiency?

4–15 *(Charles Belote)*
As a CPA, you are asked to prepare a tax return for a client. The client is anxious

to pay as little as possible and requests that you reduce his tax liability as much as you can. He assures you that he will "reward" you adequately if you can achieve the desired results.

How should you respond to the client?

4–16 Bill Stone was recently made a tax senior. In preparing the federal tax return for a new client, the Cozy Corporation, he discovers a material error in the previous year's return. A correction of this error will result in a tax liability for the client. What are his professional obligations with regard to this error?

4–17 (*Frank Nigro*)

CPA Kevin Davis, during the course of an audit engagement with client Sly Dog, discovered several irregularities. Subsequent to a lengthy conversation with Sly concerning the irregularities, Kevin withdrew from the engagement. Shortly thereafter, Kevin was contacted by CPA Jodie Wynn concerning Kevin's prior relationship with Sly Dog. She also inquired as to the circumstances which caused the termination.

Can Kevin tell Jodie about the irregularities? Won't he be violating the Rule in the AICPA Code of Professional Conduct about confidential client information?

4–18 (*Letty Lanier*)

Joe N. Corruptible has been an internal auditor with Devo, Inc. for ten years. While on a audit of the corporation's New York office, Joe discovers an unusually large expense amount labeled as "Consultant Fees."

When asked about the item, the controller, Will Easy, says that such costs are associated with certain large sales, and that the company has made many large sales this year. Not satisfied, Joe talks with Devo's president about the item. The president explains that such fees are a normal part of carrying on business with Rumulac, a third world nation.

"We think of it as a cost of sales," he replies. "We pay the foreign minister a fee for communicating Devo's bids so well to the Internal Development Ministry there. He agrees to let us add the amount to the sales price. That's simply the way everyone does business over there, and who are we to querstion their methods? Our main responsibility is to turn a good profit for our share holders, and we've done very well at that in Rumulac."

What action should Joe take?

4–19 (*Emmanuel Ekong*)

Southwest Industries, Inc., which is registered with the SEC, has asked a CPA firm to prepare an interim financial report to be presented to the stockholders at an emergency general meeting. The CPA firm has prepared audited annual financial statements for the last five years.

The financial statements are needed for internal purposes and for the shareholders of the company in voting on a proposed merger. Because the company needs the report soon, management has asked the auditors not to perform any detailed tests or review of the financial statements, but wishes to have an audited report.

Discuss the firm's professional responsibilities and its responsibilities to Southwest.

4–20 (*James Thomas*)
A CPA firm is engaged for the audit of a small manufacturing firm which has grown considerably in the last year. They need an audit in order to complete a loan application for additional capital for expansion. The firm's rapid growth caused a work overload in the accounting department and many control procedures were not being followed. Duties were no longer segregated, creditors were paid slowly, and receipts were not regularly deposited. The auditors noticed these weaknesses while preparing procedures to gain an understanding of the internal control structure, and decided to place little reliance on it.

Can the auditors still issue an unqualified opinion?

Should they do anything about the deficiencies in control that were noted?

4–21 Koestner Products, Inc. was started in Champaign, Illinois by Elmer (Bud) Koestner. The business has prospered and Bud is considering the construction of a new building to house his manufacturing operation. Bob Drabik, a local CPA, has been preparing financial statements for him quarterly, but they have never been audited. Koestner Products has an accountant who maintains the basic financial records with the help of a personal computer.

In order to finance the new building, Bud plans to get a loan from a local bank. He knows the bank will want some assurance that the financial information he provides them is correct. He asks his CPA, Bob Drabik, what his options are. Does he need an audit? Is there anything short of an audit which will satisfy the bank?

How should Bob respond?

5

RESPONSIBILITY TO COLLEAGUES

INTRODUCTION

The Biblical admonition "As ye would that men should do to you, do ye also to them likewise"[1] is an appropriate standard for relationships among accounting professionals. These relationships encompass a broad range of activities and include the relationship between the auditor and the internal professional whose financial statements he is examining, between the management consultant designing an accounting system and the controller of the concerned company, and between a division accountant and his superior at corporate headquarters. All such relationships must be carried out in an atmosphere of mutual respect and honesty.

Article I of the AICPA Code of Professional Conduct, quoted in its entirety in Chapter 4, also has relevance in connection with responsibility to colleagues. The following is from its explanatory paragraph:

> Members. . . have a continuing responsibility to cooperate with each other to improve the art of accounting, maintain the public's confidence, and carry out the profession's special responsibilities for self-governance.[2]

[1]Luke 6:31

[2]"Responsibilities," *AICPA Professional Standards*, vol. 2, ET Section 52.01. Copyright © American Institute of Certified Public Accountants, Inc.

THE AUDITOR

There are many occasions in which an auditor has formal or informal contact with his fellow professionals. He, of course, will associate with them in the various professional societies in which they are active. As clients previously audited by another are acquired, or as present clients move on to another, the successor and predecessor auditors will need to communicate and to rely upon one another. In the area of practice development which results in the acquisition of new clients, the auditor must be extremely careful not to violate the ethical code governing such activity.

Assume, for example, that you are a partner in a medium-sized regional firm. You belong to a fashionable country club and regularly play golf with the president of a corporation which has its home office in your city. After a particularly stimulating round of golf one Saturday afternoon in which you lost by one stroke to your friend, he asks if you would be willing to give him some advice on how to handle an especially difficult accounting matter. Although his company is being audited by another accounting firm, he would like your advice. Is it ethical to give it?

You would be able to accept the engagement, but you must first consult with the other accountant to ascertain that you are aware of all the available facts relevant to forming a professional judgment. If your friend is merely "shopping for an accounting principle," you would not want to be a party to it. You should explain to your friend the need to consult with the continuing accountant, request permission to do so, and request him to authorize the accountant to respond fully to your inquiries. Specific reporting standards must also be followed if your report is written.[3]

Sometimes an auditor is required to express an opinion on combined or consolidated financial statements which include a subsidiary, branch, or other component, audited by another public accountant. Should his insistence upon auditing any such component in order to express an overall opinion be interpreted as an unethical encroachment upon the practice of a colleague?

No, an auditor should insist upon auditing such a component when, in his judgment, it is necessary to warrant the expression of an opinion. Generally accepted auditing standards must always be complied with. Insistence upon auditing an unreasonably large portion of the financial statements might, however, lead to an assertion that the auditor's judgment is part of a plan or design to deceptively solicit a client. Rule 502 specifically prohibits any solicitation that is false, misleading, or deceptive.[4]

What are the guidelines for reporting on financial statements when the independent audiutor utilizes the work and reports of another independent auditor who has examined the financial statements of a component, such as a subsidiary? Should he make reference to the other auditor in his report? How does he satisfy himself that the work of the other auditor is reliable?

[3]"Reports on the Application of Accounting Principles," *AICPA Professional Standards,* vol. 1, AU Section 625.

[4]"Advertising and Other Forms of Solicitation," *AICPA Professional Standards,* vol. 2, ET Section 502.01.

The following statement is found in the professional literature:

> If the principal auditor decided to assume responsibility for the work of another auditor insofar as that work relates to the principal auditor's expression of an opinion on the financial statements taken as a whole, no reference should be made to the other auditor's work or report. On the other hand, if the principal auditor decides not to assume that responsibility, his report should make reference to the audit of the other auditor and should indicate clearly the division of responsibility between himself and the other auditor in expressing his opinion on the financial statements. Regardless of the principal auditor's decision, the other auditor remains responsible for the performance of his own work and for his own report.[5]

In satisfying himself that the other auditor's work can be relied upon, the principal auditor " should make inquiries" as to his "professional reputation and independence," and "should adopt appropriate measures to assure the coordination of his activities with those of the other auditor in order to achieve a proper review of matters affecting the consolidating or combining of accounts in the financial statements."[6]

THE MANAGEMENT CONSULTANT AND THE TAX PRACTITIONER

One area presenting ethical questions to the management consultant and the tax practitioner is that of referrals. Assume, for example, that you are a sole practitioner with an audit, tax, and management consulting practice. You have been serving a particular business since its inception, preparing the necessary tax returns and acting as a management consultant. The business has now grown to such an extent that a public issuance of stock is to be made, entailing involvement with a variety of government regulations and reports. You have no desire to review that area in depth, although you would still like to continue your service as general management consultant to the business. Should you prepare the needed reports as best you can in order not to lose your consulting job with the client?

Clearly, you have a responsibility to see that your client gets competent assistance in this case. As pointed out in an interpretation of Rule 201 of the AICPA Code of Professional Conduct, it is sometimes necessary in fairness to your client and the public, to suggest that the client engage someone else to perform the needed service, either independently or as an associate.[7]

What if you were the accountant called in to assist in this case, and after completing your assignment, the client asked if you would be willing to advise him on another aspect of the business? Can you accept such an engagement? Would it

[5]"Part of Audit Performed by Other Independent Auditors," *AICPA Professional Standards*, vol. 1, AU Section 543.03. Copyright © 1989 by the American Institute of Certified Public Accountants, Inc.

[6]Ibid., AU Section 543.10.

[7]"General Standards," *AICPA Professional Standards*, vol. 2, ET Section 201.02.

be ethical for you to make an inquiry of the client about engaging you to assist with another problem you uncovered as a part of your work on the referred job?

It would be ethical for you to extend your service beyond the specific engagement, and to make inquiry regarding an additional job. Professional courtesy, however, would dictate that you notify the referring accountant of your intentions. This is one of the instances where the practitioner must look to his own sense of fairness for an answer, rather than to a specific Rule of Conduct.

The management consultant and the tax practitioner often interface with their colleagues on the audit staff. They also may interface with the audit staff of another firm of independent certified public accountants. It goes without saying that such contacts should be carried out in an atmosphere of cordiality, with full cognizance that the work being done will be relied upon by another.

What if you, as management consultant for a particular nonaudit client, become aware that the financial statements of that client, audited by another independent CPA, deviate substantially from accepted professional standards? Do you have any ethical obligation to bring this to the attention of anyone?

A professional accountant does have an obligation to assist his colleagues in complying with the Code of Professional Conduct. Probably the first step in this case would be to determine whether the client is aware of the violation of accepted standards. Perhaps such an inquiry will correct the situation. If it reveals, however, that the deviation is being done willfully, some action may be called for. The financial statements may be referred to the Professional Ethics Division of the American Institute of Certified Public Accountants, to a state society ethics committee, or to a state board of accountancy.

THE INTERNAL PROFESSIONAL

A major area of contact between the internal professional and other professionals is provided by the external audit. The work of the controller and his staff come under intensive scrutiny by the independent certified public accountant, and it is very important that each party respect the professionalism of the other. And, of course, each party must perform his work in a manner that will justify such respect.

The possible reliance of the external auditor upon the work of the internal auditor is one instance of direct contact. The external auditor "should acquire an understanding of the internal audit function as it relates to understanding the internal control structure. The work performed by internal auditors may be a factor in determining the nature, timing, and extent" of the external auditor's procedures. If the external auditor "decides that the work by internal auditors may have a bearing on his own procedures, he should consider the competence and objectivity of internal auditors and evaluate their work."[8]

[8]"The Effect of an Internal Audit Function on the Scope of the Independent Audit," *AICPA Professional Standards*, vol. 1, AU Section 322.04. Copyright © 1989 by the American Institute of Certified Public Accountants, Inc.

"When the work of internal auditors is expected to be significant to the independent auditor's understanding of the internal control structure or the assessment of control risk, the independent auditor should, at the outset of the engagement, inform internal auditors of the reports and working papers he will need. He should also consult with internal auditors concerning work they are performing, since work not yet completed may also have a bearing on his audit. Also, work done by internal auditors will frequently be more useful to the independent auditor if plans for the work are discussed in advance."[9]

The external auditor may also use the internal auditor to provide direct assistance, such as in performing substantive tests or tests of controls. When the independent auditor employs internal auditors in this way, he "should consider their competence and objectivity and supervise and test their work to the extent appropriate in the circumstances."[10]

Assume that you are the controller of a small manufacturing company and that the company's federal income tax return is being examined by the Internal Revenue Service. What should your behavior be toward the internal professional working for the IRS? What is your obligation with regard to questions raised by the agent?

Clearly, you should behave with the same integrity and objectivity that you would in interacting with any other professional. This is not to imply that you should not work for the best interests of the company, but only that you should be honest in your answers and should not deliberately mislead or misinform. You should also not allow an untruth or misinterpretation to remain uncorrected, even though you are not directly responsible for it.

COMMUNICATION BETWEEN PREDECESSOR AND SUCCESSOR AUDITORS

In order to provide guidance on communications between precedessor and successor auditors when a change has taken place or is in process, Statement on Auditing Standards No. 7 was issued. A portion of this important statement follows:

1. The purpose of this section is to provide guidance on communications between predecessor and successor auditors when a change of auditors has taken place or is in process. The term "predecessor auditor" refers to an auditor who has resigned or who has been notified that his services have been terminated. The term "successor auditor" refers to an auditor who has accepted an engagement or an auditor who has been invited to make a proposal for an engagement. This section applies whenever an independent auditor has been retained, or is to be retained, to audit the financial statements, in accordance with generally accepted auditing standards.
2. The initiative in communicating rests with the successor auditor. The communica-

[9]Ibid., AU Section 322.09.
[10]Ibid., AU Section 322.10.

tion may be either in writing or oral. Both the predecessor and successor auditors should hold in confidence information obtained from each other. This obligation applies whether or not the successor accepts the engagement.

3. Prior to acceptance of the engagement, the successor auditor should attempt certain communications that are described in paragraphs 4 through 7. Other communications between the successor and the predecessor, described in paragraphs 8 and 9 are advisable. However, their timing is more flexible. The successor may attempt these other communications either prior to acceptance of the engagement or subsequent thereto.

COMMUNICATIONS BEFORE SUCCESSOR ACCEPTS ENGAGEMENT

4. Inquiry of the predecessor auditor is a necessary procedure because the predecessor may be able to provide the successor with information that will assist him in determining whether to accept the engagement. The successor should bear in mind that, among other things, the predecessor and the client may have disagreed about accounting principles, auditing procedures, or similarly significant matters.
5. The successor auditor should explain to his prospective client the need to make an inquiry of the predecessor and should request permission to do so. Except as permitted by the Rules of the Code of Professional Conduct, an auditor is precluded from disclosing confidential information obtained in the course of an audit engagement unless the client specifically consents. Thus, the successor auditor should ask the prospective client to authorize the predecessor to respond fully to the successor's inquiries. If a prospective client refuses to permit the predecessor to respond or limits the response, the successor auditor should inquire as to the reasons and consider the implications of that refusal in deciding whether to accept the engagement.
6. The successor auditor should make specific and reasonable inquiries of the predecessor regarding matters that the successor believes will assist him in determining whether to accept the engagement. His inquiries should include specific questions regarding, among other things, facts that might bear on the integrity of management; on disagreements with management as to accounting principles, auditing procedures, or other similarly significant matters; and on the predecessor's understanding as to the reasons for the change of auditors.
7. The predecessor auditor should respond promptly and fully, on the basis of facts known to him, to the successor's reasonable inquiries. However, should he decide, due to unusual circumstances such as impending litigation, not to respond fully to the inquiries, he should indicate that his response is limited. If the successor auditor receives a limited response, he should consider its implications in deciding whether to accept the engagement.

OTHER COMMUNICATIONS

8. When one auditor succeeds another, the successor auditor must obtain sufficient competent evidential matter to afford a reasonable basis for expressing his opinion on the financial statements he has been engaged to examine as well as for evaluating the consistency of the application of accounting principles in that year as compared with the preceding year. This may be done by applying appropriate auditing procedures to the account balances at the beginning of the period under audit and

in some cases to transactions in prior periods. The successor auditor's audit may be facilitated by (a) making specific inquiries of the predecessor regarding matters that the successor believes may affect the conduct of his audit, such as audit areas that have required an inordinate amount of time or audit problems that arose from the condition of the accounting system and records, and (b) reviewing the predecessor auditor's working papers. In reporting on his audit, however, the successor auditor should not make reference to the report or work of the predecessor auditor as the basis, in part, for his own opinion.

9. The successor auditor should request the client to authorize the predecessor to allow a review of the predecessor's working papers. It is customary in such circumstances for the predecessor auditor to make himself available to the successor auditor for consultation and to make available for review certain of his working papers. The predecessor and successor auditors should agree on those working papers that are to be made available for review and those that may be copied. Ordinarily, the predecessor should permit the successor to review working papers relating to matters of continuing accounting significance, such as the working paper analysis of balance sheet accounts, both current and noncurrent, and those relating to contingencies. Valid business reasons, however, may lead the predecessor auditor to decide not to allow a review of his working papers. Further, when more than one successor auditor is considering acceptance of an engagement, the predecessor auditor should not be expected to make himself or his working papers available until the successor has accepted the engagement.

FINANCIAL STATEMENTS REPORTED ON BY PREDECESSOR

10. If during his audit the successor auditor becomes aware of information that leads him to believe that financial statements reported on by the predecessor auditor may require revision, he should request his client to arrange a meeting among the three parties to discuss this information and attempt to resolve the matter. If the client refuses or if the successor is not satisfied with the result, the successor auditor may be well advised to consult with his attorney in determining an appropriate course of further action.[11]

THE DISCIPLINE OF INDIVIDUALS

The Americans Institute of CPAs has established specific procedures for the discipline of its members. The discipline ranges from an administrative reprimand to expulsion. Action taken by the AICPA may in turn lead to action by a state board of accountancy or other governmental authority to suspend or revoke the member's CPA certificate or license to practice. In other cases, action by the governmental authority may precede action by the institute.

Membership in the institute is suspended without a hearing if a judgment of conviction for any of the following is filed with the secretary of the institute. Membership is terminated upon the similar filing of a final judgment of conviction.

[11] "Communications Between Predecessor and Successor Auditors," *AICPA Professional Standards*, vol. 1, AU Section 315. Copyright © 1989 by the American Institute of Certified Public Accountants, Inc.

1. A crime punishable by imprisonment for more than one year.
2. The willful failure to file any income tax return which he, as an individual taxpayer, is required by law to file.
3. The filing of a false or fraudulent income tax return on his or a client's behalf.
4. The willful aiding in the preparation and presentation of a false and fraudulent income tax return of a client.[12]

Membership in the institute may also be suspended or terminated without a hearing "should a member's certificate as a certified public accountant, or license or permit to practice as such or to practice public accounting" be suspended or revoked "as a disciplinary measure by any governmental authority." In such cases, and in the case of the type of crime referred to in Item 1 above, the member has the right to petition that this provision not be applied.[13] Only "exceptional or unusual circumstances" which would make automatic suspension or termination inequitable would result in the approval of such an appeal.[14] In such a case, the matter would be transmitted to the Professional Ethics Division of AICPA to take whatever action it seemed appropriate in the circumstances.[15]

State societies and other eligible jurisdictions may enter into an agreement with the AICPA for the joint handling of disciplinary matters. A complaint regarding professional ethics might thus be submitted to the Professional Ethics Division of the Institute or to an ethics committee (or its equivalent) of a state society of certified public accountants. State societies can elect one of the following participation options:

1. Allow the AICPA Professional Ethics Division to deal with complaints against its members. Under this option, complaints received by a state society are forwarded to the AICPA. The AICPA disposes of complaints involving joint members by taking action only after submitting its findings to the state society for its review and concurrence, or nonconcurrence, in the same action. If the AICPA receives a complaint involving someone who is a member of a state society but not the AICPA, it refers its findings to that state society for its action.[16]
2. Deal with complaints against its members through its own state society ethics committee. Under this arrangement, the AICPA's Professional Ethics Division refers complaints it receives involving joint members to the state society, except those involving (a) broad national interests, (b) litigation, (c) federal government regulatory proceedings, (d) investigations by the Special Investi-

[12]"Disciplinary Suspension and Termination of Membership Without Hearing," *AICPA Professional Standards*, vol. 2, BL Section 730.01. Copyright © 1989 by the American Institute of Certified Public Accountants, Inc.

[13]Ibid.

[14]"Implementing Resolution Under Section 7.3 Disciplinary Suspension and Termination of Membership Without Hearing," *AICPA Professional Standards*, vol. 2, BL Section 730R.06.

[15]Ibid.

[16]*Plan to Restructure Accounting Standards* (New York: AICPA, 1987), p. 35. Copyright © 1989 by the American Institute of Certified Public Accountants, Inc.

gations Committee of the SEC Practice Section of the AICPA Division for CPA Firms, (e) referrals from agencies of the federal government, and (f) persons who are members of more than one state society.[17]

Under each option, copies of complaints involving technical and independence statndards and actions taken will be forwarded to the AICPA or state CPA committee that administers the reviews of the member's firm under the practice-monitoring program discussed later in this chapter.

If either the Professional Ethics Division or a state society ethics committee concludes that there is a prima facie case showing a violation of any applicable bylaws of the Institute or any rule of the Code of Professional Conduct of the Institute or of the involved state society, or showing any conduct discreditable to a certified public accountant, they will report the matter to the Joint Trial Board. The secretary of this board then summons the member involved to appear at the next convenient meeting of a panel of the board appointed to hear the case.[18]

The joint trial board consists of at least 36 members elected for a three-year term by the Council of the AICPA from among its present and former members.[19]

"After heaving the evidence presented by the Professional Ethics Division on other complainant, and by the defense, the trial board or sub-board hearing the case. . . may. . . admonish, suspend for a period of not more than two years, or expel the member. . . in any case in which the trial board or sub-board finds that a member has departed from the profession's technical standards it may also direct the member concerned to complete specified professional development courses and to report to the trial board upon such completion."[20]

In a case decided by a sub-board, the member concerned may request a review by the trial board of the decision of the sub-board. Such a review is not a matter of right, however, and an ad hoc committee appointed by the chairman of the trial board will decide whether or not to grant it.[21]

In those cases when the Professional Ethics Division concludes that "a prima facie violation of the Code of Professional Conduct or bylaws is not of sufficient gravity to warrant further formal action," it may direct the member to complete specified continuing professional education courses, or to take other remedial or corrective action. In such cases, there will be no publication of the action and the member concerned must be notified of his right to reject such direction. "In the case of such a rejection, the professional ethics executive committee shall determine whether to bring the matter to a hearing panel of the trial board for a hearing."[22]

[17]Ibid., pp. 33 and 35.

[18]"Implementing Resolution Under Section 7.4 Disciplining of Member by Trial Board," *AICPA Professional Standards,* vol. 2, BL Section 740R.01.

[19]"Implementing Resolutions Under Section 3.6 Committees," *AICPA Professional Standards,* vol. 2, BL Section 360R.06.

[20]"Implementing Resolution Under Section 7.4 Disciplining a Member by Trial Board," *AICPA Professional Standards,* vol. 2, BL Section 740R.03.

[21]Ibid.

[22]"Implementing Resolutions Under Section 3.6 Committees," *AICPA Professional Standards,* vol. 2, BL Section 360R.05.

THE DISCIPLINE OF FIRMS

The primary vehicle within the profession for the discipline of firms, as distinguished from individual members, is the AICPA Division for CPA Firms. Within this division of the AICPA, there are two sections: the SEC Practice Section and the Private Companies Practice Section. Although membership in the division is voluntary, it is expected that most firms will belong to one or both of its sections. Both sections require their members to (1) adhere to quality control standards established by the AICPA Quality Control Standards Committee, (2) submit to peer reviews of their accounting and audit practice every three years or at such additional times as designated by their executive committees, and (3) ensure that all of their professionals participate in continuing professional education.

In addition, the SEC Practice Section requires, among other things, that its members (1) rotate audit partners on SEC engagements every seven years, unless the firm has less than five SEC clients and less than ten partners, (2) ensure that a concurring review of the audit report and the financial statements by a partner other than the audit partner-in-charge of an SEC engagement is required before an issuance of the report, (3) file with the section annually specified information about the firm to be available for public inspection, (4) "report annually to the audit committee or board of directors (or its equivalent in a partnership) of each SEC audit client on the total fees received from the client for management advisory services during the year under audit and a description of the types of such services rendered," (5) adhere to the portions of the Code of Professional Conduct and Statements on Standards for Management Advisory Services dealing with independence in performing management advisory services for audit clients, and (6) when the client-auditor relationship has ceased due to resignation, declining to stand for re-election, or dismissal, report this fact directly in writing to the former client, with a simultaneous copy to the Chief Accountant of the Securities and Exchange Commission. This report shall be sent by the end of the fifth business day following the determination that the relationship has ended. [Added effective May 1, 1989]. They must also refrain from performing for clients services that are inconsistent with the firm's responsibilities to the public, or that consist of psychological testing, public opinion polls, merger and acquisition assistance for a finders fee, certain types of executive recruitment and certain types of actuarial service to insurance companies.[23]

The executive committee of each section has the authority to impose sanctions on member firms either on its own initiative or on the basis of recommendations from its peer review committee. The following types of sanctions may be imposed for failure to maintain compliance with the membership requirements.

1. Require corrective measures by the firm including consideration by the firm of appropriate actions with respect to individual firm personnel.

[23]*AICPA Division for CPA Firms SEC Practice Section SECPS Manual* (New York: American Institute of Certified Public Accountants, 1986) pp. 1-5 to 1-11. Copyright © 1989 by the American Institute of Certified Public Accountants, Inc.

2. Additional requirements for continuing professional education.
3. Accelerated or special peer reviews.
4. Admonishments, censures, or reprimands.
5. Monetary fines.
6. Suspension from membership.
7. Expulsion from membership.[24]

The SEC Practice Section has a Public Oversight Board, composed of prominent individuals of high integrity and reputation, with the following responsibilities and functions:

1. Monitor and evaluate the regulatory and sanction activities of the peer review and executive committees to assure their effectiveness.
2. Determine that the peer review committee is ascertaining that firms are taking appropriate action as a result of peer reviews.
3. Conduct continuing oversight of all other activities of the section.
4. Make recommendations to the executive committee for improvements in the operations of the section.
5. Publish an annual report and such other reports as may be deemed necessary with respect to its activities.
6. Engage staff to assist in carrying out its functions.
7. Have the right for any or all of its members to attend any meetings of the executive committee.[25]

The Executive Committee of the Private Companies Practice Section, should it so choose, has the authority to establish a Public Oversight Board for that Section.

THE DISCIPLINE OF A PROFESSION

In the following article, Wallace E. Olson, former president of the American Institute of Certified Public Accountants, addresses the many problems associated with disciplining the members and firms comprising the public accounting segment of the profession.

> One of the hallmarks of a profession is an accreditation or licensing process before an applicant is permitted to practice or hold himself out as a member of the group. In general, either the state or the federal government establishes right-to-practice requirements to assure consumers that licensees have met minimum standards.

[24]Ibid., pp. 1–15 to 1–16.
[25]Ibid., p. 1–14.

The notion that there should be an effective system for the ongoing regulation and disciplining of a profession is a natural effect of the monopoly that is granted to a qualified group under the law. It is rooted in the belief that initial qualification requirements, standing alone, are not sufficient to protect the consuming public from malpractice. The threat of punishment of licensees for wrongdoing is an essential part of the total scheme for public protection.

The sanctions provided under the licensing laws are normally restricted to suspensions or revocations of rights to practice. Redress for civil damages or punishment for criminal acts relating to malpractice must be sought under the civil liability and criminal laws, which are designed for application to a much wider range of activities than that of professionals.

Given this combination of regulation by threats of revocation of rights to practice, civil damages and criminal penalties, one might wonder why an organized profession either desires or is expected to impose on itself additional forms of discipline or sanctions. One answer might be that professions have membership organizations in the private sector designed to enhance both the quality of practice of its members and the stature of the profession in the eyes of the public. A code of ethics is an important means of achieving these objectives, and some form of disciplinary mechanism is necessary to put teeth in the code.

Another answer might be that a profession usually prefers to keep governmental intervention in its affairs at a minimum. An effective system of self-regulation is believed to be the best way to achieve this objective, although it is by no means a guarantee that a profession will be left alone to handle its affairs.

Professionals voluntarily assume the threat of disciplinary sanction by the organized group because they believe the alternative—greater governmental involvement—would be more onerous. If one accepts this premise, it follows that, to be effective, a system of self-regulation must be accompanied by a serious and continuing threat of additional forms of outside regulation.

In general, a disciplinary system is necessary to assure that practitioners adhere to the high ideals of a professional. However, if a profession is composed of professionals capable of individual self-restraint, why is a disciplinary system necessary?

Perhaps the answer is that the behavior of professionals is not much different from that of everyone else. An essential ingredient in improving the behavior of professionals, like that of all human behavior, is the threat of punishment for wrongdoing.

Even the threat of punishment has been of questionable effectiveness in curbing the misdeeds of individuals who lack respect for authority and the law. Nevertheless, most people are likely to behave better as a result of the threat of punishment from wrongdoing. Thus, "How should a profession be disciplined?" is really a question of what kinds of punishment and how great a threat of punishment of professionals is necessary to assure expected levels of performance.

This is a complex matter because it involves an evaluation of the strength of pressure that might cause a breakdown in performance and the identification of the performance that can reasonably be expected of the average practitioner. These involve subjective judgments, which make decisions about individual cases or the effectiveness of a disciplinary system difficult at best.

THE PUBLIC ACCOUNTING PROFESSION

It would be interesting to know what would happen if the public accounting professional abandoned all efforts to discipline itself. Would the quality of performance decline substantially? Would the number of alleged audit failures increase?

Would the states or the federal government rush in with legislation to establish an additional disciplinary system that would provide for sanctions, such as monetary fines, which would go beyond the present suspensions or revocations of rights to practice?

The answers to these questions are not clear, but it is safe to assume that the elimination of all self-disciplinary efforts would be unacceptable to the profession and the public alike, even though such efforts may not be wholly successful. Accordingly, assuming that a system of self-discipline is necessary, and that the combined internal and external disciplinary systems ought to be as effective as possible in protecting the public from malpractice, it is appropriate to address these questions:

1. Who should be disciplined?
2. What types of misconduct should give rise to discipline?
3. What types of sanctions should be imposed?
4. Which institutions should impose discipline and how much?

The balance of this article discusses these questions.

WHO SHOULD BE DISCIPLINED?

Because state accountancy statutes are all designed to regulate the accreditation and practice of CPAs as individuals, the provisions for suspension or revocation of a CPA certificate apply only to individuals. In some states CPA firms must also register to practice. For all practical purposes, however, the disciplinary machinery of state boards of accountancy is directed at individuals.

Most practice is carried on today in the names of firms, not in the names of individual practitioners. CPAs have surrendered their individual identities to the firm entities that sign auditors' reports, set policies and carry on multilocation practices as partnerships or professional corporations. If a substandard performance occurs, it raises questions about who was at fault. Was it a defect in the firm's policies? If not, did an individual in the firm fail to adhere to its policies? If the firm's policies were deficient, should top management be disciplined as the responsible individuals or should a sanction be imposed on the entire firm, or both?

Lately it has been recognized that the way the practice of accounting is conducted calls for a means of disciplining firms as well as individuals. Until now the only attempts of regulators to deal with firms were those of the Securities and Exchange Commission under rule 2(e) proceedings and injunctive actions. When a very large CPA firm was involved, the SEC found it impractical to suspend it from practice before the commission because of the harm such action would impose on the firm's innocent SEC clients. Therefore, alternative sanctions were developed such as suspensions of single offices of firms, mandated peer reviews and agreements not to add new SEC clients for specified periods. Of course, SEC injunctive actions against firms also spawned civil liability suits, which are a severe and effective form of discipline of firms. . . .

The AICPA has now established a division for firms with two sections, one for SEC practice and another for private companies practice. Each section can impose sanctions on its particular firms for not meeting the requirements for participation. This is a significant step because it brings firms within a self-disciplinary scheme for the first time. It represents a voluntary surrender of a considerable degree of autonomy on the part of the participating firms.

This development recognizes that an effective system of discipline for the public accounting profession must deal with both individual CPAs and CPA firms as separate entities, depending on the cause of the substandard performance giving rise to the need for disciplinary action. Thus, the answer to the question "Who should be disciplined?" seems to be individuals, firms or both.

WHAT TYPES OF MISCONDUCT SHOULD GIVE RISE TO DISCIPLINE?

At first blush it might appear to be a simple matter to determine what types of misconduct should give rise to discipline. Most people believe that they know misconduct when they see it. But when it comes to evaluating the performance of practicing CPAs, there are many degrees of misconduct that make disciplinary decisions difficult. Indeed, in deciding on the circumstances for which auditors should be held liable, even the courts have had difficulty in defining where the dividing lines should be.

Most people would agree that a conscious violation of the profession's technical standards or a knowing participation in the issuance of misleading audited financial statements calls for disciplinary action. Less clear is whether an honest oversight or mistake by an auditor should result in a sanction. Even if it should not, is there a point where the negligence is so gross or the act so reckless that a sanction should be imposed? Where should the line be drawn? Also, to what extent should it be required that harm resulted before the disciplinary process comes into play?

In most cases involving questionable technical performance, there is a further complication—the difficulty in determining the technical standard to which the practitioner should be held. For example, when a management fraud has not been detected by an auditor, it is seldom clear whether a normally prudent auditor exercising due care would have uncovered the fraud.

Often, the technical standards are not sufficiently defined to be able to measure performance. . . . The *Continental Vending* case (*U.S.* v. *Simon*) is an example of a case where a main issue was whether there was an appropriate standard that should have been applied in an audit.

A tribunal faced with making a decision about the adequacy of technical performance, whether it be a court, the SEC, a state board of accountancy, or one of the profession's . . . trial boards, often finds itself making subjective judgments about what the defendant auditor should have done under the circumstances. Such judgments are always made after it is known that a mistake was made and what caused it. It would take a body of saints to prevent such knowledge from causing a bias in the judgment about what the auditor should have done at a time when the present information was unknown.

Under these circumstances, it seems clear that the standards for determining misconduct are, to a large extent, established ad hoc by subjective judgments made with the benefit of hindsight. Broad concepts such as negligence, recklessness and scienter may be followed, but applying them to a specific set of facts is largely a subjective process. Thus, the accounting profession is in a position of having to accept, as a risk of doing business, the fact that it will be held responsible for meeting a shifting set of standards subjectively determined by hindsight, and usually by an uninformed laity, if litigation is involved. This is not to say that the standards of the profession are useless or ignored for disciplinary purposes. But compliance with them is no guarantee that under particular circumstances an auditor will be held blameless. There is simply no substitute for vigilance and good judgment when it comes to avoiding blame.

In addition to requiring adherence to technical standards, the state boards of accountancy and the profession's state and national organizations have included a series of rules on general behavior in their codes of conduct. These rules have as their principal objective fostering harmony and courtesy within the profession, ostensibly to assure that the public is well served.

Because many of the rules place a degree of restraint on unfettered competition, it has been charged in recent times that they may be in violation of the antitrust laws. Rules restricting advertising and solicitation are now seen to be improper restraints on competition unless they involve false claims or deception. Other rules. . . are likely to be subject to the same kind of attack.

Perhaps the only behavioral rules likely to survive the test of current perception about what serves the public interest are those that deal with potential conflicts of interest or rights of privacy. These include the rules on independence, receipt or payment of commissions, and confidentiality of client information.

The foregoing observations lead to the conclusion that the professional organizations and the state boards of accountancy are likely to be restricted to imposing discipline for the following types of offenses:

1. Performing services without competence or due care or failing to adhere to technical standards.
2. Knowingly engaging in deceptive practices or misrepresenting facts in the practice of public accounting.
3. Failing to adhere to rules on independence and commissions when reporting on audits of financial statements as an independent auditor.
4. Being found guilty of a felony for acts whether or not related to the practice of public accounting.
5. Violating the confidences of clients except as technical standards, the law, peer reviews or disciplinary proceedings require such disclosure.
6. Any unspecified acts, whether or not related to the practice of public accounting, that bring discredit on the entire profession.

Only the first three offenses are the bases for disciplinary sanctions by the SEC, although presumably an auditor might be found to be unfit and suspended from practice under the fourth or sixth categories. The first three offenses are also recognized by the courts as providing bases for either civil liability or criminal penalties, depending on a showing of willfulness or deliberate intent to engage in a fraud or conduct so reckless as to be its equivalent.

As previously noted, it is one thing to describe in a general way what types of misconduct should give rise to discipline but it is quite another to make judgments about whether in a specific case misconduct that should result in discipline has occurred. Nevertheless, the profession, the courts and governmental regulatory bodies must do their best to impose punishment fairly for offenses under these broad categories, however imprecise they may be.

WHAT TYPES OF SANCTIONS SHOULD BE IMPOSED?

The range of sanctions that have been imposed against members or firms of the profession include

1. Private or public censure by the profession's organizations.
2. Remedial actions including peer reviews and attendance at specified educational courses.

3. Suspension or expulsion from membership in the profession's organizations.
4. Injunctions against continuing violations of the federal securities laws.
5. Suspension or revocation of a CPA's certificate and right to practice.
6. Money damages in civil liability suits.
7. Fines and/or imprisonment for criminal acts.

Until recently, when the AICPA's division for firms was established, the sanctions that could be imposed by the profession's disciplinary actions were the least effective of those of the various disciplinary bodies. Members who are expelled from the profession's organizations may still practice if their licenses are not revoked. This is not to say that the profession's sanctions have been wholly ineffective. Practitioners have consistently taken the profession's disciplinary actions against them very seriously because of the damage such actions can do to their reputations and their abilities to recruit and hold a qualified staff. Also, the profession's sanctions are brought to the attention of state boards of accountancy, and the result can be suspension or revocation of the license to practice.

The AICPA's new division for firms has adopted a range of sanctions that includes the possible imposition of fines for failure to maintain appropriate quality controls. This goes beyond the traditional types of punishment that the profession has imposed in the past. Even the SEC and the state boards of accountancy do not have the authority to impose fines on CPAs or CPA firms.

The most severe penalties are those that can be imposed by the licensing bodies and the courts. Revocation of rights to practice and fines or imprisonment are the most extreme measures that can be taken. Only slightly less severe are the money damages resulting from civil liability suits. Even though there are widely varying judgments about when and to whom auditors should be held liable for money damages, this form of sanction has had a significant effect on improving the profession's performance. The threat of unlimited liability has caused most practitioners to take the quality of their work very seriously.

Based on experience to date, it is clear that each of the seven types of sanctions listed above is necessary to provide gradations of penalties to fit the differing degrees of professional misconduct that may be encountered in practice. The principal problem is not identifying the types of sanctions to impose. The greatest difficulty is determining how to apply, on a consistent basis, the range of sanctions to the varying degrees of misconduct.

WHICH INSTITUTION SHOULD IMPOSE DISCIPLINE AND HOW MUCH?

A major question to be resolved is whether the present forms of discipline are sufficient to assure the levels of performance that can reasonably be expected, given the nature of the functions involved. . . .

It can be argued that the threat of unlimited legal liability is sufficient to assure that the profession will take all reasonable steps to avoid audit failures. A number of practitioners have questioned whether it makes sense for the profession to add its own layer of discipline on top of legal liability, SEC sanctions and suspension or revocation of the CPA certificate by state boards of accountancy. Although this addition may not be necessary from the standpoint of needed restraining pressures, it is likely, as previously noted, that neither the profession nor the public is prepared to accept a complete abdication of disciplinary responsibility by the profession.

To the contrary, there are strong pressures to increase the amount of self-regulation and make it more effective. Presumably, this is based on the view that the profession has an obligation to protect the public through preventive measures, thereby minimizing the need for resorting to the courts for redress.

Some have said that the amount of auditors' legal liability should be limited because the threat of unlimited liability causes the profession to be excessively defensive and to shun new responsibilities out of fear of increased exposure to lawsuits. . . .

It seems certain that all the present institutions involved in disciplining the profession will continue to function for the foreseeable future. The question is not whether any will be eliminated but, rather, how they will be made more effective and what additional forms and layers of discipline will be added. If the AICPA-sponsored division for CPA firms is successful in its efforts to regulate and impose sanctions on firms, perhaps the SEC and Congress will be persuaded that additional federal regulation is unnecessary. If not, creation of a National Association of Securities Dealers type of regulatory body under the direct oversight of the SEC becomes a likely possibility.

A key problem to be resolved if more governmental regulation is to be avoided is finding a way to take disciplinary action immediately even though litigation is involved in an alleged case of substandard audit performance. Because the AICPA does not have subpoena powers, it has found litigation to be an insurmountable barrier to prompt action. It cannot compel production of witnesses or evidence, and its files are open to discovery by adverse parties in litigation.

Most CPA firms take the position that the profession should not attempt to preempt the judicial system and thereby jeopardize the due process rights of the individual involved. On the other hand, the SEC, members of Congress and other critics of the profession's disciplinary efforts find unacceptable the profession's policy of deferring action pending a determination through litigation.

Where litigation is involved, it might be expected that the threat of substantial money damages would force CPA firms to exercise reasonable precautions against malpractice. Immediate additional discipline should not be necessary. Unfortunately, much of today's criticism is based on appearances, and the critics are not always persuaded by the substance. . . .

The institution that has received the least attention is the state board of accountancy. Historically, the state boards, with few exceptions, have been ineffective in meeting their disciplinary responsibilities. This stems in part from a lack of funds and investigative staff.

Because the boards can suspend or revoke the right to practice, they offer a fertile possibility for increasing the disciplinary pressures on the profession. Perhaps the profession should turn its attention to improving the capabilities of the boards as a means of satisfying the critics. It is questionable, however, whether this would satisfy members of Congress who have a natural inclination to solve the perceived problems at the federal level through its creation, the SEC. In any event, the firms might find effective and immediate state regulation to be almost as distasteful as federal regulation and would, no doubt, opt for self-regulation. Otherwise, there would be the likely result of incurring additional sanctions at both levels of government. . . .

Whether the many layers of disciplinary pressures are all necessary is open to question, but in the present environment any argument for reduction is likely to fall on deaf ears. Suggestions for relief from unlimited legal liability are likely to be similarly received.

Under these circumstances, practitioners and firms are well advised to maintain the highest possible quality controls. If they wish to avoid sanctions that can flow from as many as five different sources for the same offense, they will take increasingly defensive positions in resolving problems with their clients. . . .[26]

QUALITY REVIEW PROGRAMS

As indicated in the discussion of the discipline of firms, one responsibility those practicing public accounting have to their colleagues is to assist in one of the various quality review programs. In addition to the mandatory peer review required of those firms in the AICPA Division for CPA Firms, quality review is required of all members of the Institute. A practice-monitoring program is carried out by the Quality Review Division of the Institute, in cooperation with state CPA societies.[27]

Quality review procedures under the program are tailored to the size of the firm and the nature of its practice. Firms that perform audits of historical financial statements or examinations of prospective financial statements must have an on-site review, whereas firms that provide only compilation or review services will have an off-site review of selected reports on those services. If none of these services are provided, the firm will not be reviewed. A set of standards for performing and reporting on quality review has been prepared by the Quality Review Executive Committee, which governs the Quality Review Division [QR Section 100].

Also impacting on quality is a bylaw of the AICPA stating that those applying for membership who first become eligible to take the CPA examination after the year 2000, shall have obtained 150 semester hours of education at an accredited college or university, including a bachelor's degree or its equivalent.[28] Finally, all members of the Institute must demonstrate for each calendar year that they have completed acceptable continuing education.[29]

The AICPA Quality Control Standards Committee is the senior technical committee of the Institute designated to issue pronouncements on quality control standards. The following nine elements of quality control are enumerated in a statement issued by the Committee.

1. *Independence.* Policies and procedures should be established to provide the firm with reasonable assurance that persons at all organizational levels maintain independence to the extent required by the rules of conduct of the AICPA. Interpretation 101-1 of the rules of conduct contains examples of instances wherein a firm's independence will be considered to be impaired.

[26]Wallace E. Olson, "How Should a Profession be Disciplined?" *Journal of Acountancy*, May 1978, pp. 59-66. Copyright © 1978 by the American Institute of Certified Public Accountants, Inc.

[27]"Implementing Resolution Under Section 2.2 Requirements for Admission to Membership," *AICPA Professional Standards*, vol. 2, BL Section 220R.01.

[28]"Requirements for Admission to Membership," *AICPA Professional Standards*, vol. 2, BL Section 220.

[29]"Implementing Resolutions Under Section 2.3 Requirements for Retention of Membership," *AICPA Professional Standards*, vol. 2, BL Section 230R.04 and 230R.06.

2. *Assigning Personnel to Engagements.* Policies and procedures for assigning personnel to engagements should be established to provide the firm with reasonable assurance that work will be performed by persons having the degree of technical training and proficiency required in the circumstances. In making assignments, the nature and extent of supervision to be provided should be taken into account. Generally, the more able and experienced the personnel assigned to a particular engagement, the less is the need for direct supervision.
3. *Consultation.* Policies and procedures for consultation should be established to provide the firm with reasonable assurance that personnel will seek assistance, to the extent required, from persons having appropriate levels of knowledge, competence, judgment, and authority. The nature of the arrangements for consultation will depend on a number of factors, including the size of the firm and the levels of knowledge, competence, and judgment possessed by the persons performing the work.
4. *Supervision.* Policies and procedures for the conduct and supervision of work at all organizational levels should be established to provide the firm with reasonable assurance that the work performed meets the firm's standards of quality. The extent of supervision and review appropriate in a given instance depends on many factors, including the complexity of the subject matter, the qualifications of the persons performing the work, and the extent of consultation available and used. The responsibility of a firm for establishing procedures for supervision is distinct from the responsibility of a person to adequately plan and supervise the work on a particular engagement.
5. *Hiring.* Policies and procedures for hiring should be established to provide the firm with reasonable assurance that those employed possess the appropriate characteristics to enable them to perform competently. The quality of a firm's work ultimately depends on the integrity, competence, and motivation of personnel who perform and supervise the work. Thus, a firm's recruiting programs are factors in maintaining such quality.
6. *Professional Development.* Policies and procedures for professional development should be established to provide the firm with reasonable assurance that personnel will have the knowledge required to enable them to fulfill responsibilities assigned. Continuing professional education and training activities enable a firm to provide personnel with the knowledge required to fulfill responsibilities assigned to them and to progress within the firm.
7. *Advancement.* Policies and procedures for advancing personnel should be established to provide the firm with reasonable assurance that those selected for advancement will have the qualifications necessary for fulfillment of the responsibilities they will be called on to assume. Practices in advancing personnel have important implications for the quality of a firm's work. Qualifications that personnel selected for advancement should possess include, but are not limited to, character, intelligence, judgment, and motivation.
8. *Acceptance and Continuance of Clients.* Policies and procedures should be established for deciding whether to accept or continue a client in order to minimize the likelihood of association with a client whose management lacks integrity. Suggesting that there should be procedures for this purpose does not imply that a firm vouches for the integrity or reliability of a client, nor does it imply that a firm has a duty to anyone but itself with respect to the acceptance, rejection, or retention of clients. However, prudence suggests that a firm be selective in determining its professional relationships.

9. *Inspection.* Policies and procedures for inspection should be established to provide the firm with reasonable assurance that the procedures relating to the other elements of quality control are being effectively applied. Procedures for inspection may be developed and performed by individuals acting on behalf of the firm's management. The type of inspection procedures used will depend on the controls established by the firm and the assignment of responsibilities within the firm to implement its quality control policies and procedures.[30]

In order to provide guidance in the establishment of quality control, some quality control policies and procedures were developed by the AICPA Quality Control Standards Committee.[31] These guidelines do not have the authority of a pronouncement by the committee, but are issued to provide guidance in the application of the standards on quality control. The guidelines are used as the requirements to be met in connection with reviews conducted under the authority of the Peer Review Committees of the AICPA Division for CPA Firms.[32] The nine elements of quality control enumerated previously are the basis for the discussion of guidelines.

QUESTIONS AND CASES

5–1 As a practicing CPA, is it ethical for you to offer your audit services to a company already being audited by another firm? What if that company approaches you about the service?

5–2 As auditor for a large conglomerate, can you ethically insist upon auditing a subsidiary already audited by another firm? What are the guidelines for reporting if you decided to rely upon the work of another auditor? How do you satisfy yourself that the work of the other auditor can be relied upon?

5–3 Is it ethical for one practitioner to refer work to another? What if a referral is made and the client then requests an extension of the service beyond the specific engagement? Should the practitioner receiving the referral seek additional engagements from the client?

5–4 Under what circumstances is it permissible for an external auditor to utilize work done by an internal auditor? Is it necessary to audit the internal auditor before relying upon his work?

5–5 What communications is a successor auditor required to attempt under generally accepted auditing standards prior to accepting an engagement? What additional communications are advisable?

[30] "System of Quality Control for a CPA Firm," *AICPA Professional Standards,* vol. 2, QC Section 10.07. Copyright © 1984 by the American Institute of Certified Public Accountants, Inc.

[31] "Quality Control Policies and Procedures for CPA Firms: Establishing Quality Control Policies and Procedures," *AICPA Professional Standards,* vol. 2, QC Section 90.

[32] *AICPA Division for CPA Firms SEC Practice Section SECPS Manual,* op. cit., p. A–17.

5–6 Membership in the AICPA may be terminated without a hearing upon the filing of a final judgment of conviction for any of four actions. What are they? What other occurrence may result in a member's suspension without a hearing?

5–7 What is the function of the Joint Trial Board of the AICPA? What roles are played by the Professional Ethics Division of the Institute and state societies?

5–8 What three membership requirements are common to both the SEC Practice Section and the Private Companies Practice Section of the AICPA Division for CPA Firms?

5–9 What are the responsibilities and functions of the Public Oversight Board of the SEC Practice Section?

5–10 What quality review programs are operated under the auspices of the AICPA? What are the nine elements of quality control applicable to all firms?

5–11 (*Joann Gidday*)
As a partner in a large regional CPA firm, you have been approached to take on a new client. The client has many subsidiaries and will issue consolidated financial statements. Some of the subsidiaries are being audited to their satisfaction by other firms, but the prospective client is unhappy with its primary auditor. If you accept the engagement you would audit the parent company plus eight of their 11 subsidiaries. You would also issue the opinion on the consolidated statements.

What procedures should you follow in determining whether to accept this engagement? If you accept the engagement, what will you do about the three subsidiaries audited by others?

5–12 (*Joan Gidday*)
You have been a member of Smith, Jones & Co., a medium-sized local CPA firm, for 5 years and now decide to open your own office within the same general geographic area. During the years of your association with Smith, Jones & Co., you developed a close professional relationship with many of their audit clients and have earned a great deal of respect from them. You are under no contract not to compete with Smith, Jones & Co. and it would be financially beneficial for you to acquire some of their clients with whom you have dealt. This would create a stable base on which to expand your practice.

Can you solicit these clients for your new practice?

5–13 Mary Sharp, CPA, has just taken over as auditor for the Sweetmark Company. During the course of the audit, she becomes aware of information that leads her to believe that the financial statements reported on by the predecessor auditor may require revision. What should she do?

5–14 (*Ken Brewer*)
Roger Waters is a CPA who performs tax assistance and management advisory services for Greene Hardware, a small local business. Will Greene, its owner, was considering opening two more stores in the area and needed an independent audit for the bank to agree to the necessary loans. Roger Waters was extremely busy and

understaffed at that time, and consequently referred Will to another CPA. After the audit was completed, Will was so pleased with the work that he requested the new firm to take the responsibility of preparing tax returns for Greene Hardware in the future. Should the new firm accept Greene Hardware as a permanent client?

5–15 Bill Blake is a certified public accountant in Lawrence, Kansas, and a member of the AICPA. The Internal Revenue Service has just completed an examination of a tax return he filed on behalf of a client, and has notified him that it plans to bring legal action against him for filing a fraudulent income tax return. Bill is aghast at this news. How would his practice be affected should he be convicted?

5–16 Conglomerate Enterprises, Inc. is a regular client of Fife & Drum, a regional CPA firm. While performing the year-end audit of Conglomerate, Phil Marston, a partner at Fife & Drum, noticed that during the last year CE had acquired Littleco, a small local business.

Phil contacted Littleco and inquired as to whether their records had been audited, and if so, by whom. The president replied "Our records are fine, you have no reason to worry about them." Phil tried a second time to obtain the information, but the President refused to answer.

What should Phil do?

5–17 (*Catherine Saye*)

Joe Fink, CPA, has been engaged by Wrong-Way, Inc., as a management consultant. During the engagement, Fink discovers that the audited financial statements of the client do not conform with generally accepted accounting principles, but the client's independent auditor had expressed an unqualified opinion on them.

What is Joe Fink's responsibility in this situation?

5–18 (*Susan Schayer*)

Karen Long is the main tax partner for Long & Whitney, Certified Public Accountants. Mrs. Zachary, President of Zachary, Inc., has been referred to Long & Whitney by Zachary's current auditors, Short & Short. Mrs. Zachary is seeking advice and information on tax planning opportunities concerning a possible merger. Short & Short did not have the technical expertise or the manpower to advise on such matters.

While reviewing the financial statements, ledgers, and prior-year tax returns, Karen noticed numerous opportunities where Zachary, Inc. could be saving tax dollars. She also noticed several errors in the financial statements; however, they were not material. Upon completing her research and review of the company, Karen had a conference with Mrs. Zachary to discuss her findings.

Mrs. Zachary was very enthusiastic about the tax planning ideas, and the two developed rapport quickly. Mrs. Zachary then asked Karen if Long & Whitney would like Zachary, Inc. as a client in the tax area. She also inquired as to whether Long & Whitney would "prefer" to handle all the CPA services for Zachary, Inc., including the audit services now being performed by Short & Short.

How should Karen respond to Mrs. Zachary's questions?

Should Karen reveal the errors she found? If so, to whom?

5–19 (*Julia Ogle*)

Lynn Loyal, CPA, recently left public accounting to work with a large corporation in the position of assistant controller. After two months of working for the company, Lynn noticed some possible problems in the payroll records. She did not have enough supporting evidence to reach any conclusions, but something seemed wrong. During a conversation with the controller about other matters, Lynn casually inquired about the payroll matter and was assured there were no problems. The controller suggested she forget the payroll question and concentrate on some other important matters. The following week the external auditors were to arrive.

Should Lynn tell the external auditors of the problems that could exist?

Would your answer be different if it were the internal audit staff?

Would your answers be different if Lynn had found real evidence that indicated the problem did indeed exist?

5–20 (*Sylvia Hutchison*)

Julius Caesaro, CPA, was engaged to perform an audit of the annual financial statements of Cleopatro Company. During the course of his examination of records, he discovered that certain items were misstated on the previous year's income tax return, which resulted in large tax advantages for Cleopatro Company. The tax return had been prepared by Mr. Caesaro's good friend, Anthony Markos, CPA. It appeared to Mr. Caesaro that the discrepancies on the tax return resulted from a deliberate effort to manipulate facts and figures with the sole intent of (illegally) reducing taxes.

Mr. Caesaro cannot decide what, if anything, he should do about this discovery. He does not want to offend either his audit client or his friend and colleague, Mr. Markos. Indeed, he is not sure of the exact root of the problem—whether Mr. Markos took it upon himself to juggle figures, whether the errors resulted from oversight or honest mistake by one or both parties, or whether there was from the beginning a Markos-Cleopatro collusion to deceive the tax authorities.

Can you give Mr. Caesaro any guidelines for action?

6

OTHER RESPONSIBILITIES AND PRACTICES

INTRODUCTION

It is impossible to list every possible circumstance in which the professional accountant may face an ethical question. His responsibilities and practice are so varied that he must be alert at all times to see that his motives and behavior are on the highest possible level.

Article II, entitled The Public Interest, one of the principles from The Code of Professional Conduct of the American Institute of Public Accountants, encompasses many of the responsibilities and practices not previously addressed:

> Members should accept the obligation to act in a way that will serve the public interest, honor the public trust, and demonstrate commitment to professionalism.[1]

The following paragraphs elaborate on this principle:

> A distinguishing mark of a profession is acceptance of its responsibility to the public. The accounting profession's public consists of clients, credit grantors, govern-

[1]*AICPA Professional Standards,* vol. 2, ET Section 53. Copyright © 1988 by the American Institute of Certified Public Accountants, Inc.

ments, employers, investors, the business and financial community, and others who rely on the objectivity and integrity of certified public accountants to maintain the orderly functioning of commerce. This reliance imposes a public interest responsibility on certified public accountants. The public interest is defined as the collective well-being of the community of people and institutions the profession serves.

In discharging their professional responsibilities, members may encounter conflicting pressures from among each of those groups. In resolving those conflicts, members should act with integrity, guided by the precept that when members fulfill their responsibility to the public, clients' and employers' interest are best served.

Those who rely on certified public accountants expect them to discharge their responsibilities with integrity, objectivity, due professional care, and a genuine interest in serving the public. They are expected to provide quality services, enter into fee arrangements, and offer a range of services—all in a manner that demonstrates a level of professionalism consistent with these Principles of the Code of Professional Conduct.

All who accept membership in the American Institute of Certified Public Accountants commit themselves to honor the public trust. In return for the faith that the public reposes in them, members should seek continually to demonstrate their dedication to professional excellence.[2]

THE AUDITOR

For over half a century prior to March 31, 1978, members of the organized public accounting profession in the United States were prohibited by their Code of Professional Ethics from advertising. From March 31, 1978 until March 31, 1979, the prohibition extended only to advertising or other forms of solicitaiton that were "false, misleading, or deceptive," and to "a direct uninvited solicitation of a specific potential client." Effective March 31, 1979, the latter prohibition was removed. In 1983, an additional prohibition against solicitation by the use or coercion, overreaching or harassing conduct was added.[3]

Assume that your firm is relatively small but over the years has developed great expertise in working with small- to medium-sized retail businesses. You not only audit these companies, but prepare their tax returns and serve as their management consultant. Would it be proper for you to advertise your special competence in this area?

Yes, there is no longer a prohibition against advertising your special competence or expertise in a particular area. You must be careful, however, that your advertising is not "false, misleading, or deceptive."

What if your firm is asked by a local chapter of the National Association of Accountants to place an ad in their monthly newsletter as a means of financing that publication? Could you do so? Would there be any restriction on the size of your ad, its style, or placement?

Yes, you could place the ad, as long as it is not false, misleading, or decep-

[2]Ibid.

[3]"Advertising and Other Forms of Solicitation," *AICPA Professional Standards*, vol. 2, ET Section 502.01. Copyright © 1988 by the American Institute of Certified Public Accountants, Inc.

tive. There are no restrictions as to the frequency of placement, size, artwork, or type style. Some examples of acceptable content are:

1. Information about the member and the member's firm, such as:
   a. Names, addresses, telephone numbers, number of partners, shareholders or employees, office hours, foreign language competence, and date the firm was established.
   b. Services offered and fees for such services, including hourly rates and fixed fees.
   c. Educational and professional attainments, including date and place of certifications, schools attended, dates of graduation, degrees received, and memberships in professional associations.
2. Statements of policy or position made by a member or a member's firm related to the practice of public accounting or addressed to a subject of public interest.

Commissions

The acceptance by a member of the AICPA in public practice of a payment for the referral of products or services of others to a client has long been prohibited. Such action was considered to create a conflict of interest that results in a loss of objectivity and independence. The payment by a member to obtain a client has also been prohibited. It was believed that a client should not have to pay a fee for which he did not receive commensurate services.

If the terms of a 1988 agreement with the Federal Trade Commission are finalized, the AICPA could no longer prohibit the payment or acceptance of a referral fee (compensation for recommending or referring any service of a CPA to any person), although it could impose a requirement that any AICPA member (a) who accepts a referral fee shall disclose that fact to the member's client or (b) who pays a referral fee to obtain a client shall disclose that fact to the client.

The terms of the agreement also provide that, with one exception, the AICPA could not prohibit the rendering of professional services for, or the receipt of, a commission (compensation, except a referral fee, for recommending or referring any product or service to be supplied by another person). The exception would be where the CPA also performs one of the following attest services for the client:

1. Any audit.
2. Any review of a financial statement.
3. Any compilation of a financial statement when the CPA expects, or reasonably might expect, that a third party will use the compilation and the CPA does not disclose a lack of independence.
4. Any examination of prospective financial information.

In these situations, the AICPA could prohibit a commission during the period of the attest services engagement and the period covered by any historical financial statements involved in such attest services. The AICPA could also impose a requirement that any AICPA member who has been paid or expects to be paid shall disclose that fact to any person to whom the CPA recommends or refers a product or service to which the commission relates.

Suppose, for example, that you have a small audit and tax practice, while your wife is an insurance agent. From time to time, in the course of your practice, you come upon clients who need insurance. Would it be ethical for you to refer these clients to your wife?

Your return in this case would be the economic benefit you derive from your wife's commission—a form of commission itself. Under the terms of the FTC agreement, the question would then be whether you have performed attest services for the client. If so, a commission would be prohibited and you could not make the referral.

Could you accept a commission from a computer dealer for recommending a particular computer system to your client? Again, under the terms of the FTC agreement, the answer would hinge on whether you perform attest services for the client. If your only service is in a management advisory services capacity, the commission would be acceptable.

If the FTC agreement is not finalized, the commission in each of the above cases would be unethical, whether or not attest services were performed for the client.

THE MANAGEMENT CONSULTANT AND THE TAX PRACTITIONER

The advertising question is of significance to the management consultant and the tax practitioner, as well as to the auditor. Suppose, for example, that your firm wished to sponsor a radio program on taxation issues during tax season. Listeners could call in with questions, and you would present a tax tip of interest to small businessmen in the area. Or what if your management consulting group wanted to sponsor a seminar on cash flow analysis to show businessmen how to better budget and control their cash flows. Are either of these activities acceptable?

CPAs engage in a variety of activities to enhance their reputations and professional stature with the objective of expanding their clientele. Such indirect forms of solicitation, which include giving speeches, conducting seminars, distributing professional literature, and writing articles and books, are normally considered to be in the public interest and are permitted. Sponsoring a radio program would probably also fall in this category.

Are there any ground rules for determining if a particular piece of advertising is "false, misleading, or deceptive?" Is it permissible, for example, for you as a successful management consultant to quote your satisfied clients? Can you compare the quality of your services in a particular area with those of your competitors? You might point out, for example, that 90 percent of your tax staff served previously with the Internal Revenue Service, as compared with a 25 percent rate for other firms.

One of the official interpreations of Rule 502 offers some guidance on these questions. Examples of activities that would be prohibited are those that:

1. Create false or unjustified expectations of favorable results.
2. Imply the ability to influence any court, tribunal, regulatory agency, or similar body or official.
3. Consist of self-laudatory statements that are not based on verifiable facts.
4. Make comparisons with other CPAs that are not based on verifiable facts.
5. Contain a representation that specific professional services in current or future periods will be performed for a stated fee, estimated fee or fee range when it was likely at the time of the representation that such fees would be substantially increased and the prospective client was not advised of that likelihood.
6. Contain any other representations that would be likely to cause a reasonable person to misunderstand or be deceived.[4]

If the terms of the FTC agreement quoted in the preceding section are finalized, activities (3) and (4) previously stated would no longer be prohibited.

Thus, you *could* quote your satisfied clients, and you *could* compare the quality of your services with those of your competitors. If the FTC agreement is not finalized, such a comparison would have to be based on verifiable facts. A statement that 90 percent of your tax staff served previously with the IRS might be challenged as implying the ability to influence a governmental body.

Form of Practice

The form of your practice is also governed by the Code of Professional Conduct. Suppose, for example, that your firm engages in a great deal of write-up work and provides accounting services to many clients. You have the opportunity to acquire a 75 percent interest in a corporation which offers data processing services to the public. You would be able to better serve your own clients if you had control of this data processing installation. Would such a step be a violation of the Code?

Rule 505 states that "a member may practice public accounting only in the form of a proprietorship, a partnership, or a professional corporation whose characteristics conform to resolutions of Council."[5] These characteristics are:

1. Ownership. All shareholders of the corporation or association shall be persons engaged in the practice of public accounting as defined by the Code of Professional Conduct. Shareholders shall at all times own their shares in

[4]Ibid., ET Section 502.03.
[5]"Form of Practice and Name," *AICPA Professional Standards*, vol. 2, ET Section 505.01.

their own right, and shall be the beneficial owners of the equity capital ascribed to them.

2. Transfer of Shares. Provision shall be made requiring any shareholder who ceases to be eligible to be a shareholder to dispose of all of his shares within a reasonable period to a person qualified to be a shareholder or to the corporation or association.
3. Directors and Officers. The principal executive officer shall be a shareholder and a director, and to the extent possible, all other directors and officers shall be certified public accountants. Lay directors and officers shall not exercise any authority whatsoever over professional matters.
4. Conduct. The right to practice as a corporation or association shall not change the obligation of its shareholders, directors, officers and other employees to comply with the Code of Professional Conduct established by the American Institute of Certified Public Accountants.[6]

The data processing corporation does not appear to have the requisite characteristics of a professional corporation. A member, however, may have a financial interest in a commercial corporation which performs for the public services of a type performed by public accountants and whose characteristics do not conform to resolutions of Council, provided such interest is not material to the corporation's net worth, and the member's interest in and relation to the corporation is solely that of an investor.[7] The proposed 75 percent material interest in the data processing corporation would, therefore, be a violation of this provision. Your interest would certainly be material to the corporation's net worth, and your relation to the corporation would not be solely that of an investor.

It is, however, permissible for a member in public practice to operate a separate business that offers clients one or more types of services rendered by public accountants. In such a case, the member is considered to be in the practice of public accounting in the conduct of that business and would simply be required to observe all the Rules of the Code of Professional Conduct in its operation.[8]

THE INTERNAL PROFESSIONAL

One responsibility of the internal professional which places his integrity and reputation squarely on the line is his signature on management representation letters. The chief financial officer of a corporation, as well as its chief executive officer, are normally asked to sign these letters on behalf of management.

One type of management representation letter is required by the indepen-

[6]"Council Resolution Concerning Professional Corporations or Associations," *AICPA Professional Standards,* vol. 2, ET Appendix B. Copyright © 1988 by the American Institute of Certified Public Accountants, Inc.

[7]"Form of Practice and Name," *AICPA Professional Standards,* vol. 2, ET Section 505.02.

[8]Ibid., ET Section 505.03.

dent auditor as part of his examination. These representations, involving some matters which are the direct responsibility of the internal professional accountant, comprise part of the evidential matter the auditor obtains. They "ordinarily confirm oral representations given to the auditor, indicate and document the continuing appropriateness of such representations, and reduce the possibility of misunderstanding concerning matters that are the subject of the representations."[9] The casual signing of such a letter by an internal professional, without substantive knowledge that all of the statements in it are correct, would certainly be an act discreditable to the profession. A CPA acting in such a fashion would be in violation of Rule 501,[10] and a CMA would certainly be in violation of the high standard of his calling.

Another management representation letter which the internal professional is likely to have to sign and vouch for is one advocated by the Commission on Auditors' Responsibilities (Cohen Commission, 1978), the Financial Executives Institute (1978), the Treadway Commission (1987), and the Securities and Exchange Commission 1979 and 1988). The FEI's committee on corporate reporting has recommended that financial statements be accompanied by a management report. The committee stated that "we believe that such reports will further public understanding of the respective roles of management and the outside auditor, and the 'report' should emphasize that the primary responsibility for financial statements and representations related thereto rests with management, and not with the Certified Public Accountant, whose role is one of independent verification." Included in such a report would be comments on the system of internal accounting controls, the preparation and presentation of the financial statements in conformity with generally accepted accounting principles appropriate in the circumstances, and the quality of the data in the statements, all of which fall within the purview of the internal professional.[11] The Treadway Commission called specifically for management's assessment of the effectiveness of the company's internal controls.

Other Occupations

Can an internal professional concurrently engage in another occupation? For example, would it be ethical for the assistant controller of a manufacturing company to accept engagements as a systems consultant for other companies? Could an internal professional working for the Internal Revenue Service moonlight as a tax consultant?

Perhaps the guiding standard in arriving at an answer to these questions can be borrowed from Rule 102, which governs CPAs:

> In the performance on any professional service, a member shall maintain objectivity and integrity, shall be free of conflicts of interest, and shall not knowingly misrepresent facts or subordinate his or her judgment to others.[12]

[9] "Client Representations," *AICPA Professional Standards,* vol. 1, AU Section 333.02.

[10] "Acts Discreditable," *AICPA Professional Standards,* vol. 2, ET Section 501.

[11] "FEI Calls for 'Management Reports' in Annual Reports," *Journal of Accountancy,* August 1978, pp. 14, 20.

[12] "Integrity and Objectivity," *AICPA Professional Standards,* vol. 2, ET Section 102.01.

The decision would be clear-cut in the case of the Internal Revenue Service employee. Certainly, moonlighting as a tax consultant would create a conflict of interest with his primary job. As one working for the tax collection agency, he could not at the same time counsel the one being taxed. The case of the assistant controller is not quite so easy. So long as the companies with which he consults are not in competition with his own company, and his employer does not object, there would appear to be no reason why he could not engage in such activity. If he is a CPA, he would, of course, need to abide by all of the other Rules in the Code of Professional Conduct in connection with his consulting practice.

SCOPE OF PRACTICE

One of the principles in the AICPA Code of Professional Conduct addresses the issue of Scope of Practice. Article VI is entitled Scope and Nature of Services:

> The public interest aspect of certified public accountants' services requires that such services be consistent with acceptable professional behavior for certified public accountants. Integrity requires that service and the public trust not be subordinated to personal gain and advantage. Objectivity and independence require that members be free from conflicts of interest in discharging professional responsibilities. Due care requires that services be provided with competence and dilligence.
>
> Each of these Principles should be considered by members in determining whether or not to provide specific services in individual circumstances. In some instances, they may represent an overall constraint on the nonaudit services that might be offered to a specific client. No hard-and-fast rules can be developed to help members reach these judgments, but they must be satisfied that they are meeting the spirit of the Principles in this regard.
>
> In order to accomplish this, members should:
>
> - Practice in firms that have in place internal quality control procedures to ensure that services are competently delivered and adequately supervised.
> - Determine, in their individual judgments, whether the scope and nature of other services provided to an audit client would create a conflict of interest in the performance of the audit function for that client.
> - Assess, in their individual judgments, whether an activity is consistent with their role as professionals (for example, is such activity a reasonable extension or variation of existing services offered by the member or others in the profession?)[13]

Concern is often centered on firms with both an audit practice and a management advisory services practice. Some have argued strongly that some of these services are not really the practice of public accounting, that some of them impair auditor independence and are in essence incompatible occupations.

The Public Oversight Board of the SEC Practice Section has taken the position that "mandatory limitations on the scope of services should be predicated only

[13]"Scope and Nature of Services," *AICPA Professional Standards*, vol. 2, ET SEction 57. Copyright © 1989 by the American Institute of Certified Public Accountants, Inc.

on the determination that certain services, or the role of the firm performing certain services, will impair the member's independence in rendering an opinion on the fairness of a client's financial statements or present a strong likelihood of doing so."[14] The Board further states that the profession "should be careful not to impose unnecessarily prophylactic rules with regard to MAS and independence" because of the "many potential benefits to be realized by permitting auditors to perform MAS for audit clients.[15]

Many avenues are available to insure the objectivity and independence of auditors performing management advisory services. Various sections of the AICPA Code of Professional Conduct and of the Statements on Standards for Management Advisory Services address these issues. In addition, disclosure of the extent and nature of management advisory services carried out by an individual firm is now required for those firms who are members of the SEC Practice Section. Members of the Section, as a requirement of membership, must disclose their gross fees for accounting and auditing, tax, and MAS expressed as a percentage of total gross fees. In addition, they must disclose the gross fees for both MAS and tax services performed for SEC audit clients expressed as a percentage of total fees charged to all SEC audit clients.[16]

Peer review is, of course, required for all members of the AICPA Division for CPA firms, thus providing an avenue for determining adherence to the prescribed principle of objectivity and independence.

In addition to prohibiting psychological testing, public opinion polls, and mergers and acquisition for a finder's fee, the Executive Committee of the SEC Practice Section, with the support of the Public Oversight Board, has prohibited certain types of executive recruiting services. These types of services are perceived by some as having a strong likelihood of impairing independence. In addition, certain limitations have been set forth relative to the rendering of actuarially oriented advisory services to audit clients. These positions are set forth in Appendix A of the SEC Practice Section SECPS Manual

EXECUTIVE RECRUITING SERVICES

> The hiring of persons for managerial, executive, or director positions is a function which is properly the client's responsibility. Accordingly, the role of a member firm in this function should be limited. In serving an audit client whose securities are registered with the SEC, a member firm should not:
>
> 1. Accept an engagement to search for, or seek out, prospective candidates for managerial, executive, or director positions with its audit clients. This would not preclude giving the name of a prospective candidate previously known to someone in the member firm, provided such knowledge was not obtained as a result of the performance of executive recruiting services for another client.
> 2. Engage in psychological testing, other formal testing or evaluation programs, or

[14]Public Oversight Board, *Scope of Services by CPA Firms* (New York: American Institute of Certified Public Accountants, 1979), p. 4.

[15]Ibid.

[16]*AICPA Division for CPA Firms SEC Practice Section SECPS Manual,* AICPA, pp. 1-8 and 1-9.

undertake reference checks of prospective candidates for an executive or director position.

3. Act as a negotiator on the client's behalf, for example, in determining position status or title, compensation, fringe benefits, or other conditions of employment.
4. Recommend, or advise the client to hire, a specific candidate for a specific job. However, a member firm may, upon request by the client, interview candidates and advise the client on the candidate's competence for financial, accounting, or control positions.

When a client seeks to fill a position within its organization that is related to its system of accounting, financial, or administrative controls, the client will frequently approach employees of the member firm directly as candidates or seek referral of the member firm's employees who may be considering employment outside of the profession. Such employment from time to time is an inevitable consequence of the training and experience that the public accounting profession provides to its staff, is beneficial to all concerned, including society in general, and therefore is not proscribed.

INSURANCE ACTUARIAL SERVICES

Actuarial skills are both accounting and auditing related. The bodies of knowledge supporting the actuarial and accounting professions have a substantial degree of overlap. Both professions involve the analysis of various factors of time, probability and economics, and the quantification of such analysis in financial terms. The results of their work are significantly interrelated. The professions are logical extensions of each other: indeed, they have practiced jointly for many years and even shared the same professional society in Scotland prior to their becoming established in the United States.

The work of actuarial specialists generally is necessary to obtain audit satisfaction in support of insurance policy and loss reserves. To assist them in meeting their audit responsibilities, a number of CPA firms have hired qualified actuaries of their own.

The actuarial function is basic to the operation and management of an insurance company. Management's responsibility for this function cannot be assumed by the CPA firm without jeopardizing the CPA firm's independence. Because of the special significance of the CPA firm's appearance of independence when auditing publicly held insurance companies:

1. The CPA firm should not render actuarially oriented advisory services involving the determination of policy reserves and related accounts to its audit clients unless such clients utilize their own actuaries or third party actuaries to provide management with the primary actuarial capabilities. This does not preclude the use of the CPA firm's actuarial staff in connection with the auditing of such reserves.
2. Whenever the CPA firm renders actuarially oriented advisory services, it must satisfy itself that it is acting in an advisory capacity and that the responsibility for any significant actuarial methods and assumptions is accepted by the client.
3. The CPA firm should not render actuarially oriented advisory services when the CPA firm's involvement is continuous since such a relationship might be perceived as an engagement to perform a management function.

Subject to the above limitations it is appropriate for the CPA firm to render certain actuarially oriented advisory services to its audit clients. Such services include:

1. Assisting management to develop appropriate methods, assumptions, and amounts for policy and loss reserves and other actuarial items presented in financial reports based on the company's historical experience, current practices and future plans.
2. Assisting management in the conversion of financial statements from a statutory basis to one conforming with generally accepted accounting principles.
3. Analyzing actuarial considerations and alternatives in federal income tax planning.
4. Assisting management in the financial analyses of various matters such as proposed new policies, new markets, business acquisitions and reinsurance needs.[17]

MANAGEMENT ADVISORY SERVICES: COMPATIBILITY AND INDEPENDENCE

Stanley R. Klion, an experienced management consultant, discusses in the following article the relationship of management advisory services to the audit practice of a CPA firm, as well as the value of such services to clients, shareholders, and society at large. Although the article is biased in favor of MAS, the major issues relative to independence and objectivity are raised.

It is likely that few other professions in modern times have been exposed to public scrutiny to the degree that the accounting profession is at present. Indeed, it seems fair to suggest that the profession is at the most critical stage in its history. Every aspect of it is under review—from its professional organizational structure to its independence and ethics to the basic principles by which it performs its various functions.

And if the accounting profession in its entirety is under attack, certainly management advisory services have not escaped notice. MAS practitioners find themselves defending the scope of their practice, the impact of their activities on audit independence, indeed their very reason for being. I cannot speak for all of the 7,000 to 8,000 full-time MAS practitioners who work in a CPA environment;. . . But I have been actively involved in MAS for more than twenty years with a large international CPA firm, and I have served three terms on the AICPA MAS executive committee, . . . Accordingly, I believe I can speak from personal experience and knowledge of the realities of MAS practice. In my view, it is important that the position set forth in this article be presented because the bulk of the public pronouncements, articles, research reports and the like, has presented what I believe to be a distorted and erroneous appraisal of MAS activities.

Let's start with my conclusions:

1. *MAS practice is an integral part of the public accounting profession* and has been since it was organized more than eighty years ago. Today, there is hardly a practice unit, from the national firms to the sole practitioner, that does not provide business counsel to its clients. Businessmen look to their CPAs for business insight and advice because the CPA has demonstrated his competence in this field for many years.
2. *The critical relationship between the CPA as an MAS practitioner and his client relates to his role as an advisor* rather than to the subject matter or technical component of any particular engagement.

[17]Ibid., pp. 1–17 and 1–19.

3. *MAS capabilities are increasingly important in enhancing the quality of audits,* and the absence or proscription of such skills in a CPA environment will adversely affect audit performance.
4. *There are demonstrable advantages to clients in obtaining MAS from their CPAs.*
5. *Examination of the impact of MAS activities on auditors' independence has yet to produce the first hard instance of compromise,* although this question has been one of the most thoroughly researched subjects in the profession. . . .

Let's look at each of these matters in turn.

MAS PART OF THE PUBLIC ACCOUNTING PROFESSION

From the beginning of the accounting profession, the businessman has looked to his CPA to provide business advice and insight in a number of areas. Obviously, the CPA renders bookkeeping and accounting advice, but he is also the source of counsel on a great many business management matters, including organization, costing, inventory control, data processing, internal control, administrative procedures and other business functions. In many cases, the businessman also looks to the accountant to assist him in locating accounting and administrative personnel. These services were, and continue to be, sought because the CPA is in the unique position of serving many business enterprises, and his clients wish to avail themselves of the knowledge and experience that the CPA obtains through his exposure to business needs and concerns. To this day, this generalized description of services rendered by a CPA to his clients probably refers to the bulk of the accounting profession in public practice.

There is nothing sinister or devious in a businessman's seeking such counsel from his CPA; indeed, as the businessman profits from this advice, stockholders and society should be the better for it. In turn, the CPA carefully guards the integrity and independence of this relationship. His reputation and livelihood depend on his ability to advise clients in confidence and with competence. One result of this "advice-giving" has been the expansion of the number of individuals or groups of MAS practitioners to be found in CPA practice units of all sizes.

In our economic system, such growth can take place only if the services rendered serve a specific need and are of a quality to demand their expansion. To suggest, as did one witness before the late Senator Lee Metcalf's Subcommittee on Reports, Accounting and Management of the Senate Committee on Governmental Affairs, that the CPA takes unfair advantage of his overall client relationship to render such services is to deny the logic that the client makes the final judgment on obtaining counsel from among all the sources available; the MAS practitioner does not provide it as a right. Were the CPA not considered a prime source of MAS, clearly these services would not have grown as they have. If the business community may look only to certain persons for its business counseling and not to others, irrespective of competence, competition is not fostered; it is restricted. And one need only attend any bidders' conference of a public or private sector request for proposal to dismiss the erroneous allegation that real competition does not exist within the profession and between CPA firms and other providers of MAS.

Current professional literature recognizes the wide variety of services rendered by CPAs to their clients. Structured services are described fully. . . . The need for such services, both informal and structured, is best tested in the marketplace. When the services cease to be of value, the businessman will cease to obtain them from his CPA.

THE ROLE OF THE MAS PRACTITIONER

The role of the CPA in providing advisory services is the most efficient criterion for identifying the types of MAS that are appropriate for CPAs to render to both audit and nonaudit clients. Basically, this role is to provide advice and technical assistance but to avoid assuming the responsibilities of client management to make decisions. . . .

Attempts to establish relatively objective criteria based on factors other than role have been fruitless. Typically, these other factors have involved either the functional or the technical aspects of the services provided. The functional aspects relate to the client's operational functions, e.g., finance, manufacturing, engineering, marketing, industrial relations, etc. Technical aspects are concerned with the particular academic discipline or skill on which the service is based, e.g., systems analysis, data processing, management sciences, etc. Because most MAS engagements involve many different operational functions and a variety of technical disciplines, useful advisory services might cease if they were to be curtailed in these terms. Even such traditional and relatively uncontroversial services as the design of a management information or inventory control system might not be performed properly if the CPA's fact-finding and recommendations for procedural improvements were confined to the client's accounting or finance department and could not extend to the marketing, distribution, engineering and manufacturing functions. Similarly, the CPA's services would probably be of limited value if he restricted the skills he applies to those traditionally associated with a narrow definition of accounting, ignoring the benefits his client might often realize from the use of, for example, sophisticated mathematical techniques.

It is important to recognize that the role of MAS practitioners is to counsel and to make recommendations to their clients. It is not to participate in management decision-making. A proper understanding of this relationship should lay to rest the concern of some that MAS somehow compromises the independence of the auditor.

ENHANCING THE QUALITY OF AUDITS

The performance of MAS enhances the quality of audits. In most CPA firms, audits of clients and sophisticated information systems depend significantly on the technical skills of the personnel employed and trained primarily for MAS work. MAS assistance in designing or improving clients' control systems results in more reliable financial information. It is not uncommon for work performed as part of an MAS engagement to lead directly to improvements in financial statements or in the auditing procedures applied to them.

When an auditor (or auditing firm) provides MAS to a client, the reliability of the client's financial statements and the quality and effectiveness of the audit are directly enhanced in five ways:

1. *Controls incorporated in the design of a financial information system.* Because of the CPA's "control consciousness," financial information systems designed and installed by CPAs can be expected to have better controls and greater auditability than systems designed by others. This is equally true for information systems that are oriented primarily toward operations but that produce accounting by-products, such as inventory management or production planning and scheduling systems.

   A reasonable extension of this concept strongly indicates that other advisory services, when performed by auditors, can effectively enhance the client's financial controls. For example, the auditor's assistance can be particularly valuable in evaluating the technical qualifications of senior accounting personnel because of the CPA's own technical competence and his strong motivation to have highly qualified personnel prepare the financial statements on which he will express an opinion.

2. *Correction of control deficiencies.* A key audit procedure is the study and evaluation of internal control. It would be counterproductive to prohibit the auditor from communicating to the client any weaknesses or defects he observes. It would be just as unsound to prohibit the auditor from making specific recommendations for improvement, because no one is better qualified to do so. Any restrictions on the auditor's assistance in implementing the improvements would also be illogical. The auditor's affirmative participation in such circumstances results in improved controls on financial information and, consequently, in improved reliability of financial statements.
3. *Effective conduct of the audit.* MAS work enables the auditor to understand better his client and the client's operations and information systems. This increased familiarity results in more effective audit procedures, more perceptive analytical reviews and greater sensitivity to problem areas that deserve intensive scrutiny.
4. *Utilization of MAS technical skills.* The auditor's need to rely on specialized competencies not normally included in a narrow definition of accountancy has increased greatly in recent years, and this growth can be expected to continue. It might be argued that the auditor is responsible for providing those skills, either from within his organization or from outside experts, regardless of inconvenience. Auditors normally do just that. However, their ability or inclination to do so could be seriously diminished if they are unable to maintain the needed skills within their own organizations while, at the same time, they are held professionally responsible for the results.

   Computer auditing provides the most obvious example. Some CPA firms customarily call on their MAS personnel to provide the needed technical skills. Others have computer audit specialists, but even these firms often involve their MAS personnel in particularly difficult or sensitive investigations because of the MAS staff's broader technical knowledge and experience. Moreover, computer audit software, typically employed in audits of even modest sophistication, is the direct result of MAS competence resident in the various firms that develop or use this important audit tool.

   Accounting firms would find it uneconomical, and even impossible, to maintain sufficient expertise within their organizations if such personnel could not be used on, and stimulated by, consulting assignments. And securing appropriate assistance from an outside expert is often an unsatisfactory last resort because of cost, decentralized responsibility, lack of direct control over the outside expert's activities and uncertainty about his full understanding of the audit function. Indeed, it is ironic that, at the very time when the SEC is seeking to have auditors report publicly on their clients' systems of internal control and become involved in forecasting, there is a movement afoot to cut back or proscribe the specific talents that auditors require to perform these activities.
5. *Enhancement of the auditor's image.* If the profession would limit its professional services to only those that constitute an essential part of audits, it would become much narrower and more highly specialized than it is today. The resultant deterioration of the image of the CPA profession would diminish its auditing effectiveness in two distinct ways.

   The first would be to discourage the entry of many highly qualified graduates into auditing firms. Graese stated it well in 1967, and I believe it is not less true today: "To anyone who has engaged in college recruiting, particularly at the graduate level, it goes without saying that the embracing of management [advisory] services by the CPA firms has been a major factor in enhancing the general status of the CPA profession. Any profession, in order to survive, needs to attract promising young men to its ranks."*

The second detrimental effect of the CPA's diminished image concerns financial statement users' perceptions of the auditor's overall competence. It could be difficult for auditors to maintain a useful level of credibility if the public viewed their function as simply limited to vouching and confirming transaction samples, checking the logic and arithmetic of transaction compilations and evaluating the application of generally accepted accounting principles. Such auditors might appear to be operating in an artificial environment, insulated from the real world of business. Their credibility in attesting to the overall fairness of presentation, and in relating their conclusions to the broad economic and operating factors affecting their clients' financial health, could be sharply diminished.

In contrast, the knowledge that businesses frequently turn to their auditors for advice and assistance in translating information about economic events into usable management information reinforces the image of auditors as competent, knowledgeable and constructive professionals.

ADVANTAGES TO CLIENTS

When a client requires MAS, he can turn to his auditor, to another consulting organization or do without the services. Here are five benefits that, in most cases, the auditor can best provide:

1. *Familiarity with client.* The accounting firm is already familiar with the client and his objectives, operations, finances, organization and personnel. MAS personnel have ready access to additional details, either by referring to workpapers or by direct contact with audit personnel. At the very least, this enables the consulting project to get under way more quickly and more efficiently. In many circumstances, it will result in a more responsible and effective end product.
2. *Confidence of client.* The final objective of most consulting engagements is some sort of action. If such action does not occur, the engagement is of questionable value. Accordingly, the consultant who is most effective at stimulating appropriate action is the one who usually produces the greatest client benefit.

   A consultant's effectiveness at stimulating action is directly related to the client's confidence in him. All things being equal, the client's confidence in his accounting firm, usually built up, maintained and reinforced over years of professional association, will usually exceed his confidence in a firm that lacks this continuing relationship.
3. *Follow-through.* Since the accounting firm continues in close contact with the client after completion of the consulting engagement, it will have greater opportunity to monitor and appraise the implementation of the recommended course of action. This follow-through is critical to successful results.
4. *Incentive for quality.* In most instances a recurring annual audit fee is of much greater commercial value to the accounting firm than the fee for a consulting engagement.

*C. E. Graese, "Management Services and the Independence Issue," *New York Certified Public Accountant,* June 1967, p. 436. This article reprinted with permission from *The CPA Journal,* published by the New York State Society of Certified Public Accountants.

Therefore, good business practice compels the accountant to avoid overselling his services or undertaking a job for which he lacks competence. And he has a powerful incentive to produce work of the highest quality, regardless of whether the cost of the engagement exceeds his original expectations.

5. *Audits of efficiency, economy and program results.* Although the majority of CPA firms are not at present involved in government auditing for efficiency and effectiveness, those firms that do participate extensively, and those that expect to in the future, must have the necessary skills. . . .

CPAs traditionally have recognized that they often supplement the GAO's audit staff in conducting government audits, especially of state and local entities and programs and of grant recipients. It is doubtful that CPA firms could maintain the necessary technical competencies if it were not for the requirements of their MAS practice. . . .

MAS ACTIVITIES AND AUDITORS' INDEPENDENCE

The fundamental issue encountered in evaluating the relationship of MAS to the audit function is the possibility that, by providing MAS to an audit client, a CPA might somehow jeopardize either the substance or the appearance of his independence as auditor.

Independence traditionally has been defined by the CPA profession as the ability to act with integrity and objectivity. In this sense, integrity is equivalent to honesty or to trustworthiness and incorruptibility even in the face of strong pressures. Objectivity is lack of bias and resistance of any conscious or subconscious influences toward action, inaction, conclusions or statements that are based on anything other than an impartial evaluation of the best available evidence.

Few aspects of the practice of accountancy have been questioned more frequently or scrutinized more closely than the potential effects of MAS on audit independence. . . .

Many of the researchers who questioned the independence of an auditor who performs MAS seem to have started with the hypothesis that auditing and MAS are somehow incompatible. Using questionnaires, information was compiled on the attitudes of informed users of financial statements toward this hypothesis. . . .

Despite more than fifteen years of research—much of which conducted by persons, however sincere their motives, with an apparent preconception about the impropriety of MAS—the record of MAS practice as it relates to audit independence is unblemished: *Not a single compromising instance has been presented.* Both equity and reason would seem to suggest that the question has been answered adequately.

As to the argument that MAS created the appearance of lack of independence of the auditor, no relationship between the offeror and the user of professional services can be totally immune from such perceptions. Payment of fees, personal friendship, joint service in community activities—these and many other factors might conceivably affect the auditor's independence, however slightly. But given the ethical and professional constraints placed on practitioners by the AICPA, the state CPA societies and the state boards of accountancy, the internal control procedures of auditing firms regarding MAS activities and the integrity and objectivity that are the cornerstones of every professional's reputation and career, one must ask, What more is necessary? At what point may the profession provide services requested by and beneficial to its clientele? The continuing unsubstantiated suggestion that there is something vaguely wrong with MAS activities must adversely affect the MAS practitioner. Ultimately, these allegations, although unproved, will produce a result that scholarly research has failed to justify: the diminution of MAS skills in auditing firms to the detriment of all who are involved—the professional, his client, shareholders and society at large.

Academicians, congressional committees, AICPA commissions—all have set out to examine the problem. None have found a substantiation of the allegation that MAS activities impair independence. The profession should be permitted to practice its skills in a free marketplace, subject to current regulations, ethical codes and practice standards—unless hard evidence is produced that our independence has actually been impaired. So far, no such evidence has been produced. From the intensity of recent scrutiny, I suspect that none will be. Therefore, it is time for the profession to move ahead with MAS—not retreat.[18]

DUAL PRACTICE OF LAW AND ACCOUNTING

Another question arising in connection with incompatible occupations is whether or not it is ethical to practice law and accounting concurrently. One possible basis under the AICPA Code of Professional Conduct for charging that the practice of law is incompatible with the practice of accounting is that it creates a "conflict of interest" or that it "impairs the member's objectivity."[19] It might also be asserted that it impairs the auditor's independence and thus is a violation of another section of the code (Rule 101).

The assertion that the dual practice of law and accounting, in and of itself, creates a conflict of interest, impairs a member's objectivity, or impairs his independence is probably not supportable. While it is easy to imagine particular circumstances that would cause a conflict or impairment, it is equally easy to imagine other circumstances with no such effect.

A management consulting engagement for an accounting client might, for example, be conducted concurrently with the preparation of legal documents for another client, with no code violation. Similarly, an accounting tax practitioner might at the same time practice law in the area of trusts and estates. On the other hand, a conflict of interest and an impairment of objectivity and independence would clearly result if a lawyer/accountant served as legal counsel for a company bringing action against his audit client. There would also be a serious question as to whether an auditor's independence could be maintained if he served as legal counsel for his client. Thus, while the AICPA Code of Professional Conduct does not prohibit the dual practice of law and accounting, it does raise some serious questions about the nature of the practice.

The American Bar Association, likewise, does not prohibit dual practice. Furthermore, the ABA Model Rules no longer prohibit a lawyer from stating on a

[18]Stanley R. Klion, "MAS Practice: Are the Critics Justified?" *Journal of Accountancy*, June 1978, pp. 72–78. Copyright © 1978 by the American Institute of Certified Public Accountants, Inc.

[19]"Integrity and Objectivity," *AICPA Professional Standards*, vol. 2, ET Section 102.01.

letterhead, office sign, or business card that he is qualified in a different professional field, such as accounting. Most states, also, allow listing of dual professions, although some still restrict it. [See ABA/BNA Lawyers' Manual on Professional Conduct, pp. 81:3012 adn 81:3013]. It is clear that dual practice should be approached cautiously and with careful attention to the ethical codes of both professions.

THE SMALL CLIENT AND REPRESENTATION LETTERS

The representation letter required by auditors from their clients, which was discussed earlier in the chapter in the context of the responsibility of the internal professional, is of particular concern to the small practitioner and his client. In the following article, the author discusses the usefulness of such a letter in establishing the client's responsibility for his own financial statements, as well as in establishing the auditor's independence. The desirability of an engagement letter is also discussed.

Your field work is completed; you have just finished reviewing the pencil copy of the annual financial statements with your client. Before you leave his office, you give him the client representation letter for his signature. You put on your hat and coat and stand, briefcase resting on the edge of the desk, waiting for the final document which will allow you to complete the audit and have the report typed for distribution to banks and other credit grantors.

"Wait a minute," says the client. "I am not 'responsible for the fair presentation in the. . . financial statements of financial position, results of operations and changes in financial position in conformity with generally accepted accounting principles.'* You are. You prepare my unaudited quarterly financial statements, and you prepare my audited annual financial statements. You decide what accounting principles to use—I don't. I don't know what generally accepted accounting principles are, let alone whether my statements are prepared in conformity with them. I won't sign the letter unless you eliminate this section."

You close your briefcase, remove your hat and coat and sit down. Patiently, you say, "Although I have prepared the financial statements, they are yours. They are your representation prepared from your books and records which summarize transactions you initiated or participated in. I must have your signature of this letter or I cannot issue a clean opinion on your financial statements."

Your client thinks for a moment and responds, "I run a $5 million a year manufacturing company; I purchase, I sell and I supervise production. I have a head bookkeeper and four clerks who keep my books and records. I depend on you to review their work, correct their errors and tell them how to record unusual transactions. I rely on you for financial and tax advice. If you want me to sign that letter, you'll have to give me a better explanation of why I must sign it, and then you'll have to modify it. I suggest you do some research and come back in a day or two."

Frustrated and disgruntled, you once again put on your hat and coat and depart for your office and your library. Clearly, a major question must be answered.

*Statement on Auditing Standards No. 19, *Client Representations* (New York: AICPA, 1977), p. 8. [AICPA Professional Standards, vol. 2, AU Section 333]

WHOSE STATEMENTS ARE THEY?

While the client may have doubts as to who is responsible for the content of his financial statements, the literature leaves no doubt. As far back as 1939, the American Institute of Accountants stated that "the function of the independent certified public accountant is to examine a concern's accounting records and supporting data. . . . to the extent necessary to enable him to form an opinion as to whether or not the financial statements *as submitted* present fairly. . . . " (Emphasis added.)*

It further stated that "management itself has the direct responsibility for the maintenance of an adequate and effective system of acocunts, for the proper recording of transactions in the books of account. . . . It is also charged with the primary responsibility. . . for the substantial accuracy and adequacy of statements of position and operations. . . ."†

The above statements were issued by the AIA committee on auditing procedure. To further reinforce the concept that the financial statements were representations of management, the Institute committee on accounting procedure stated in 1939 that "underlying all committee opinions is the fact that the accounts of a company are primarily the responsibility of management. The responsibility of the auditor is to express his opinion concerning the financial statements. . . ."‡

In its first codification of auditing procedures issued in 1951, the Institute stated that "the independent auditor's knowledge of them [the company's accounting transactions] is a secondary one, based on his examination. Accordingly, even though the form of the statements may show the influence of the accountant—it can do so only if the company accepts, and adopts, the form of disclosure advised by the accountant—the substance of the financial statements of necessity constitutes the representations of the company."§

While the above statements may appear to be directed to those companies with the human resources necessary to prepare financial statements, their implications are clear:

"In the case of some concerns the statements may, in fact, be prepared by the auditor from the books after giving effect to the results of his examination, in which event he will naturally discuss with the client any adjustments which may have been made in the figures as shown on the face of the books, and the form of presentation to be used. As to any such adjustments, the auditor will naturally seek to obtain concurrence of the client. In either event, the statements are regarded as the representations of the client. In the former event [prepared by company personnel] they are not only theoretically so but even physically so. In the latter event [prepared by company auditor] they are so becasue the client adopts them as his and decides whether they shall be promulgated."**

The Securities and Exchange Commission has taken an even more rigorous position than the accounting profession on management responsibility for the books and records and financial statements of the company. It considers the accountant's independence lost if he performs any bookkeeping services whatsoever. Thus, the commission has stated:

*Statement on Auditing Procedure No. 1, *Extensions of Auditing Procedure* (New York: AIA, 1939), pp. 3–4.

†Ibid., p. 4

‡Accounting Research Bulletin No. 1 (New York: AIA, 1939). See also Accounting Research Bulletin No. 43 (New York: AICPA, 1953), Introduction, par. 11.

§*Codification of Statements on Auditing Procedure* (New York: AIA, 1951), p. 12.

**Walter A. Staub, *Auditing Developments During the Present Century* (Cambridge, Mass.: Harvard University Press, 1942), p. 68.

"The fundamental and primary responsibility for the accuracy of information filed with the Commission and disseminated among the investors rests upon management. Management does not discharge its obligations in this respect by the employment of independent public accountants, however, reputable. Accountants' certificates are required not as a substitute for management's accounting of its stewardship, but as a check upon that accounting."*

The SEC and the accounting profession both have recognized the primacy of management's financial reporting obligations. The small or closely held business that retains an accountant to perform both auditing and accounting services must recognize that although the CPA may suggest adjusting entries and often prepare the financial statements, his knowledge of the transactions is a secondary one.

CLIENT'S WRITTEN REPRESENTATIONS

Before Statement on Auditing Standards No. 19, *Client Representations,* generally accepted auditing standards, with one exception, did not explicitly require the independent auditor to obtain written representations from management. This exception pertained to representations as to whether any events occurred subsequent to the date of the financial statements that would require adjustment of or disclosure in the financial statements.† However, written representation letters were often used by auditors, particularly for client representations on inventories and liabilities. Thus, a pamphlet issued by the American Institute of Accountants in 1950 said:

"The CPA generally secures considerable information by discussing with officers and employees of the company various questions that arise during the audit. These inquiries generally involve points which are not completely clear from the records. . . . Not infrequently, the more important of these explanations are reduced to writing in a statement signed by responsible officers of the company."‡

In 1941, Statement on Auditing Procedure No. 4 explained the need for client representations:

"Whether or not a written representation is required from the client, the information would necessarily have to be obtained where pertinent, and oral representations be made by the client. Reducing these to writing has the advantage of confirming the statements made and avoiding any misunderstanding regarding them. Moreover, they have the effect of reminding the client or the management of the client company that *the primary responsibility for the correctness of the statements rests with the client rather than the auditor and of insuring that the client realizes this primary responsibility*. . . . There seems to be little or no feeling that the representations of the client . . . reduce the examination the auditor should make or relieve him of his responsibility." (Emphasis added.)§

Thus, the practice of obtaining written client representations served the dual purpose of confirming management's oral representations and reinforcing the fact that the financial statements were in fact those of management.

**Interstate Hosiery Mills, Inc.,* 4 SEC 706, 721 (1939).

†Statement on Auditing Standards No. 1, *Codification of Auditing Standards and Procedures* (New York: AICPA, 1973), Section 560.12(d). Also see SAP No. 47, *Subsequent Events* (1971); SAP No. 33, *Auditing Standards and Procedures* (a codification) (1963); and SAP No. 25, *Events Subsequent to the Date of Financial Statements* (1954).

‡*Audits by Certified Public Accountants* (New York: AIA, 1950), p. 29.

§SAP No. 4, *Clients' Written Representations Regarding Inventories, Liabilities, and Other Matters* (New York: AIA, 1941), p. 26.

AUDITOR INDEPENDENCE AND SAS NO. 19

SAS No. 19 requires the auditor to obtain certain specific written representations from the client including management's acknowledgment of its responsibility for the financial statements: "Management's refusal to furnish a written representation that the auditor believes is essential constitutes a limitation on the scope of the auditor's examination sufficient to preclude an unqualified opinion."*

Inherent in the audit function is the recognition that the financial statements are those of the one being audited. Management's acknowledgment of this fact is always essential.

There is a direct and significant relationship between client responsibility for the financial statements and auditor independence:

"A part of the rationale which underlies any rule on independence is that managerial and decision-making functions are the responsibility of the client and not of the independent accountant. It is felt that if the independent accountant were to perform functions of this nature, he would develop, or appear to develop, a mutuality of interest with his client which would differ only in degree, but not in kind, from that of an employee. And where this relationship appears to exist, it may be logically inferred that the accountant's professional judgment toward the particular client might be prejudiced in that he would, in effect, be auditing the result of his own work, thereby destroying the objectivity sought by shareholders [and credit grantors]. Consequently, the performance of such functions is fundamentally inconsistent with an impartial examination. *However, it is the role of the accountant to advise management and to offer professional advice on their problems. Therefore, the problem posed by this dilemma is to ascertain the point where advice ends and managerial responsibility begins.*" (Emphasis added.)†

One method of delineating the thin line between accounting services and managerial responsibility is to require management to acknowledge in writing its responsibility for the company's books and records and for the information developed from such records.

The conflict between independence and accounting services is a significant one in the relationship of the independent accountant with his small or closely held clients. The relationship is often closer than that which exists between the independent accountant and large, publicly held clients. For the small or closely held business, the independent accountant provides significant financial and accounting services and advice. Therefore, it is essential that the client recognize that although he receives and accepts accounting advice from his accountant, the responsibility for accepting such advice is his.

The AICPA code of professional ethics recognizes the close relationship between the independent accountant and the small or closely held client. In an interpretation of rule 101—the rule pertaining to independence—the code states: "The client must accept the responsibility for the financial statements as his own. A small client may not have anyone in his employ to maintain accounting records and may rely on the CPA for this purpose. Nevertheless, the client must be sufficiently knowledgeable of the enterprise's activities and financial condition and the applicable accounting principles so that he can reasonably *accept such responsibility, including, specifically, fairness of valuation and presentation and adequacy of disclosure. When*

*Statement on Auditing Standards No. 19, par. 11.

†Accounting Series Release 126, "Guidelines and Examples of Situations Involving the Independence of Accountants" (Securities and Exchange Commission, July 1972).

necessary, the CPA must discuss accounting matters with the client to be sure that the client has the required degree of understanding." (Emphasis added.)*

The interpretation goes on to state that "the CPA, in making an examination of financial statements prepared from books and records which he has maintained completely or in part, *must conform to generally accepted auditing standards.*" (Emphasis added.)†

The independent accountant recommends, perhaps even decides, which generally accepted accounting principles should be applied; he indicates the method of recording certain transactions and, in some engagements, posts to the general ledger of the client. At the conclusion of his work, if he is to express an unqualified opinion on his client's financial statements, the accountant must establish his independence of the client. The client, by means of a written representation, must acknowledge responsibility for the fair presentation of its financial statements in conformity with generally accepted accounting principles. The client, however, may justifiably claim reliance on the accountant for such presentation and refuse to acknowledge his responsibility. The auditor has a duty to his client to educate the client on the nature and extent of the client's responsibility.

ENGAGEMENT LETTERS

It is especially important for the independent accountant to establish early in the engagement that the financial statements which he will report on are those of his client even though he will be the preparer. There is no better instrument for early clarification of this matter than the engagement letter.

Engagement letters are not required by generally accepted auditing standards; however, they are essential for the clear understanding of the services to be rendered by the independent accountant. In the past, they have been used sparingly by accountants with small or closely held clients; however, they are now used more often as accountants have become more aware of the hazards of litigation.

Engagement letters, if properly prepared and presented, improve client relations and avoid client misunderstandings. They enumerate the services to be performed and the responsibilities to be assumed by the independent accountant. They also cover the obligations and responsibilities of the client's accounting staff. However, engagement letters do not always indicate that the financial statements and the accounting principles underlying them are the sole responsibility of management.

Most engagement letters specify the inability of the accountant to uncover all frauds. They specify fee arrangements and terms of payment of such fees, and they indicate that the financial statements of the company will be examined by the accountant to express an opinion on such statements.

Because the engagement letter is the initial formalization of the terms of retention of the accountant by the client, it is suggested that a paragraph such as the following be added to the letter:

"Although we may prepare or help prepare the financial statements of XYZ Corp., these financial statements are solely the representations of management. Although we may advise as to which accounting principles should be applied to the financial

*"Ethics By-Laws Quality Control as of July 1, 1977," *AICPA Professional Standards*, vol. 2 (New York: AICPA, 1977), p. 4413. [ET Section 101.5]

†Ibid., p. 4414.

statements and the method of application, the selection and method of application is a determination made solely by management."

The implications and ramifications of the above must be discussed with the client at the time of the signing of the engagement letter.

Although client responsibility for the financial statements must be established at the beginning of the engagement, it must not be allowd to stop at that point. Thus, during the year, as accounting decisions are made, the responsibility for such decisions must be noted and acknowledged.

PROCEDURES DURING THE YEAR

Many decisions about accounting principles are made during the year. Depreciation methods may be determined at the time assets are acquired; decisions to capitalize or to charge to income start-up and similar costs may be made when such costs are incurred; and the method of reporting long-term construction contracts may be determined at inception of the contract. All such decisions should be reviewed with the client, formalized in work sheets and acknowledged by the client. If the application of an accounting principle will have a material effect on the financial statements, it is suggested that the accountant write to the client explaining the principle and its effects and request a return written acknowledgment.

Before starting the engagement, the accountant should prepare a list of the accounting principles that were applied last year and that will be applied during the current year. This list and its implications should be reviewed with the client and his written acknowledgment obtained.

However, many decisions as to appropriate accounting principles are not made until the end of the year. The treatment of investment tax credits, the reporting of long-term leases and the valuation of inventories are examples of such decisions. Again, when these decisions are made, it is of utmost importance that they be acknowledged by the client.

As a final step in the acknowledgment procedure, it is suggested that at year-end a list be prepared of all significant accounting policies applied during the year. The partner in charge of the examination should review this with the client and present the effects of each principle's application. At the conclusion of this meeting, the partner should obtain from the client written acknowledgment that the client reviewed, understood and accepted such principles for application in his financial statements. Since disclosure of accounting policies is required in financial statements, this step can be combined with the review of the financial statements with the client.

DISCLOSURE OF ACCOUNTING PRINCIPLES

Accounting Principles Board Opinion No. 22, *Disclosure of Accounting Policies*, paragraph 8, states: "When financial statements are issued purporting to present fairly financial position, changes in financial position, [changed to cash flow for fiscal years ending after 7/15/88] and results of operations in accordance with generally accepted accounting principles, a description of all significant accounting policies of the reporting entity should be included as an integral part of the financial statements."

In paragraph 12, the opinion states that "disclosure of accounting policies should identify and describe the accounting principles followed by the reporting entity and the methods of applying those principles. . . ." It emphasizes who determines the accounting principles to be applied when, in paragraph 6, it states that "the *accounting policies* of a reporting entity are the specific accounting principles and the methods of applying those principles that are judged by the management of the entity to be the most appropriate in the circumstances to present fairly. . . ."

Thus, it can be seen that disclosure of accounting policies is an integral part of financial statements and that the determination of such accounting policies is the responsibility of management.

Opinion No. 22 merely reinforced that which has been stated in other authoritative literature—the financial statements, and the principles applied in their preparation, are the representations and responsibility of management. Requiring written acknowledgment of this by management merely reduces to writing that which is understood and accepted by most sophisticated users of financial statements. Thus, Opinion 22 presents no extra burden. It is a convenient way of assuring that the client reviews, understands and approves significant accounting policies.

THE OFFICIAL ANSWER TO THE CLIENT'S QUESTION

Both generally accepted auditing standards and generally accepted accounting principles recognize the primacy of management's responsibility for financial statements.

Paragraph 11 of the introduction to Accounting Research Bulletin No. 43 emphasizes that underlying the development of all accounting principles is the fact that the accounts of the company and the financial statements it issues are the responsibility of management. Paragraph 6 of Opinion No. 22 acknowledges this concept of management responsibility by noting that accounting principles of a reporting entity are those judged by the management of that entity to be most appropriate in the circumstances. Thus, generally accepted accounting principles clearly establish the concept that financial statements are solely the representation and responsibility of the company.

Auditing literature acknowledges the accounting and advisory services performed by the independent accountant; it also recognizes the dichotomy of these services from its results—the financial statements of the enterprise. Thus, "it should be clearly understood that owners or management are responsible for the financial statements; the auditor is responsible for his report and opinion. . . . The auditor may assist, advise, and persuade management with respect to form and content of financial statements, but he cannot compel management to accept his recommendations.*

The independent accountant has the additional problem of establishing and maintaining his independence as interpreted under rule 101 of the code of professional ethics. Interpretation 101-3 states that, "with regard to accounting judgments, if third parties have confidence in a member's judgment in performing an audit, it is difficult to contend that they would have less confidence where the same judgment is applied in the process of preparing the underlying accounting records.**

The interpretation clearly recognizes and defends the important internal services provided by the independent accountant. Nonetheless, it emphasizes that the client must accept the responsibility for the financial statements. To obtain this acceptance, the independent accountant must "when necessary. . . . discuss accounting

*Norman J. Lenhart and Philip L. Defliese, *Montgomery's Auditing*, 8th ed. (New York: The Ronald Press Company, 1957), p. 95. Copyright © 1957 by John Wiley & Sons, Inc. Reprinted with permission.

†*AICPA Professional Standards*, vol. 2, p. 4413. [ET Section 101.05]

matters with the client to be sure that the client has the required degree of understanding."*

Thus, before expressing an opinion on financial statements, the auditor must formally establish his independence and his client's responsibility for those financial statements. The formal medium for establishing this condition is the client representation letter as described in SAS No. 19.

THE CLOSING CONFERENCE WITH THE CLIENT

Having concluded your research, you are now ready to return to the client with the representation letter. However, you do recognize that, to some degree, you are at fault. During the year, you did not ascertain that your client had the required degree of understanding about accounting matters. Further, you did not discuss with him the adoption of accounting principles; you decided which principles to adopt. Therefore, you are now prepared to spend a significant amount of time reviewing with the client all significant accounting matters of the past year. You have now modified the client representation letter so that all significant accounting policies are enumerated. These will have to be explained to the client.

Your meeting has been set for late in the afternoon and, as you enter your client's office, you can see a clear desk; it is obvious he is prepared to devote his full attention to the problem at hand.

As you pull photocopies of articles and pronouncements from your briefcase, your client remarks, "I see you're well prepared. What did your research uncover?"

You report the results of your research, giving him copies of articles when appropriate. You conclude by acknowledging your error and handing him the modified representation letter.

The client reads it, pauses for a moment and says, "Okay, let's review it."

Three hours later, exhausted but with the signed representation letter in your briefcase, you prepare to leave. Your client says, "I'm sorry I put you through this, but you accountants created the problem. I always thought that since you reviewed my records quarterly, maintained subsidiary records in your workpapers, prepared all tax returns and financial statements, and suggested appropriate accounting principles, my financial statements were your responsibility. I am willing to accept your rules, but I think your profession must reach out to people like me—the small business people—to explain to us in nontechnical terms exactly what it is you do and what it is you are responsible for. I assure you that in the future, if the financial statements are my responsibility, you and I will be spending more time together.

CONCLUSION

A long-established belief in practice and in law is that a company's financial statements are the responsibility of management. The AICPA code of professional ethics confronts the problem of auditor independence when accounting services as well as auditing services are provided. The client representation letter, as required by SAS No. 19, is the instrument by which management's responsibility for financial statements is acknowledged and auditor independence is firmly established. The letter gives management a final opportunity to consider the effects of its

*Ibid.

representations and its decisions on the financial statements. The accounting profession has not been sufficiently vocal in communicating to its major constituency—small business people—the importance and necessity of client representation letters.

It is suggested that the engagement letter, the initial formalization of the terms of retention of the accountant by the client, emphasize the client's responsibility for its financial statements. However, this emphasis is not enough. Throughout the year, it is essential that the accountant and his client discuss the choices of accounting principles and the effects of such choices on the financial statements. This constant communication should ultimately eliminate questions as to who is responsible for the statements. It is the client.[20]

QUESTIONS AND CASES

6–1 Is it ethical for a CPA firm to place an advertisement in the newspaper? In the yellow pages? Are there any restrictions as to the frequency of placement, size, artwork, or type style?

6–2 Assume that you have a thriving tax practice. Would it be ethical for you to pay a small commission to any present client who refers a new client to you?

6–3 If you have particular expertise in SEC matters, could you ethically advertise this competence? Could you refer to yourself as a specialist in that area?

6–4 Give three examples of advertising practices that would be prohibited under the AICPA Code of Professional Conduct.

6–5 What characteristics must a professional corporation have in order for it to be an acceptable form of practice under the AICPA Code of Professional Conduct?

6–6 What is the responsibility of an internal professional with respect to management representation letters? What role should such an accounting professional play in connection with the "management report" advocated by the Commission on Auditors' Responsibilities (Cohen Commission), the Financial Executives Institute, the Treadway Commission, and the SEC?

6–7 Could a CMA working as an internal professional ethically engage in another occupation? Should the CMA, for example, accept management consulting engagements apart from his regular employment?

6–8 If your firm were a member of the SEC Practice Section of the AICPA Division for Firms, what guidelines would you need to follow in providing executive recruiting services? Can you ethically accept an engagement to search for prospective candidates for managerial positions with your audit clients?

6–9 State the case for and against retaining management advisory services as an integral part of the public accounting profession. Is there any empirical evidence regarding

[20]Martin Benis, "The Small Client and Representation Letters," *Journal of Accountancy*, Sept. 1978, pp. 78–84. Copyright © 1978 by the American Institute of Certified Public Accountants, Inc.

the independence of an auditor whose firm also provides management advisory services?

6–10 Is it ethical to practice law and accounting concurrently? What is the view of the American Bar Association?

6–11 Are financial statements prepared for a small client the statements of management or of the auditor? What responsibility does the auditor have in this regard when dealing with small clients? What role does a client representation letter play?

6–12 What is an "engagement letter?" Discuss its desirability and usefulness.

6–13 (*Darren Ash*)
Brates and Charter, CPAs, is a local public accounting firm in Gainesville, Georgia. Bill Brates, the senior partner, has been approached by a company, Hall Real Estate Investment Corporation, that sells limited partnership interests in various kinds of properties. He is approached with the proposal that:

1. Brates investigate this investment venture to the extent he deems necessary and inform or recommend the investment to appropriate clients of Brates and Charter.
2. The company (Hall) will make a payment to Brates and Charter, such payment being roughly equal to 5% of any amount invested by the firm's clients who invest because of Brate's recommendation.

Would such an arrangement violate the AICPA Code of Professional Conduct? Would it make any difference if the firm's clients are told of the arrangement?

6–14 Bill Wilkie is a CPA in Kankakee, Illinois. His practice includes auditing, tax work, and managerial consulting. His former college roommate, Jim Rush, was an insurance major in college and has just moved to Kankakee. The two decide to form a separate financial planning business. Part of their income will be derived from commissions on the sale of insurance and investments. Will Bill Wilkie be in violation of the AICPA Code of Professional Conduct?

6–15 (*John Warner*)
Barney and Fred are CPAs working in the capital city of a southern state. They both work in the state comptroller's office. Because of their meager salaries, they have formed a partnership and perform many of the audits for the smaller surrounding municipalities. The state requires the cities to have these audits in order to qualify for state funds.

In a solicitation letter to the city officials of Bedrock, Barney and Fred stated that although the financial statements would solely be the representation of city officials, due to their relationship with the comptroller's office they are particularly well qualified to do governmental audits, and there would be no problem in preparing financial statements that would be acceptable to state officials.

Can Barney and Fred ethically perform these audits. Are there any ethical problems with their solicitation letter?

6–16 (*Doug Cruickshank*)
Burt Lockwood has an accounting practice in a small town. In a recent advertisement in the local paper, Burt stated the following information:

Burt Lockwood, CPA
Member of
American Institute of Certified Public Accountants
Providing Tax and Consulting Services
"My satisfied clients say that
my services have saved
hundreds of dollars for them"
Inquiries welcome

Shortly after running the advertisement, Bob Scala, a local businessman called Burt. Bob had a complex tax problem that he wanted Burt to handle. Burt told Bob that the problem was within his competence to solve and that he would probably be able to save him over $500.

Once Burt started working on the problem, he found that he would need legal advice. He called on his friend Chuck Lombardo, a local tax attorney, to help him with the problem. After discussing the problem with Chuck, the two agreed that Chuck should take the case since the problem was primarily of a legal rather than accounting nature. In return for the referral, Chuck said that in the future he would refer any of his clients with accounting problems to Burt. What ethical questions are raised in this situation?

6–17 (*Denise Cummins*)
Situation 1
Jason Parker was a CPA with Arthur Waterhouse & Co. for seven years, and rose to the rank of manager in the MAS department. For about a year, Jason has considered starting his own computer advising company. Two months ago, he left AW and set up Parker Consulting in an office at his home. The company has been doing very well and Jason has not had time to attend to many of the necessary details. He has not ordered new business cards, but since he has almost 650 left from his days with AW, he has been giving them out and marking out the business address and phone number when he gives one to a potential client. The card looks somewhat like this:

Jason Parker, CPA
Member AICPA

Home:	Business:
130 Oak Street	Arthur Waterhouse & Co.
Atlanta, Ga. 30066	2600 Georgia Pacific
404–449–4979	Atlanta, Ga. 30303
	404–620–6826

Is Jason bound by the Code of Professional Conduct in his dealings with clients of Parker Consulting? What if he marks out the *CPA* and *Member AICPA* on his business card?

Situation 2

Suppose that while Jason was employed by AW, he was asked by several of his clients to aid them in recruiting executives for their firms. He decided that instead of using his computer skills, he would capitalize on his friendships with numerous key personnel in about 100 major companies. Therefore, he leaves AW and establishes an executive search company, Parker Placements. After two months of operation, Jason runs an ad in the paper which includes the following information and comments:

1. The president's experience as a CPA provides the firm with inside contacts in over 100 businesses.
2. A list of several of the firms in which insiders are known.
3. A placement rate of 82%.

Is Jason bound by the Code of Ethics? Is his advertisement acceptable?

6–18 Union South, Inc., a large regional insurance company, hired the accounting firm of Baker and Long to audit their financial statements. The firm is a member of the SEC Practice Section of the AICPA Division for CPA firms. As part of the audit, Baker and Long provided actuarially oriented advisory services involving the determination of policy reserves and related accounts. Since Union South, Inc. does not have its own actuarial staff, the company will primarily use the auditor's work.

Is it all right for Baker and Long to perform these advisory services? Are there any constraints on their practice in this area? What if Baker and Long is not a member of the SEC Practice Section?

6–19 Johnson and Worthy, CPAs, were hired to audit the financial statements of Lakers, Inc. At the completion of the field work, Johnson and Worthy gave Lakers, Inc. the client representation letter to sign. However, the management of Lakers, Inc. refused to sign the letter because they believe Johnson and Worthy are responsible for the financial statements. If the management of Lakers, Inc. refuses to sign the letter, what should Worthy and Johnson do?

6–20 (*Charles Belote*)

A CPA sole practitioner wishes to go into business with his former college roommate. The CPA has been in practice locally for several years. The individual he intends to have join him is not a CPA, but operates a financial statement write-up service in the community. The addition of the write-up work would be of considerable financial benefit to the CPA. The two individuals decide to practice as a professional corporation under the name of Better Bookkeeping Company. Are there any problems with this plan?

6–21 (*Ken Brewer*)

Bobby Merritt graduated from a widely recognized and reputable college with a degree in accounting as well as a degree in computer science. At the time of his graduation the market was very much in need of computer science personnel, but Bob chose to enter the field of accounting with a medium-sized firm. At nights, however, he continued to take courses in computer systems and soon received a Master's degree in this area of study. Bob's knowledge of these systems made him very valuable to the CPA firm that employed him, especially when called upon to study the feasibility of installing data processing systems.

Bob developed a close friendship with Pete Cross, another computer student, while in graduate studies. Pete is opening a computer service for companies in the area and has requested that Bob join him in this endeavor. This would involve a partnership in the service company, but Bob would still like to continue his work as a CPA. Would this be in violation of the AICPA Code of Professional Conduct?

6–22 (*Jessica Blume*)

The firm of Smith and White is located in a small city. There are only two other firms in the city. Smith and White do not offer management advisory services because at this time they do not have the necessary personnel. The other two firms are larger than Smith and White and do offer management advisory services.

One of the other firms, Jones and Blanke, has proposed that if Smith and White will refer all their clients desiring management advisory services to them, they will give Smith and White a fee of 10% of billings on the engagements Jones and Blanke obtain. Is the proposal ethical?

Appendix 1

AICPA Code of Professional Conduct and Interpretations of Rules of Conduct[1]

COMPOSITION, APPLICABILITY, AND COMPLIANCE

The Code of Professional Conduct of the American Institute of Certified Public Accountants consists of two sections—(1) the Principles and (2) the Rules. The Principles provide the framework for the Rules, which govern the performance of professional services by members. The Council of the American Institute of Certified Public Accountants is authorized to designate bodies to promulgate technical standards under the Rules, and the bylaws require adherence to those Rules and standards.

[1]*AICPA Professional Standards,* vol. 2, ET Sections 50, 90, 100, 200, 300, 500 and Appendixes A and B.

The Code of Professional Conduct was adopted by the membership to provide guidance and rules to all members—those in public practice, in industry, in government, and in education—in the performance of their professional responsibilities.

Compliance with the Code of Professional Conduct, as with all standards in an open society, depends primarily on members' understanding and voluntary actions, secondarily on reinforcement by peers and public opinion, and ultimately on disciplinary proceedings, when necessary, against members who fail to comply with the Rules.

OTHER CATEGORIES

Interpretations of Rules of Conduct consist of interpretations which have been adopted, after exposure to state societies, state boards, practice units and other interested parties, by the professional ethics division's executive committee to provide guidelines as to the scope and application of the Rules but are not intended to limit such scope or application. A member who departs from such guidelines shall have the burden of justifying such departure in any disciplinary hearing. *Interpretations* which existed before the adoption of the Code of Professional Conduct on January 12, 1988, will remain in effect until further action is deemed necessary by the appropriate senior technical committee.

Ethics Rulings consist of formal rulings made by the professional ethics division's executive committee after exposure to state societies, state boards, practice units and other interested parties. These rulings summarize the application of Rules of Conduct and Interpretations to a particular set of factual circumstances. Members who depart from such rulings in similar circumstances will be requested to justify such departures. *Ethics Rulings* which existed before the adoption of the Code of Professional Conduct on January 12, 1988, will remain in effect until further action is deemed necessary by the appropriate senior technical committee.

Publication of an Interpretation or Ethics Rulings in *The Journal of Accountancy* constitutes notice to members. Hence, the effective date of the pronouncement is the last day of the month in which the pronouncement is published in *The Journal of Accountancy*. The professional ethics division will take into consideration the time that would have been reasonable for the member to comply with the pronouncement.

ET Section 51

Preamble

.01 Membership in the American Institute of Certified Public Accountants is voluntary. By accepting membership, a certified public accountant assumes an obligation of self-discipline above and beyond the requirements of laws and regulations.

.02 These principles of the Code of Professional Conduct of the American Institute of Certified Public Accountants express the profession's recognition of its responsibilities to the public, to clients, and to colleagues. They guide members in the performance of their professional responsibilities and express the basic tenets of ethical and professional conduct. The Principles call for an unswerving commitment to honorable behavior, even at the sacrifice of personal advantage.

ET Section 52

Article I—Responsibilities

In carrying out their responsibilities as professionals, members should exercise sensitive professional and moral judgments in all their activities.

.01 As professionals, certified public accountants perform an essential role in society. Consistent with that role, members of the American Institute of Certified Public Accountants have responsibilities to all those who use their professional services. Members also have a continuing responsibility to cooperate with each other to improve the art of accounting, maintain the public's confidence, and carry out the profession's special responsibilities for self-governance. The collective efforts of all members are required to maintain and enhance the traditions of the profession.

ET Section 53

Article II—The Public Interest

Members should accept the obligation to act in a way that will serve the public interest, honor the public trust, and demonstrate commitment to professionalism.

.01 A distinguishing mark of a profession is acceptance of its responsibilities to the public. The accounting profession's public consists of clients, credit grantors, governments, employers, investors, the business and financial community, and others who rely on the objectivity and integrity of certified public accountants to maintain the orderly functioning of commerce. This reliance imposes a public interest responsibility on certified public accountants. The public interest is defined as the collective well-being of the community of people and institutions the profession serves.

.02 In discharging their professional responsibilities, members may encounter conflicting pressures from among each of those groups. In resolving those conflicts, members should act with integrity, guided by the precept that when members fulfill their responsibility to the public, clients' and employers' interests are best served.

.03 Those who rely on certified public accountants expect them to discharge their responsibilities with integrity, objectivity, due professional care, and a genuine interest in serving the public. They are expected to provide quality services, enter into fee arrangements, and offer a range of services—all in a manner that demonstrates a level of professionalism consistent with these Principles of the Code of Professional Conduct.

.04 All who accept membership in the American Institute of Certified Public Accountants commit themselves to honor the public trust. In return for the faith that the public reposes in them, members should seek continually to demonstrate their dedication to professional excellence.

ET Section 54

Article III—Integrity

To maintain and broaden public confidence, members should perform all professional responsibilities with the highest sense of integrity.

.01 Integrity is an element of character fundamental to professional recognition. It is the quality from which the public trust derives and the benchmark against which a member must ultimately test all decisions.

.02 Integrity requires a member to be, among other things, honest and candid within the constraints of client confidentiality. Service and the public trust should not be subordinated to personal gain and advantage. Integrity can accommodate the inadvertent error and the honest difference of opinion; it cannot accommodate deceit or subordination of principle.

.03 Integrity is measured in terms of what is right and just. In the absence of specific rules, standards, or guidance, or in the face of conflicting opinions, a member should test decisions and deeds by asking: "Am I doing what a person of integrity would do? Have I retained my integrity?" Integrity requires a member to observe both the form and the spirit of technical and ethical standards; circumvention of those standards constitutes subordination of judgment.

.04. Integrity also requires a member to observe the principles of objectivity and independence and of due care.

ET Section 55

Article IV—Objectivity and Independence

A member should maintain objectivity and be free of conflicts of interest in discharging profesional responsibilities. A member in public practice should be independent in fact and appearance when providing auditing and other attestation services.

.01 Objectivity is a state of mind, a quality that lends value to a member's services. It is a distinguishing feature of the profession. The principle of objectivity imposes the obligation to be impartial, intellectually honest, and free of conflicts of interest. Independence precludes relationships that may appear to impair a member's objectivity in rendering attestation services.

.02 Members often serve multiple interests in many different capacities and must demonstrate their objectivity in varying circumstances. Members in public practice render attest, tax, and management advisory services. Other members prepare financial statements in the employment of others, perform internal auditing services, and serve in financial and management capacities in industry, education, and government. They also educate and train those who aspire to admission into the profession. Regardless of service or capacity, members should protect the integrity of their work, maintain objectivity, and avoid any subordination of their judgment.

.03 For a member in public practice, the maintenance of objectivity and independence requires a continuing assessment of client relationshis and public responsibility. Such a member who provides auditing and other attestation services should be independent in fact and appearance. In providing all other services, a member should maintain objectivity and avoid conflicts of interest.

.04 Although members not in public practice cannot maintain the appearance of independence, they nevertheless have the responsibilty to maintain objectivity in rendering professional services. Members employed by others to prepare financial statements or to perform auditing, tax, or consulting services are charged with the same responsibility for objectivity as members in public practice and must be scrupulous in their application of generally accepted accounting principles and candid in all their dealings with members in public practice.

ET Section 56

Article V—Due Care

A member should observe the profession's technical and ethical standards, strive continually to improve competence and the quality of services, and discharge professional responsibility to the best of the member's ability.

.01 The quest for excellence is the essence of due care. Due care requires a member to discharge professional responsibilities with competence and diligence. It imposes the obligation to perform professional services to the best of a member's ability with concern for the best interest of those for whom the services are performed and consistent with the profession's responsibility to the public.

.02 Competence is derived from a synthesis of education and experience. It begins with a mastery of the common body of knowledge required for designation as a certified public accountant. The maintenance of competence requires a commitment to learning and professional improvement that must continue throughout a member's professional life. It is a member's individual responsibility. In all engagements and in all responsibilities, each member should undertake to achieve a level of competence that will assure that the quality of the member's services meets the high level of professionalism required by these Principles.

.03 Competence represents the attainment and maintenance of a level of understanding and knowledge that enables a member to render services with facility and acumen. It also establishes the limitations of a member's capabilities by dictating that consultation or referral may be required when a professional engagement exceeds the personal competence of a member or a member's firm. Each member is responsible for assessing his or her own competence—of evaluating whether education, experience, and judgment are adequate for the responsibility to be assumed.

.04 Members should be diligent is discharging responsibilities to clients, employers, and the public. Diligence imposes the responsibility to render services promptly and carefully, to be thorough, and to observe applicable technical and ethical standards.

.05 Due care requires a member to plan and supervise adequately any professional activity for which he or she is responsible.

ET Section 57

Article VI—Scope and Nature of Services

A member in public practice should observe the Principles of the Code of Professional Conduct in determining the scope and nature of services to be provided.

.01 The public interest aspect of certified public accountants' services requires that such services be consistent with acceptable professional behavior for certified public accountants. Integrity requires that service and the public trust not be subordinated to personal gain and advantage. Objectivity and independence require that members be free from conflicts of interest in discharging professional responsibilities. Due care requires that services be provided with competence and diligence.

.02 Each of these Principles should be considered by members in determining whether or not to provide specific services in individual circumstances. In some instances, they may represent an overall constraint on the nonaudit services that might be offered to a specific client. No hard-and-fast rules can be developed to help members reach these judgments, but they must be satisfied that they are meeting the spirit of the Principles in this regard.

.03 In order to accomplish this, members should

- Practice in firms that have in place internal quality-control procedures to ensure that services are competently delivered and adequately supervised.
- Determine, in their individual judgments, whether the scope and nature of other services provided to an audit client would create a conflict of interest in the performance of the audit function for that client.
- Assess, in their individual judgments, whether an activity is consistent with their role as professionals (for example, Is such activity a reasonable extension or variation of existing services offered by the member or others in the profession?)

ET Section 91

Applicability

As adopted
January 12, 1988

.01 The bylaws of the American Institute of Certified Public Accountants require that members adhere to the Rules of the Code of Professional Conduct. Members must be prepared to justify departures from these Rules.

.02 Interpretation Addressing the Applicability of the AICPA Code of Professional Conduct. For purposes of the Applicability Section of the Code, a "member" is a member or international associate of the American Institute of CPAs.

1. The Rules of Conduct that follow apply to all professional services performed except (a) where the wording of the rule indicates otherwise and (b) that a member who is practicing outside the United States will not be subject to discipline for departing from any of the rules stated herein as long as the member's conduct is in accord with the rules of the organized accounting profession in the country in which he or she is practicing. However, where a member's name is associated with financial statements under circumstances that would entitle the reader to assume that United States practices were followed, the member must comply with the requirements of Rules 202 and 203.
2. A member may be held responsible for compliance with the rules by all persons associated with him or her in the practice of public accounting who are either under the member's supervision or are the member's partners or shareholders in the practice.
3. A member shall not permit others to carry out on his or her behalf, either with or without compensation, acts, which if carried out by the member, would place the member in violation of the rules.

[Paragraph added, August, 1989.]

ET Section 92

Definitions

As adopted
January 12, 1988

[Pursuant to its authority under the bylaws (BL §360.01) to interpret the Code of Professional Conduct, the Professional Ethics Executive Committee has issued the following definitions of terms appearing in the code effective November 30, 1989.]

.01 Client. (This replaces the previous definition of "Client" at paragraph .01.) A client is any person or entity, other than the member's employer, that engages a member or a member's firm to perform professional services or a person or entity with respect to which professional services are performed. The term "employer" for these purposes does not include those entities engaged in the practice of public accounting.

.02 Council. The Council of the American Institute of Certified Public Accountants.

.03 Enterprise. (This replaces the previous definition of "Enterprise" at paragraph .03.) For purposes of the Code, the term "enterprise" is synonymous with the term "client."

.04 Financial statements. Statements and footnotes related thereto that purport to show financial position which relates to a point in time or changes in financial position which relate to a period of time, and statements which use a cash or other incomplete basis of accounting. Balance sheets, statements of income, statements of retained earnings, statements of changes in financial position, and statements of changes in owners' equity are financial statements.

Incidental financial data included in management advisory services reports to support recommendations to a client and tax returns and supporting schedules do not, for this purpose, constitute financial statements; and the statement, affidavit, or signature of preparers required on tax returns neither constitutes an opinion on financial statements nor requires a disclaimer of such opinion.

.05 Firm. A proprietorship, partnership, or professional corporation or association engaged in the practice of public accounting, including individual partners or shareholders thereof.

.06 Institute. The American Institute of Certified Public Accountants.

.07 Interpretations of rules of conduct. Pronouncements issued by the division of professional ethics to provide guidelines concerning the scope and application of the rules of conduct.

.08 Member. A member, associate member, or international associate of the American Institute of Certified Public Accountants.

.09 Practice of public accountings. (This replaces the previous definition of "Practice of public accounting" at paragraph .09.) The practice of public accounting consists of the performance for a client, by a member or a member's firm, while holding out as CPA(s), of the professional services of accounting, tax, personal financial planning, litigation support services, and those professional services for which standards are promulgated by bodies designated by Council, such as Statements of Financial Accounting Standards, Statements on Auditing Standards, Statements on Standards for Accounting and Review Services, Statements on Standards for Management Advisory Services, Statements of Governmental Accounting Standards, Statement on Standards for Attestation Engagements, and Statement on Standards for Accountants' Services on Prospective Financial Information.

However, a member or a member's firm, while holding out as CPA(s), is not considered to be in the practice of public accounting if the member or the member's firm does not perform, for any client, any of the professional services described in the preceding paragraph.

.10 Professional services. (This replaces the previous definition of "Professional services" at paragraph .10.) Professional services include all services performed by a member while holding out as a CPA.

.11 Holding out. In general, any action initiated by a member that informs others of his or her status as a CPA, or AICPA-accredited specialist constitutes holding out as a CPA. This would include, for example, any oral or written representation to another regarding CPA status, use of the CPA designation on business cards or letterhead, the display of a certificate evidencing a member's CPA designation, or listing as a CPA in local telephone directories.

ET Section 101

Independence

.01 Rules 101—Independence. A member in public practice shall be independent in the performance of professional services as required by standards promulgated by bodies designated by Council.
[As adopted January 12, 1988.]

Interpretations under Rule 101—Independence

Interpretations and Ethics Rulings which existed before the adoption of the Code of Professional Conduct on January 12, 1988, will remain in effect until further action is deemed necessary by the appropriate senior technical committee.

.02 101-1—Interpretation of Rule 101. Independence shall be considered to be impaired if, for example, a member had any of the following transactions, interests, or relationships:

A. During the period of a professional engagement or at the time of expressing an opinion, a member or a member's firm
   1. Had or was committed to acquire any direct or material indirect financial interest in the enterprise.
   2. Was a trustee of any trust or executor or administrator of any estate if such trust or estate had or was committed to acquire any direct or material indirect financial interest in the enterprise.
   3. Had any joint, closely held business investment with the enterprise or with any officer, director, or principal stockholders thereof that was material in relation to the member's net worth or to the net worth of the member's firm.
   4. Had any loan to or from the enterprise or any officer, director, or principal stockholder of the enterprise. This proscription does not apply to the follow-

ing loans from a financial institution when made under normal lending procedures, terms, and requirements:

a. Loans obtained by a member or a member's firm that are not material in relation to the net worth of such borrower.

b. Home mortgages.

c. Other secured loans, except loans guaranteed by a member's firm which are otherwise unsecured.

B. During the period covered by the financial statements, during the period of the professional engagement, or at the time of expressing an opinion, a member or a member's firm

1. Was connected with the enterprise as a promoter, underwriter or voting trustee, as a director or officer, or in any capacity equivalent to that of a member of management or of an employee.
2. Was a trustee for any pension or profit-sharing trust of the enterprise.

The above examples are not intended to be all-inclusive.

[Paragraph added by adoption of the Code of Professional Conduct on Janaury 12, 1988.]

.03 101-1 [to be renumbered]—Honorary directorships and trusteeships. Members are often asked to lend the prestige of their names to not-for-profit organizations that limit their activities to those of a charitable, religious, civic or similar nature by being named as a director or a trustee. A member who permits his name to be used in this manner and who is associated with the financial statements of the organization would not be considered lacking in independence under Rule 101 so long as (1) his position is purely honorary, (2) it is identified as honorary in all letterheads and externally circulated materials in which he is named as a director or trustee, (3) he restricts his participation to the use of his name, and (4) he does not vote or otherwise participate in management functions.

It is presumed that organizations to which members lend only the prestige of their names will have sufficiently large boards of directors or trustees to clearly permit the member to limit his participation consistent with the foregoing restriction. [Formerly paragraph .02, renumbered by adoption of the Code of Professional Conduct on January 12, 1988.]

.04 101-2—Former practitioners and firm independence. For purposes of this interpretation, a former practitioner is defined as a proprietor, partner, shareholder, or equivalent who leaves by resignation, termination, retirement, or sale of all or part of the practice.

For purposes of determining a firm's compliance with Rule 101 and its interpretations, a former practitioner is not included in the term "a member or a member's firm" (see Ethics Interpretation 101-9, ET section 101.11) provided that

1. Payment of the amounts due to the former practitioner for his or her

interest in the firm and for unfunded, vested retirement benefits according to the payment schedule in effect should be such that they do not cause a substantial doubt about the firm's ability to continue as a going concern for a reasonable period of time. In addition, such amounts including all retirement benefits should be fixed, both as to the amount and payment dates. Such amounts due a former practitioner may be paid over a reasonable period of time, and a reasonable rate of interest may be paid on any unpaid balances. Retirement benefits may be adjusted only for inflation.

2. The former practitioner does not participate in the firm's business or professional activities whether or not compensated for such participation. This proscription does not apply to consultations on an advisory basis for a reasonable period of time during the transition period upon leaving the firm.

3. The former practitioner does not appear to participate in the activities of or be associated with his or her former firm. An appearance of participation or association results from such actions as inclusion of the former practitioner's name under the firm's name in an office building directory, inclusion of the former practitioner's name as a member of the firm in membership lists of business, professional or civic organizations, or inclusion of the former practitioner's name in the firm's internal directory without being designated as retired. The former practitioner will not be considered as participating or associating with his or her former firm solely because the former practitioner is provided an office, either in the firm's suite or in a separate location, and related office amenities such as secretarial and telephone services. (However, see 4. below for restrictions regarding office space and amenities for a former practitioner who accepts a position of significant influence with a client.)

4. A former practitioner in a position of significant influence with the client must no longer be provided with office space and related amenities by his or her former firm.

[Replaces previous Interpretation 101-2, *Retired Partners and Firm Independence,* August, 1989]

.05 101-3—Accounting services. Members in public practice are sometimes asked to provide manual or automated bookkeeping or data processing services to clients who are of insufficient size to employ an adequate internal accounting staff. Computer systems design and programming assistance are also rendered by members either in conjunction with data processing services or as a separate engagement. Members who perform such services and who are engaged in the practice of public accounting are subject to the bylaws and Rules of Conduct.

On occasion members also rent "block time" on their computers to their clients but are not involved in the processing of transactions or maintaining the client's accounting records. In such cases the sale of block time constitutes a business rather than a professional relationship and must be considered together with all other relationships between the member and his client to determine if their aggregate impact is such as to impair the member's independence.

When a member performs manual or automated bookkeeping services, concern may arise whether the performance of such services would impair his audit independence—that the performance of such basic accounting services would cause his audit to be lacking in a review of mechanical accuracy or that the accounting judgments made by him in recording transactions may somehow be less reliable than if made by him in connection with the subsequent audit.

Members are skilled in, and well accustomed to, applying techniques to control mechanical accuracy, and the performance of the record-keeping function should have no effect on application of such techniques. With regard to accounting judgments, if third parties have confidence in a member's judgment in performing an audit, it is difficult to contend that they would have less confidence where the same judgment is applied in the process of preparing the underlying accounting records.

Nevertheless, a member performing accounting services for an audit client must meet the following requirements to retain the appearance that he is not virtually an employee and therefore lacking in independence in the eyes of a reasonable observer.

1. The CPA must not have any relationship or combination of relationships with the client or any conflict of interest which would impair his integrity and objectivity.

2. The client must accept the responsibility for the financial statements as his own. A small client may not have anyone in his employ to maintain accounting records and may rely on the CPA for this purpose. Nevertheless, the client must be sufficiently knowledgeable of the enterprise's activities and financial condition and the applicable accounting principles so that he can reasonably accept such responsibility, including, specifically, fairness of valuation and presentation and adequacy of disclosure. When necessary, the CPA must discuss accounting matters with the client to be sure that the client has the required degree of understanding.

3. The CPA must not assume the role of employee or of management conducting the operations of an enterprise. For example, the CPA shall not consummate transactions, have custody of assets or exercise authority on behalf of the client. The client must prepare the source documents on all transactions in sufficient detail to identify clearly the nature and amount of such transactions and maintain an accounting control over data processed by the CPA such as control totals and document counts. The CPA should not make changes in such basic data without the concurrence of the client.

4. The CPA, in making an examination of financial statements prepared from books and records which he has maintained completely or in part, must conform to generally accepted auditing standards. The fact that he has processed or maintained certain records does not eliminate the need to make sufficient audit tests.

When a client's securities become subject to regulation by the Securities and Exchange Commission or other federal or state regulatory body, responsibility for maintenance of the accounting records, including accounting classification decisions, must be assumed by accounting personnel employed by the client. The assumption of this responsibility must commence with the first fiscal year after which the client's securities qualify for such regulation. [Formerly paragraph .04, renumbered by adoption of the Code of Professional Conduct on January 12, 1988.]

[.06] [101–4] [Deleted] [Formerly paragraph .05, renumbered by adoption of the Code of Professional Conduct on January 12, 1988.]

.07 101–5—The Meaning of Certain Terminology Used in Interpretation 101–A–4 [ET section 101.02]. This interpretation defines certain terms used in Interpretation 101–A–4 of the Institute's ethics code. The rule prohibits loans to a member from his client, except for certain specified kinds of loans from a client financial institution when made under "normal lending procedures, terms, and requirements."

TERMINOLOGY

For purposes of Interpretation 101–A–4, the following are defined:

Loan

A loan is considered to be a financial transaction, the characteristics of which generally include, but are not limited to, an agreement that provides for repayment terms and a rate of interest.

Financial Institution

A financial institution is considered to be an entity that, as part of its normal business operations, makes loans to the general public.

Normal Lending Procedures, Terms, and Requirements

"Normal lending procedures, terms, and requirements" relating to a member's loan from a financial institution are defined as lending procedures, terms, and requirements that are reasonably comparable with those relating to loans of a similar character committed to other borrowers during the period in which the loan to the member is committed. Accordingly, in making such comparison and in evaluating whether a loan was made under "normal lending procedures, terms, and requirements," the member should consider all the circumstances under which the loan was granted, including—

1. The amount of the loan in relation to the value of the collateral pledged as security and the credit standing of the member or the member's firm.
2. Repayment terms.
3. Interest rate, including "points."

4. Requirement to pay closing costs in accordance with the lender's usual practice.
5. General availability of such loans to the public.

Related prohibitions that may be more restrictive are prescribed by certain state and federal agencies having regulatory authority over such financial institutions. Broker-dealers, for example, are subject to regulation by the Securities and Exchange Commission. [Formerly paragraph .06, renumbered by adoption of the Code of Professional Conduct on January 12, 1988. References revised to reflect issuance of AICPA Code of Professional Conduct on January 12, 1988.]

[Revised, November 30, 1987, by the Professional Ethics Executive Committee.]

.08 101-6—The effect of actual or threatened litigation on independence. Rule 101 and its interpretations prohibit the expression of an opinion on financial statements of an enterprise unless a member and his firm are independent with respect to the enterprise. In some circumstances, independence may be considered to be impaired as a result of litigation or the expressed intention to commence litigation.

Litigation between client and auditor

In order for the auditor to fulfill his obligation to render an informed, objective opinion on the client company's financial statements, the relationship between the management of the client and the auditor must be characterized by complete candor and full disclosure regarding all aspects of the client's business operations. In addition, there must be an absence of bias on the part of the auditor so that he can exercise dispassionate professional judgment on the financial reporting decisions made by the management. When the present management of a client company commences, or expresses an intention to commence, legal action against the auditor, the auditor and the client management may be placed in adversary positions in which the management's willingness to make complete disclosures and the auditor's objectivity may be affected by self-interest.

For the reasons outlined above, independence may be impaired whenever the auditor and his client company or its management are in threatened or actual positions of material adverse interests by reason of actual or intended litigation. Because of the complexity and diversity of the situations of adverse interests which may arise, however, it is difficult to prescribe precise points at which independence may be impaired. The following criteria are offered as guidelines:

1. The commencement of litigation by the present management alleging deficiencies in audit work for the client would be considered to impair independence.

2. The commencement of litigation by the auditor against the present management alleging management fraud or deceit would be considered to impair independence.
3. An expressed intention by the present management to commence litigation against the auditor alleging deficiencies in audit work for the client is considered to impair independence if the auditor concludes that there is a strong possibility that such a claim will be filed.
4. Litigation not related to audit work for the client (whether threatened or actual) for an amount not material to the member's firm[2] or to the financial statements of the client company would not usually be considered to affect the relationship in such a way as to impair independence. Such claims may arise, for example, out of disputes as to billings for services, results of tax or management services advice or similar matters.

Litigation by security holders

The auditor may also become involved in litigation ("primary litigation") in which he and the client company or its management are defendants. Such litigation may arise, for example, when one or more stockholders bring a stockholders' derivative action or a so-called "class action" against the client company or its management, its officers, directors, underwriters and auditors under the securities laws. Such primary litigation in itself would not alter fundamental relationships between the client company or its management and auditor and therefore should not be deemed to have an adverse impact on the auditor's independence. These situations should be examined carefully, however, since the potential for adverse interests may exist if cross-claims are filed against the auditor alleging that he is responsible for any deficiencies or if the auditor alleges fraud or deceit by the present management as a defense. In assessing the extent to which his independence may be impaired under these conditions, the auditor should consider the following additional guidelines:

1. The existence of cross-claims filed by the client, its management, or any of its directors to protect a right to legal redress in the event of a future adverse decision in the primary litigation (or, in lieu of cross-claims, agreements to extend the statute of limitations) would not normally affect the relationship between client management and auditor in such a way as to impair independence, unless there exists a significant risk that the cross-claim will result in a settlement or judgment in an amount material to the member's firm[3] or to the financial statements of the client.
2. The assertion of cross-claims against the auditor by underwriters would

[2]Because of the complexities of litigation and the circumstances under which it may arise, it is not possible to prescribe meaningful criteria for measuring materiality; accordingly, the member should consider the nature of the controversy underlying the litigaton and all other relevant factors in reaching a judgment.

[3]See footnote 2.

not usually impair independence if no such claims are asserted by the company or the present management.

3. If any of the persons who file cross-claims against the auditor are also officers or directors of other clients of the auditor, the auditor's independence with respect to such other clients would not usually be impaired.

Other third-party litigation

Another type of third-party litigation against the auditor may be commenced by a lending institution, other creditor, security holder or insurance company who alleges reliance on financial statements of the client examined by the auditor as a basis for extending credit or insurance coverage to the client. In some instances, an insurance company may commence litigation (under subrogation rights) against the auditor in the name of the client to recover losses reimbursed to the client. These types of litigation would not normally affect the auditor's independence with respect to a client who is either not the plaintiff or is only the nominal plaintiff, since the relationship between the auditor and client management would not be affected. They should be examined carefully, however, since the potential for adverse interests may exist if the auditor alleges, in his defense, fraud, or deceit by the present management.

If the real party in interest in the litigation (e.g., the insurance company) is also a client of the auditor ("the plaintiff client"), the auditor's independence with respect to the plaintiff client may be impaired if the litigation involves a significant risk of a settlement or judgment in an amount which would be material to the member's firm or to the financial statements of the plaintiff client. If the auditor concludes that such litigation is not material to the plaintiff client or his firm and thus his independence is not impaired, he should nevertheless ensure that professional personnel assigned to the audit of either of the two clients have no involvement with the audit of the other.

Effects of impairment of independence

If the auditor believes that the circumstances would lead a reasonable person having knowledge of the facts to conclude that the actual or intended litigation poses an unacceptable threat to the auditor's independence he should either (a) disengage himself to avoid the appearance that his self-interest would affect his objectivity, or (b) disclaim an opinion because of lack of independence. Such disengagement may take the form of resignation or cessation of any audit work then in progress pending resolution of the issue between the parties.

Termination of impairment

The conditions giving rise to a lack of independence are usually eliminated when a final resolution is reached and the matters at issue no longer affect the relationship between auditor and client. The auditor should carefully review the conditions of such resolution to determine that all impairments to his objectivity have been removed.

Actions permitted while independence is impaired

If the auditor was independent when his report was initially rendered, he may re-sign such report or consent to its use at a later date while his independence is impaired provided that no post-audit work is performed by such auditor during the period of impairment. The term "post-audit work," in this context, does not include inquiries of subsequent auditors, reading of subsequent financial statements, or such procedures as may be necessary to assess the effect of subsequently discovered facts on the financial statements covered by his previously issued report. [Formerly paragraph .07, renumbered by adoption of the Code of Professional Conduct on January 12, 1988.]

[.09] [101-7] [Deleted] [Formerly paragraph .08, renumbered by adoption of the Code of Professional Conduct on January 12, 1988.]

.10 101-8—Effect on independence of financial interests in nonclients having investor or investee relationships with a member's client.

Introduction

Interpretation 101-1 under Rule 101, *Independence* [ET section 101.02], provides in part that "A member or a firm of which he is a partner or shareholder shall not express an opinion on financial statements of an enterprise unless he and his firm are independent with respect to such enterprise. Independence will be considered to be impaired if for example, (A)... during the period of his professional engagement, or at the time of expressing his opinion, he or his firm... had or was committed to acquire any direct or material indirect financial interest in the enterprise... (B) during the period covered by the financial statements, during the period of the professional engagement, or at the time of expressing an opinion, he or his firm... was connected with the enterprise... in any capacity equivalent to that of a member of management..."

This interpretation deals with the effect on the appearance of independence of financial interests in nonclients that are related in various ways to a client. Some of the relationships discussed herein result in a financial interest in their client, while others would place the member in a capacity equivalent to that of a member of management.

Situations in which the nonclient investor is a partnership are not covered in this interpretation because the interests of the partnership are ascribed directly to the partners. A member holding a direct financial interest in a partnership that invests in his client has, as a result, a direct financial interest in the client, which impairs his independence.

Terminology

The following specially identified terms are used in this Interpretation as indicated:

1. *Client.* The enterprise with whose financial statements the member is associated.
2. *Member.* In this Interpretation the term "member" means those individuals identified in the term "he and his firm" as defined in Interpretation 101–9 [section 101.11].
3. *Investor.* In this Interpretation the term "investor" means (a) a parent or (b) another investor (including a natural person but not a partnership) that holds an interest in another company ("investee"), but only if the interest gives such other investor the ability to exercise significant influence over operating and financial policies of the investee. The criteria established in paragraph 17 of Accounting Principles Board Opinion Number 18 [AC section 182.104] shall apply in determining the ability of an investor to exercise such influence.
4. *Investee.* In this Interpretation, the term "investee" means (a) a subsidiary or (b) an entity that is subject to significant influence from an investor. A limited partnership in which a client-investor holds a limited partnership interest would not be considered an "investee" subject to this interpretation unless the limited partner were in a position to exercise significant influence over operating and financial policies of the limited partnership.
5. *Material Investee.* An investee is presumed to be material if:
   (a) the investor's aggregate carrying amount of investment in and advances to the investee exceeds 5% of the investor's consolidated total assets, or
   (b) the investor's equity in the investee's income from continuing operations before income taxes exceeds 5% of the investor's consolidated income from continuing operations before income taxes.

When the investor is a nonclient and its carrying amount of investments in and advances to the client investee is not readily available, the investor's proportionate share of the client investee's total assets may be used in the calculation described in (a) above.

If the income of an investor or investee from continuing operations before income taxes of the most recent years is clearly not indicative of the past or expected future amounts of such income, the reference point for materiality determinations should be the average of the incomes from continuing operations before income taxes of the preceding 3 years.

If a member has a financial interest in more than one nonclient investee of a client investor, the investments in and advances to such investees, and the equity in the income from continuing operations before income taxes of all such investees must be aggregated for purposes of determining whether such investees are material to the investor.

The 5% guidelines for identifying a material investee are to be applied to financial information available at the beginning of the engagement. A minor change in the percentage resulting from later financial information, which a member does not and could not be expected to anticipate at the beginning, may be ignored.

6. *Material financial interest.* A financial interest is presumed to be material to a member if it exceeds 5% of the member's net worth. If the member has financial interests in more than one investee of one investor, such interests must be aggregated for purposes of determining whether the member has a material financial interest as described in the preceding sentence.

Interpretation

Where a nonclient investee is material to a client investor, any direct or material indirect financial interest of a member in the nonclient investee would be considered to impair the member's independence with respect to the client. Likewise, where a client investee is material to a nonclient investor, any direct or material indirect financial interest of a member in the nonclient investor would be considered to impair the member's independence with respect to the client.

The remainder of this Interpretation discusses whether, in the other situations listed below, a member's financial interest in nonclient investor or nonclient investee of an audit client will impair the member's independence.

These situations are discussed in the following sections:

(1) Nonclient investee is not material to the client investor.
(2) Client investee is not material to nonclient investor.

Other relationships, such as those involving brother-sister common control or client-nonclient joint ventures, may affect the appearance of independence. The member should make a reasonable inquiry to determine whether such relationships exist, and where they do, careful consideration should be given to whether the financial interests in question would lead a reasonable observer to conclude that the specified relationships pose an unacceptable threat to the member's independence.

In general, in brother-sister common control situations, an immaterial financial interest of a member in the nonclient investee would not impair the independence of a member with respect to the client investee provided the member could not significantly influence the nonclient investor. In like manner in a joint venture situation, an immaterial financial interest of a member in the nonclient investor would not impair the independence of the member with respect to the client investor provided that the member could not significantly influence the nonclient investor.

If a member does not and could not reasonably be expected to have knowledge of the financial interests or relationships described in this interpretation, such lack of knowledge would preclude an impairment of independence.

(1) NONCLIENT INVESTEE IS NOT MATERIAL TO CLIENT INVESTOR

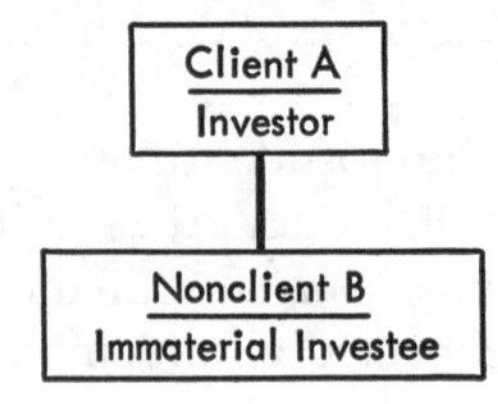

An immaterial financial interest of a member in Nonclient B (investee) would not be considered to impair the member's independence with respect to Client A (investor). A material financial interest of a member in Nonclient B would be considered to impair the member's independence with respect to Client A. The reason for this is that through its ability to influence Nonclient B, Client A could enhance or diminish the value of the member's financial interest in Nonclient B by an amount material to the member's net worth without a material effect on its own financial statements. As a result, the member would not appear to be independent when reporting on the financial statements of Client A.

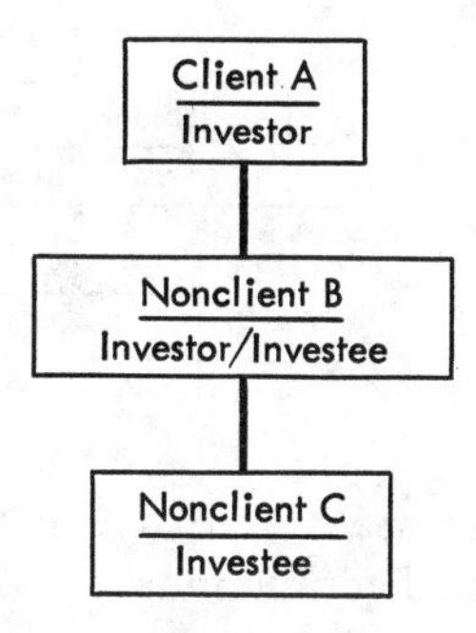

If Nonclient B (investee of Client A) had an investee, Nonclient C, the determination as to whether a financial interest in Nonclient C would be considered to impair the member's independence would be based on the same rules as above for Nonclient B, except that the materiality of Nonclient C is measured in relation to Client A, rather than to Nonclient B.

(2) CLIENT INVESTEE IS NOT MATERIAL TO NONCLIENT INVESTOR

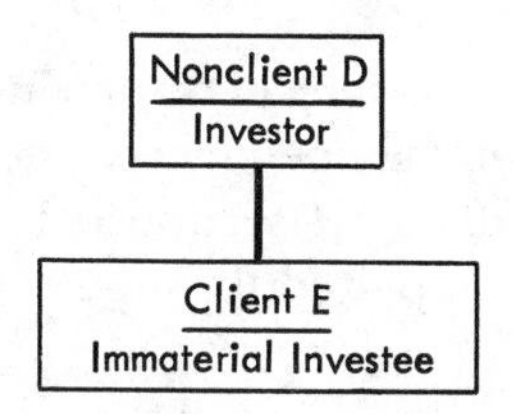

Except as indicated in the next paragraph, a financial interest of a member in Nonclient D (investor) would not be considered to impair the member's independence with respect to Client E (investee) even if the financial interest in Nonclient D were material to the member's net worth. The reason for this is that, since Client E is immaterial to Nonclient D, the member would not appear to be in a position to enhance his investment in Nonclient D.

If the member's financial interest in Nonclient D (investor) is sufficiently large to allow the member to significantly influence the actions of Nonclient D, the member's independence would be considered to be impaired. The reason for this is that a financial interest sufficient to allow the member to significantly influence the actions (operating and financial policies, intercompany transactions, etc.) of the investor could permit the member to exercise a degree of control over the client that would place the member in a capacity equivalent to that of a member of management. Such relationships would be considered to impair independence under Interpretation 101(B) (1) [ET section 101.02].

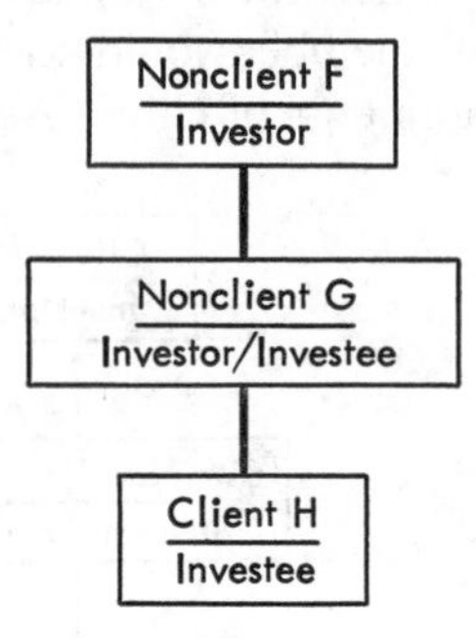

If Client H were an investee of Nonclient G, who was an investee of another investor, Nonclient F, the determination as to whether a financial interest in Nonclient F would be considered to impair the member's independence would be based on the same rules as above for Nonclient G, except that the materiality of Client H is measured in relation to Nonclient F, rather than to Nonclient G. [Formerly paragraph .09, renumbered by adoption of the Code of Professional Conduct on January 12, 1988.]

[Revised, December 31, 1983, by the Professional Ethics Executive Committee. References changed to reflect the issuance of the AICPA Code of Professional Conduct on January 12, 1988.]

.11 101-9—The meaning of certain independence terminology and the effect of family relationships on independence. This interpretation defines certain terms used in Interpreation 101.1 [ET section 101.02] and, in doing so, also explains how independence may be impaired through certain family relationships.

TERMINOLOGY

He and His Firm

For purposes of Interpretation 101-1 [ET section 101.02], "he and his firm" includes—

1. An individual member performing professional services requiring independence.
2. The proprietor or all partners or shareholders.

3. All full- and part-time professional employees* participating in the engagement.
4. All full- and part-time managerial employees* located in an office participating in a significant portion of the engagement.
5. Any entity (for example, partnership, corporation, trust, joint venture, pool, and so forth) whose operating, financial, or accounting policies can be "significantly influenced" (as discussed below) by one of the persons described in (1) through (4) or by two or more of such persons if they choose to act together.

For purposes of Interpretation 101–1B [ET section 101.02], "he and his firm" does not include an employee solely because he was formerly associated with the client in any capacity described in Interpretation 101–1B [ET section 101.02] if such employee has disassociated himself from the client and does not participate in the engagement for the client covering any period of his association with the client.

Likewise, for the purposes of Interpretation 101–1B [ET section 101.02], "he and his firm" includes a professional employee who is associated with the client in any capacity described in Interpretation 101–1B [ET section 101.02] if the professional employee is located in an office participating in a significant portion of the engagement.

Managerial Employee

A managerial employee is a professional employee who either—

1. Has a position generally similar to that of a partner, including an employee having the final authority to sign, or give final approval to the issuance of, reports in the firm's name or
2. Has a management position, in contrast with a nonmanagement position, with the firm.

The organizations of firms vary; therfore, whether an employee has a management position depends on his normal responsibilities and how he or the position itself is held out to clients and third parties. The following are some, but not necessarily all, of the responsibilities that suggest that an employee has a management position:

1. Continuing responsibility for the overall planning and supervision of engagements for specified clients.
2. Authority for determining that an engagement is complete subject to final partner approval if required.
3. Responsibility for client relationships (for example, negotiating and collecting fees for engagements, marketing the firm's services).

*Refers to employees irrespective of their functional classification (for example, audit, tax, management advisory services).

4. Responsibility for such administrative functions as assignment of personnel to engagements, hiring, and training of personnel.
5. Existence of profit sharing as a significant feature of total compensation.

Significant Influence

A person or entity can exercise significant influence over the operating, financial, or accounting policies of another entity if, for example, the person or entity—

1. Is connected with the entity as a promoter, underwriter, or voting trustee.
2. Is connected with the entity in a policy-making position related to the entity's primary operating, financial, or accounting policies, such as chief executive officer, chief operating officer, chief financial officer, chief accounting officer, and the key assistants who can influence their decisions.
3. Is connected with the entity in a capacity equivalent to that of a general partner.
4. Is connected with the entity as a director other than honorary.
5. Meets the criteria established in paragraph 17 of Accounting Principles Board Opinion No. 18 [AC section 182.104], *The Equity Method of Accounting for Investments in Common Stock,* to determine the ability of an investor to exercise such influence.
6. Holds 20 percent or more of the limited partnership interests if the entity is a limited partnership.

The foregoing examples are not necessarily all-inclusive.

EFFECT OF FAMILY RELATIONSHIPS

Spouses and Dependent Persons

The term "he and his firm" includes spouses (whether or not dependent) and dependent persons (whether or not related) for all purposes of complying with Rule 101 subject to the following exception.

The exception is that the independence of the member and his firm will not normally be impaired solely because of employment of a spouse or dependent person by a client if the employment is in a position that does not allow "significant influence" (as discussed above) over the client's operating, financial, or accounting policies. However, if such employment is in a position where the person's activities are "audit sensitive" (even though not a position of significant influence), the member should not participate in the engagement.

Generally, a person's activities would be considered audit sensitive if such activities are normally an element of or subject to significant internal accounting controls. For example, the following positions, which are not intended to be all-inclusive, would normally be considered audit sensitive (even though not positions of significant influence): cashier, internal auditor, general accounting clerk, purchasing agent, or inventory warehouse supervisor.

Nondependent Close Relatives

The term "he and his firm" excludes nondependent close relatives of the persons described in (1) through (4) of that definition. Nevertheless, in circumstances discussed below, the independence of a member or a firm can be impaired because of a nondependent close relative.

Close relatives are nondependent children, stepchildren, brothers, sisters, grandparents, parents, parents-in-law, and their respective spouses.

The independence of a member and his firm is impaired with respect to the enterprise if—

1. A proprietor, partner, shareholder, or professional employee, any of whom are participating in the engagement, has a close relative who (a) can exercise significant influence over the operating, financial, or accounting policies of the client; (b) is otherwise employed in a position where the person's activities are "audit sensitive"; or (c) has a financial interest in the client that is material to the close relative and of which the proprietor, partner, shareholder, or professional employee has knowledge.
2. A proprietor, partner, shareholder, or managerial employee, any of whom are located in an office participating in a significant portion of the engagement, has a close relative who can exercise significant influence over the operating, financial, or accounting policies of the client.

OTHER CONSIDERATIONS

Members must be aware that it is impossible to enumerate all circumstances wherein the appearance of a member's independence might be questioned by third parties because of family or dependent person relationships. In situations involving assessment of the association of any relative or dependent person with a client, members must consider whether the strength of personal and business relationships between the member and the relative or dependent person, considered in conjunction with the specified association with the client, would lead a reasonable person aware of all the facts, and taking into consideration normal strength of character and normal behavior under the circumstances, to conclude that the situation poses an unacceptable threat to the member's objectivity and appearance of independence. [Formerly paragraph .10, renumbered by adoption of the Code of Professional Conduct on January 12, 1988. References changed to reflect the issuance of the AICPA Code of Professional Conduct on January 12, 1988.]

[Revised, December 31, 1986 by the Professional Ethics Executive Committee.]

.12 101-10—The effect on independence of relationships proscribed by Rule 101 and its interpretations with nonclient entities included with a member's client in the financial statements of a government reporting entity. Rule 101 and its interpretations provide, in part, the following: "A member or a firm of which he is a partner or shareholder shall not express an opinion on financial statements of an enterprise unless he and his firm are independent with respect to such enterprise. Independence will be considered to be impaired if, for example: (A) During the period of his professional engagement, or at the time of expressing his opinion, he or his firm. . . had or was committed to acquire any direct or material indirect financial interest in the enterprise. . . (B) During the period covered by the financial statements, during the period of the professional engagement, or at the time of expressing an opinion, he or his firm. . . was connected with the enterprise. . . in any capacity equivalent to that of a member of management. . . ."

This interpretation deals with the effect on the appearance of independence of members having a relationship of a type specified in Rule 101 with nonclients that are related in various ways to clients in the state and local government sector.*

Under Statement 3, "Defining the Governmental Reporting Entity," by the National Council on Governmental Accounting (NCGA), financial statements should be issued for the governmental reporting entity, which consists of the combined financial statements of an oversight entity and one or more component unit entities. The basic criterion for including an entity as a component unit in a governmental reporting entity for general-purpose financial statements is the exercise of oversight responsibility for such units by the oversight entity. Oversight responsibility is derived from the oversight entity's significant influence on the component unit and includes, but is not limited to, financial interdependency, selection of governing authority, designation of management, ability to significantly influence operations, and accountability for fiscal matters.

Since the provisions of NCGA Statement 3 indicate that it need not be applied to immaterial items, it is presumed, for purposes of this interpretation, that all component units included in the governmental reporting entity's financial statements were included because they are material to the reporting entity, unless the member can demonstrate otherwise.

Therefore, because the oversight entity can exercise significant influence over the component units included in the reporting entity financial statements, Rule 101 is applicable and requires a member issuing a report on the combined financial statements of a governmental reporting entity to be independent of the oversight entity and of each component unit included in the reporting entity financial statements.

Similarly, a member who is the auditor of a material component unit, but is not the auditor of the oversight entity, should be independent of the oversight entity and each of the other component units because of the significant influence of the oversight entity over all the component units.

*As set forth under Section 91 of the Code entitled "Applicability," nothing in this interpretation should inhibit a member from performing his/her statutory duties as a governmental auditor.

However, a member who is the auditor of an immaterial component unit need be independent of only that component because it is immaterial to the reporting entity. If this same member also audited other immaterial component units which, when aggregated, are material to the reporting entity, the member should be independent of the oversight entity and of the component units that the member audits and all other component units included in the financial statements of the reporting entity.

A member expressing an opinion on the financial statements of a governmental reporting entity should take reasonable steps to seek satisfaction concerning the independence of auditors of component units. (See AU section 543.) [Formerly paragraph .11, renumbered by adoption of the Code of Professional Conduct on January 12, 1988. References changed to reflect the Issuance of the AICPA Code of Professional Conduct on January 12, 1988.]

.13 101-11—Independence and attest engagements.

Introduction

Rule 101, *Independence*, provides that "a member in public practice shall be independent in the performance of professional services as required by standards promulgated by bodies designated by Council." The Statement on Standards for Attestation Engagements [AT Section 100] requires independence in the performance of engagements covered by that Statement.

[Definitions]

Assertion. Any declaration, or a set of related declarations taken as a whole, by a party responsible for it.

Asserter. The person(s) or entity responsible for an assertion.

Attest Engagement. An engagement in which a practitioner is engaged to issue or does issue a written communciation that expresses a conclusion about the reliability of a written assertion that is the responsibility of another party.

Attest Engagement Team. Includes proprietors, partners, and shareholders who participate in the acceptance or performance of the attest engagement and full- or part-time professional employees who participate in the acceptance or the performance of the attest engagement, including individuals who provide consultation or supervisory services for the attest engagement.

[Applicability]

This interpretation does not apply to attest engagements covered by Statements on Auditing Standards, Statements on Standards for Accounting and Review Services, Statements on Standards for Accountants' Services on Prospective Financial Information, and such other pronouncements as may be determined from time to time by the Professional Ethics Executive Committee.

Interpretation

Independence will be considered to be impaired if, during the period of the attest engagement or at the time the written conclusion is issued—

1. An individual on the attest engagement team or his or her spouse, dependent or firm[4] has a relationship with the asserter that is proscribed by interpretation 101–1 of rule 101 [ET section 101.02].
2. An individual on the engagement team has a nondependent close relative[5] who has either a position of significant influence with, or a financial interest material to the close relative in the asserter.
3. An owner, partner, or shareholder of the firm who is located in an office participating in a significant portion of the attest engagement, or the spouse or dependent of such an owner, partner, or shareholder, has either a position of significant influence with, or a financial interest material to such person in the asserter.
4. The firm, an individual on the attest engagement team (or his or her spouse or dependent), or an owner, partner, or shareholder in an office performing a significant portion of the engagement, contributed to the development of the subject matter of the assertion (the subject) or stands to gain financially directly from the success of the subject.
5. An individual on the attest engagement team knows or could reasonably be expected to know that any owner, partner, or shareholder located in other offices of the firm (a) contributed to the development of the subject or stands to gain financially directly from the success of the subject, or (b) has a position of significant influence with the asserter.

In determining whether a relationship with an asserter is one that is proscribed under interpretation 101–1 [ET section 101.02], the following guidance is provided:

- Interpretation 101–6, "The Effect of Actual or Threatened Litigation on Independence [ET section 101.08]," is not applicable unless the litigation relates to the attest engagement or is material to the firm or to the financial statements of the asserter.
- Interpretation 101–9, "The Meaning of Certain Independence Terminology and the Effect of Family Relationships on Independence [ET section 101.11]," is not applicable because the applicability of this interpretation is stated herein.

[Effective February 28, 1990.]

[4]For the purpose of this interpretation, *firm* shall mean the sole proprietorship, partnership, or professional corporation of which an individual on the attest engagement team is an owner, partner, shareholder, or employee; it does not include owners, partners, shareholders, or employees as individuals.

[5]For the purpose of this interpretation, this term shall mean the same as in interpretation 101–9, "The Meaning of Certain Independence Terminology and the Effect of Family Relationships on Independence [ET section 101.11]."

ET Section 102

Integrity and Objectivity

.01 Rule 102—Integrity and objectivity. In the performance of any professional service, a member shall maintain objectivity and integrity, shall be free of conflicts of interest, and shall not knowingly misrepresent facts or subordinate his or her judgment to others.

[As adopted January 12, 1988.]

Interpretations under Rule 102—Integrity and Objectivity

Interpretations and Ethics Rulings which existed before the adoption of the Code of Professional Conduct on January 12, 1988, will remain in effect until further action is deemed necessary by the appropriate senior technical committee.

.02 102-1—Knowing misrepresentations in the preparation of financial statements or records. A member who knowingly makes, or permits or directs another to make, false and misleading entries in an entity's financial statements or records shall be considered to have knowingly misrepresented facts in violation of rule 102.

.03 102-2—Conflicts of Interest. A conflict of interest may occur if a member performs a professional service for a client or employer and the member or his or her firm has a significant relationship with another person, entity, product, or service that could be viewed as impairing the member's objectivity. If this significant relationship is disclosed to and consent is obtained from such client, employer, or other appropriate parties, the rule shall not operate to prohibit the performance of the professional service. When making the disclosure, the member should consider Rule 301, "Confidential Client Information."

Certain professional engagements require independence. Independence impairments under Rule 101 and its interpretation cannot be eliminated by such disclosure and consent.

ET Section 201

General Standards

.01 Rule 201—General standards. A member shall comply with the following standards and with any interpretations thereof by bodies designated by Council.

A. *Professional Competence.* Undertake only those professional services that the member or the member's firm can reasonably expect to be completed with professional competence.
B. *Due Professional Care.* Exercise due professional care in the performance of professional services.
C. *Planning and Supervision.* Adequately plan and supervise the performance of professional services.
D. *Sufficient Relevant Data.* Obtain sufficient relevant data to afford a reasonable basis for conclusions or recommendations in relation to any professional services performed.

[As adopted January 12, 1988.]

Interpretations under Rule 201—General Standards

Interpretaitons and Ethics Rulings which existed before the adoption of the Code of Professional Conduct on January 12, 1988, will remain in effect until further action is deemed necessary by the appropriate senior technical committee.

.02 201-1—Competence. A member who accepts a professional engagement implies that he has the necessary competence to complete the engagement according to professional standards, applying his knowledge and skill with reasonable care and diligence, but he does not assume a responsibility for infallibility of knowledge or judgment.

Competence in the practice of public accounting involves both the technical qualifications of the member and his staff and his ability to supervise and evaluate the quality of the work performed. Competence relates both to knowledge of the profession's standards, techniques and the technical subject matter involved, and to the capability to exercise sound judgment in appying such knowledge to each engagement.

The member may have the knowledge required to complete an engagement professionally before undertaking it. In many cases, however, additional research or consultation with others may be necessary during the course of the engagement. This does not ordinarily represent a lack of competence, but rather is a normal part of the professional conduct of an engagement.

However, if a CPA is unable to gain sufficient competence through these means, he should suggest, in fairness to his client and the public, the engagement of someone competent to perform the needed service, either independently or as an associate.

[.03] [201-2] [Deleted]

[.04] [201-3] [Deleted]

.05 201-4—Definition of the term engagement as used in rule 201—general standards. The term "engagement" as used in Rule 201 includes (1) any engagement during which a member is required to issue or does issue a written communication that expresses a conclusion about the reliability of a written assertion that is the responsibility of another party, (2) any engagement that requires a member to comply with a statement on auditing standards in the performance of that engagement, or (3) any engagement involving prospective financial statements that are, or reasonably might be, expected to be used by another (third) party in which a member either (a) submits such statements that he has assembled or assisted in assembling to his client or others or (b) reports on such statements.

To assure compliance with the General Standards A through D in Rule 201, a member who performs an engagement of the type described in (1) above should follow the Statement on Standards for Attestation Engagements. Similarly, a member who performs an engagement of the type described in (2) above should follow the applicable Generally Accepted Auditing Standards and the related Statements on Auditing Standards. To assure compliance with General Standards A through D in Rule 201, a member who performs an engagement described in (3) above should follow the Statement on Standards for Accountants' Services on Prospective Financial Information.

ET Section 202

Compliance With Standards

.01 Rule 202—Compliance with standards. A member who performs auditing, review, compilation, management advisory, tax, or other professional services shall comply with standards promulgated by bodies designated by Council. [As adopted January 12, 1988.]

Interpretation under Rule 202—Compliance With Standards

Interpretations and Ethics Rulings which existed before the adoption of the Code of Professional Conduct on January 12, 1988, will remain in effect under futher action is deemed necessary by the appropriate senior technical committee.

[.02] [202-1] [Deleted]

ET Section 203

Accounting Principles

.01 Rule 203—Accounting principles. A member shall not (1) express an opinion or state affirmatively that the financial statements or other financial data of any entity are presented in conformity with generally accepted accounting principles or (2) state that he or she is not aware of any material modifications that should be made to such statements or data in order for them to be in conformity with generally accepted accounting principles or (2) state that he or she is not aware of any material modifications that should be made to such statements or data in order for them to be in conformity with generally accepted accounting principles, if such statements or data contain any departure from an accounting principle promulgaged by bodies designated by Council to establish such principles that has a material effect on the statements or data taken as a whole. If, however, the statements or data contain such a departure and the member can demonstrate that due to unusual circumstances the financial statements or data would otherwise have been misleading, the member can comply with the rule by describing the departure, its approximate effects, if practicable, and the reasons why compliance with the principle would result in a misleading statement.

[As adopted January 12, 1988.]

Interpretations under Rule 203—Accounting Principles

Interpretations and Ethics Rulings which existed before the adoption of the Code of Professional Conduct on January 12, 1988, will remain in effect under futher action is deemed necessary by the appropriate senior technical committee.

.02 203-1—Departures from established accounting principles. Rule 203 was adopted to require compliance with accounting principles promulgated by the body designated by Council to establish such principles. There is a strong presumption that adherence to officially established accounting principles would in nearly all instances result in financial statements that are not misleading.

However, in the establishment of accounting principles it is difficult to anticipate all of the circumstances to which such principles might be applied. This rule therefore recognizes that upon occasion there may be unusual circumstances where the literal application of pronouncements on accounting principles would have the effect of rendering financial statements misleading. In such cases, the proper accounting treatment is that which will render the financial statements not misleading.

The question of what constitutes unusual circumstances as referred to in Rule 203 is a matter of professional judgment involving the ability to support the position that adherence to a promulgated principle would be regarded generally by reasonable men as producing a misleading result.

Examples of events which may justify departures from a principle are new legislation or the evolution of a new form of business transaction. An unusual degree of materiality or the existence of conflicting industry practices are examples of circumstances which would not ordinarily be regarded as unusual in the context of Rule 203.

.03 203-2—Status of FASB interpretations. Council is authorized under Rule 203 to designate a body to establish accounting principles and has designated the Financial Accounting Standards Board as such body. Council also has resolved that FASB Statements of Financial Accounting Standards, together with those Accounting Research Bulletins and APB Opinions which are not superseded by action of the FASB, constitute accounting principles as contemplated in Rule 203.

In determining the existence of a departure from an accounting principle established by a Statement of Financial Accounting Standards, Accounting Research Bulletin or APB Opinion encompassed by Rule 203, the division of professional ethics will construe such Statement, Bulletin or Opinion in the light of any interpretations thereof issued by the FASB.

[0.4] [203-3] [Deleted]

ET Section 301

Confidential Client Information

.01 Rule 301—Confidential client information. A member in public practice shall not disclose any confidential client information without the specific consent of the client.

This rule shall not be construed (1) to relieve a member of his or her professional obligations under rules 202 and 203, (2) to affect in any way the member's obligation to comply with a validly issued and enforceable subpoena or summons, (3) to prohibit review of a member's professional practice under AICPA or state CPA society authorization, or (4) to preclude a member from initiating a complaint with or responding to any inquiry made by a recognized investigative or disciplinary body.

Members of a recognized investigative or disciplinary body and professional practice reviewers shall not use to their own advantage or disclose any member's confidential client information that comes to their attention in carrying out their official responsibilities. However, this prohibition shall not restrict the exchange of information with a recognized investigative or disciplinary body or affect, in any way, compliance with a validly issued and enforceable subpoena or summons.

Interpretations under Rule 301—Confidential client information

Interpretations and Ethics Rulings which existed before the adoption of the Code of Professional Conduct on January 12, 1988, will remain in effect under futher action is deemed necessary by the appropriate senior technical committee.

[.02] [301-1] [Deleted]

.03 301-2—Disclosure of confidential client information in certain circumstances. Rule 301 provides that "A member in public practice shall not disclose any confidential client information without the specific consent of the client." The rule provides four exemptions that permit AICPA members to disclose confidential client information without the client's specific consent.

Consistent with the AICPA's jurisdiction only over AICPA members, exemptions (1), (2), and (3) pertain to bodies designated by the AICPA to set standards or acknowledge the legal process to which members are subject.

Exemption (4) in Rule 301 provides that Rule 301 shall not be construed "to preclude a member from initiating a complaint with or responding to any inquiry from a recognized investigative or disciplinary body."

In keeping with the AICPA's jurisdiction solely over AICPA members and the other three exemptions in Rule 301, exemption (4) of the rule pertains to the disciplinary and investigative processes of the AICPA. Exemption (4) allows but does not require members to file complaints with the AICPA and other participants in the Joint Ethics Enforcement Program even though the complaint may necessitate disclosing confidential client information without the specific consent of the client. The concluding paragraph of the rule is evidence of this intent as it asserts that members of recognized investigative or disciplinary bodies and professional practice reviewers shall not use to their own advantage or disclose any members's confidential client information.

Consistent with this perceived intent of exemption (4), it is interpreted to state the following: Rule 301 shall not be construed to preclude a member from initiating a complaint with or responding to any inquiry made by a recognized investigative or disciplinary body of the AICPA or other participant in the Joint Ethics Enforcement Program.

In addition, the exemption (2) is interpreted to provide that Rule 301 should not be construed to prohibit or interfere with a member's compliance with applicable laws and government regulations.

.04 301-3—Confidential Information and the Purchase, Sale, or Merger of a Practice. Rule 301 prohibits a member in public practice from disclosing any confidential client information without the specific consent of the client. The rule provides that it shall not be construed to prohibit the review of a member's professional practice under AICPA or state CPA society authorization.

For purposes of Rule 301, a review of a member's professional practice is hereby authorized to include a review in conjunction with a prospective purchase, sale, or merger of all or part of a member's practice. The member must take appropriate precautions (for example, through a written confidentiality agreement) so that the prospective purchaser does not disclose any information obtained in the course of the review, since such information is deemed to be confidential client information.

Members reviewing a practice in connection with a prospective purchase or merger shall not use to their advantage nor disclose any member's confidential client information that comes to their attention.

[Effective February 28, 1990.]

ET Section 302

Contingent Fees

.01 Rule 302—Contingent fees. Professional services shall not be offered or rendered under an arrangement whereby no fee will be charged unless a specified finding or result is attained, or where the fee is otherwise contingent upon the findings or results of such services. However, a member's fees may vary depending, for example, on the complexity of services rendered.

Fees are not regarded as being contingent if fixed by courts or other public authorities, or, in tax matters, if determined based on the results of judicial proceedings or the findings of governmental agencies.
[As adopted January 12, 1988.]

Interpretation under Rule 302—Contingent Fees

Interpretations and Ethics Rulings which existed before the adoption of the Code of Professional Conduct on January 12, 1988, will remain in effect under futher action is deemed necessary by the appropriate senior technical committee.

.02 302-1—Meaning of the phrase "the findings of governmental agencies" as stated in rule 302 of the rules of conduct. Rule 302 of the Rules of Conduct provides that fees are not regarded as being contingent "in tax matters, if determined based on the results of judicial proceedings or the findings of governmental agencies."

For the purposes of rule 302, in tax matters, the phrase "the findings of governmental agencies" refers to the resolution of a controversy with a governmental agency and does not refer to the preparation of original returns, amended returns, claims for refund, and requests for private letter rulings.

ET Section 501

Acts Discreditable

.01 Rule 501—Acts discreditable. A member shall not commit an act discreditable to the profession.
[As adopted January 12, 1988.]

Interpretations under Rule 501—Acts Discreditable

Interpretations and Ethics Rulings which existed before the adoption of the Code of Professional Conduct on January 12, 1988, will remain in effect under futher action is deemed necessary by the appropriate senior technical committee.

.02 501-1—Client's records and accountant's workpapers. Retention of client records after a demand is made for them is an act discreditable to the profession in violation of Rule 501. The fact that the statutes of the state in which a member practices may specifically grant him a lien on all client records in his possession does not change the ethical standard that it would be a violation of the Code to retain the records to enforce payment.

A member's working papers are his property and need not be surrendered to the client. However, in some instances a member's working papers will contain data which should properly be reflected in the client's books and records but which for convenience have not been duplicated therein, with the result that the client's records are incomplete. In such instances, the portion of the working papers containing such data constitutes part of the client's records, and copies should be made available to the client upon request.

If a member is engaged to perform certain work for a client and the engagement is terminated prior to the completion of such work, the member is required to return or furnish copies of only those records originally given to the member by the client.

Examples of working papers that are considered to be client's records would include:

a. Worksheets in lieu of books of original entry (e.g., listings and distributions of cash receipts or cash disbursements on columnar working paper).
b. Worksheets in lieu of general ledger or subsidiary ledgers, such as accounts receivable, job cost and equipment ledgers or similar depreciation records.
c. All adjusting and closing journal entries and supporting details. (If the supporting details are not fully set forth in the explanation of the journal entry, but are contained in analyses of accounts in the accountant's working papers, then copies of such analyses must be furnished to the client).
d. Consolidating or combining journal entries and worksheets and supporting detail used in arriving at final figures incorporated in an end product such as financial statements or tax returns.

Any working papers developed by the member incident to the performance of his engagement which do not result in changes to the clients' records or are not in themselves part of the records ordinarily maintained by such clients, are considered to be solely "accountant's working papers" and are not the property of the client, e.g.:

> The member may make extensive analyses of inventory or other accounts as part of his selective audit procedures. Even if such analyses have been prepared by client personnel at the request of the member, they nevertheless are considered to be part of the accountant's working papers.
>
> Only to the extent such analyses result in changes to the client's records would the member be required to furnish the details from his working papers in support of the journal entries recording such changes unless the journal entries themselves contain all necessary details.

Once the member has returned the client's records to him or furnished him with copies of such records and/or necessary supporting data, he has discharged his obligation in this regard and need not comply with any subsequent requests to again furnish such records.

If the member has retained in his files copies of a client's records already in possession of the client, the member is not required to return such copies to the client.

.03 501-2—Discrimination in employment practices. Discrimination based on race, color, religion, sex, age or national origin in hiring, promotion or salary practices is presumed to constitute an act discreditable to the profession in violation of Rule 501.

.04 501-3—Failure to follow standards and/or procedures or other requirements in government audits. Engagements for audits of government grants, government units or other recipients of government monies typically require that such audits be in compliance with government audit standards, guides, procedures, statutes, rules, and regulations, in addition to generally accepted auditing standards. If a member has accepted such an engagement and undertakes an obligation to follow specified government audit standards, guides, procedures, statutes, rules and regulations, in addition to generally accepted auditing standards, he is obligated to follow such requirements. Failure to do so is an act discreditable to the profession in violation of Rule 501, unless the member discloses in his report the fact that such requirements were not followed and the reasons therefor.

.05 501-4—Negligence in the preparation of financial statements or records. A member who, by virtue of his negligence, makes, or permits or directs another to make, false and misleading entries in the financial statements or records of an entity shall be considered to have committed an act discreditable to the profession in violation of rule 501.

.05 501-5—Failure to follow requirements of government bodies, commissions, or other regulatory agencies in performing attest or similar services. Many governmental bodies, commissions, or other regulatory agencies have established requirements such as audit standards, guides, rules, and regulations that members are required to follow in performing attest or similar services for clients subject to their jurisdiction. For example, the Securities and Exchange Commission, Federal Communications Commission, state insurance commissions, and other regulatory agencies have established such requirements.

When a member agrees to perform an attest or similar service for the purpose of reporting to such bodies, commissions, or regulatory agencies, the member should follow such requirements, in addition to generally accepted auditing standards (where applicable). Failure to substantially follow such requirements is an act discreditable to the profession, unless the member discloses in his or her report that such requirements were not followed and the reasons therefore. Not following such requirements could require the member to modify his or her report.

If the agency rerquires additional disclosures of the auditor, they must be made in accordance with the disclosure requirements established by the governmental body, commission or other regulatory agency. Failure to substantially follow such requirements is an act discreditable to the profession.

ET Section 502

Advertising and Other Forms of Solicitation

.01 Rule 502—Advertising and other forms of solicitation. A member in public practice shall not seek to obtain clients by advertising or other forms of solicitation in a manner that is false, misleading, or deceptive. Solicitation by the use of coercion, over-reaching, or harassing conduct is prohibited.
[As adopted January 12, 1988.]

Interpretations under Rule 502—Advertising and Other Forms of Solicitation

Interpretations and Ethics Rulings which existed before the adoption of the Code of Professional Conduct on January 12, 1988, will remain in effect under futher action is deemed necessary by the appropriate senior technical committee.

[.02] [502-1] [Deleted]

.03 502-2—False, misleading or deceptive acts in advertising or solicitation. Advertising or other forms of solicitation that are false, misleading, or deceptive are not in the public interest and are prohibited. Such activities include those that—

1. Create false or unjustified expectations of favorable results.
2. Imply the ability to influence any court, tribunal, regulatory agency, or similar body or official.
3. Consist of self-laudatory statements that are not based on verifiable facts.
4. Make comparisons with other CPAs that are not based on verifiable facts.
5. Contain a representation that specific professional services in current or future periods will be performed for a stated fee, estimated fee or fee range when it was likely at the time of the representation that such fees would be substantially increased and the prospective client was not advised of that likelihood.

6. Contain any other representations that would be likely to cause a reasonable person to misunderstand or be deceived.

[Revised, December 31, 1986 by the Professional Ethics Executive Committee.]

[.04] [502-3] [Deleted]

[.05] [502-4] [Deleted]

.06 502-5—Engagements obtained through efforts of third parties. Members are often asked to render professional services to clients or customers of third parties. Such third parties may have obtained such clients or customers as the result of their advertising and solicitation efforts.

Members are permittted to enter into such engagements. The member has the responsibility to ascertain that all promotional efforts are within the bounds of the Rules of Conduct. Such action is required because the members will receive the benefits of such efforts by third parties, and members must not do through others what they are prohibited from doing themselves by the Rules of Conduct.

ET Section 503

Commissions

.01 Rule 503—Commissions. The acceptance by a member in public practice of a payment for the referral of products or services of others to a client is prohibited. Such action is considered to create a conflict of interest that results in a loss of objectivity and independence.

A member shall not make a payment to obtain a client. This rule shall not prohibit payments for the purchase of an accounting practice or retirement payments to individuals formerly engaged in the practice of public accounting or payments to their heirs or estates.

Interpretation under Rule 503—Commissions

Interpretations and Ethics Rulings which existed before the adoption of the Code of Professional Conduct on January 12, 1988, will remain in effect under futher action is deemed necessary by the appropriate senior technical committee.

.02 503-1—Fees in payment for services. Rule 503, which prohibits payment of a commission to obtain a client, was adopted to avoid a client's having to pay fees for which he did not receive commensurate services. However, payment of fees to a referring public accountant for professional services to the successor firm or to the client in connection with the engagement is not prohibited.

ET Section 505

Form of Practice and Name

.01 Rule 505—Form of practice and name. A member may practice public accounting only in the form of a proprietorship, a partnership, or a professional corporation whose characteristics conform to resolutions of Council.

A member shall not practice public accounting under a firm name that is misleading. Names of one or more past partners or shareholders may be included in the firm name of a successor partnership or corporation. Also, a partner or shareholder surviving the death or withdrawal of all other partners or shareholders may continue to practice under such name which includes the name of past partners or shareholders for up to two years after becoming a sole practitioner.

A firm may not designate itself as "Members of the American Institute of Certified Public Accountants" unless all of its partners or shareholders are members of the Institute.

[As adopted January 12, 1988.]

Interpretations under Rule 505—Form of Practice and Name

Interpretations and Ethics Rulings which existed before the adoption of the Code of Professional Conduct on January 12, 1988, will remain in effect under futher action is deemed necessary by the appropriate senior technical committee.

.02 505-1—Investment in commercial accounting corporation. A member in the practice of public accounting may have a financial interest in a commercial corporation which performs for the public services of a type performed by public accountants provided such interest is not material to the corporation's net worth, and the member's interest in and relation to the corporation is solely that of an investor.

.03 505-2—Application of rules of conduct to members who operate a separate business. Members in public practice who participate in the operation of a separate business that offers to clients one or more types of services rendered by public accountants will be considered to be in the practice of public accounting in the conduct of that business. In such a case, members will be required to observe all of the Rules of Conduct in the operation of the separate business.

In addition, members who are not otherwise in public practice must observe the Rules of Conduct in the operation of their business if they hold out to the public as being a CPA or public accountant and at the same time offer to clients one or more types of services rendered by public accountants.

ET Appendix A

Council Resolution Designating Bodies to Promulgate Technical Standards

(As amended January 12, 1988.)

Financial Accounting Standards Board

WHEREAS: In 1959 the Council designated the Accounting Principles Board to establish accounting principles, and

WHEREAS: The Council is advised that the Financial Accounting Standards Board (FASB) has become operational, it is

RESOLVED: That as of the date hereof the FASB, in respect of statements of financial accounting standards finally adopted by such board in accordance with its rules of procedure and the bylaws of the Financial Accounting Foundation, be, and hereby is, designated by this Council as the body to establish accounting principles pursuant to rule 203 and standards on disclosure of financial information for such entities outside financial statements in published financial reports containing financial statements under rule 202 of the Rules of the Code of Professional Conduct of the American Institute of Certified Public Accountants provided, however, any accounting research bulletins or opinions of the accounting principles board issued or approved for exposure by the acocunting principles board prior to April 1, 1973, and finally adopted by such board on or before June 30, 1973, shall constitute statements of accounting principles promulgated by a body designated by Council as contemplated in rule 203 of the Rules of the Code of Professional Conduct unless and until such time as they are expressly superseded by action of the FASB.

Governmental Accounting Standards Board

WHEREAS: The Governmental Accounting Standards Board (GASB) has been established by the board of trustees of the Financial Accounting Foundation (FAF) to issue standards of financial accounting and reporting with respect to activities and transactions of state and local governmental entities, and

WHEREAS: The American Institute of Certified Public Accountants is a signatory to the agreement creating the GASB as an arm of the FAF and has supported the GASB professionally and financially, it is

RESOLVED: That as of the date hereof, the GASB, with respect to statements of governmental accounting standards adopted and issued in July 1984 and subsequently in accordance with its rules of procedure and the bylaws of the FAF, be, and hereby is, designated by the Council of the American Institute of Certified Public Accountants as the body to establish financial accounting principles for state and local governmental entities pursuant to rule 203, and standards on disclosure of financial information for such entities outside financial statements in published financial reports containing financial statements under rule 202.

AICPA COMMITTEES AND BOARDS

WHEREAS: The membership of the Institute has adopted rules 201 and 202 of the Rules of the Code of Professional Conduct, which authorizes the Council to designate bodies to promulgate technical standards with which members must comply, and therefore it is

Accounting and Review Services Committee

RESOLVED: That the AICPA accounting and review services committee is hereby designated to promulgate standards under rules 201 and 202 with respect to unaudited financial statements or other unauditied financial information of an entity that is not required to file financial statements with a regulatory agency in connection with the sale or trading of its securities in a public market.

Auditing Standards Board

RESOLVED: That the AICPA auditing standards board is hereby designated as the body authorized under rules 201 and 202 to promulgate auditing and attest standards and procedures.

RESOLVED: That the auditing standards board shall establish under statements on auditing standards the responsibilities of members with respect to standards for disclosure of financial information outside financial statements in published financial reports containing financial statements.

Management Advisory Services Executive Committee

RESOLVED: That the AICPA management advisory services executive committee is hereby designated to promulgate standards under rules 201 and 202 with respect to the offering of management advisory services, provided, however, that such standards do not deal with the broad question of what, if any, services should be proscribed.

AND FURTHER RESOLVED: That any Institute committee or board now or in the future authorized by the Council to issue enforceable standards under rules 201 and 202 must observe an exposure process seeking comment from other affected committees and boards, as well as the general membership.

Attestation Standards

RESOLVED: That the AICPA accounting and review services committee, auditing standards board, and management advisory services executive committee are hereby designated as bodies authorized under rules 201 and 202 to promulgate attestation standards in their respective areas of responsibility.
[Added by Council, May 1988]

ET Appendix B

Council Resolution Concerning Professional Corporations or Associations

(As amended January 12, 1988.)

RESEOLVED: that the characteristics of a professional corporation as referred to in Rule 505 of the Code of Professional Conduct are as follows:

1. *Ownership.* All shareholders of the corporation or association shall be persons engaged in the practice of public accounting as defined by the Code of Professional Conduct. Shareholders shall at all times own their shares in their own right and shall be the beneficial owners of the equity capital ascribed to them.
2. *Transfer of Shares.* Provision shall be made requiring any shareholder who ceases to be eligible to be a shareholder to dispose of all of his or her shares within a reasonable period to a person qualified to be a shareholder or to the corporation or association.
3. *Directors and Officers.* The principal executive officer shall be a shareholder and a director, and to the extent possible, all other directors and officers shall be certified public accountants. Lay directors and officers shall not exercise any authority whatsoever over professional matters.
4. *Conduct.* The right to practice as a corporation or association shall not change the obligation of its shareholders, directors, officers, and other employees to comply with the Code of Professional Conduct established by the American Institute of Certified Public Accountants.

Appendix 2

Statements on Standards for Management Advisory Services[1]

Statements on Standards for Management Advisory Services are issued by the AICPA Management Advisory Services Executive Committee, the senior technical committee of the Institute designated to issue pronouncements in connection with management advisory services. Members should be aware that they may be called upon to justify departures from these statements.

MS Section 11

Definitions and Standards for MAS Practice

Effective for MAS rendered after May 1, 1982, unless otherwise indicated

.01 CPAs have historically served as business advisors and consultants, performing functions that are described as "management advisory services (MAS)." In general, management advisory services consist of advice and assistance concerning such matters as an entity's organization, personnel, planning, finances, operations, systems, controls, and other aspects of current or proposed activities. Such services are often closely related to the auditing, tax, and accounting and review services that CPAs provide.

.02 A management advisory service may range from a response to an inquiry based only on the knowledge and experience of the individual practitioner consulted to one involving an extensive project. For the purpose of Statements on Standards for Management Advisory Services, all such services are categorized as either MAS consultations or MAS engagements.[2] Professional Practices for each of these two forms of MAS will be different; standards for each of them will be provided in this and subsequent statements.[3]

[1]*AICPA Professional Standards,* vol. 2, MS Sections 11, 21, and 31. Copyright © 1982 by the American Institute of Certified Public Accountants, Inc.

[2]MAS consultations were referred to as MAS "informal advice" prior to the issuance of this statement.

[3]A series of Statements on Management Advisory Services was issued in the past to provide practical advice on MAS. They are not enforceable under the AICPA Rules of Conduct. Some of the material in those statements may be incorporated into future MAS standards and practice aids. Until then, practitioners may continue to consult such statements, although it should be recognized that future publications may contain guidance that differs from the views expressed in those statements.

PURPOSE

.03 This statement is the first in a series that will

a. Provide guidance to enable members to comply with rule 201 [ET section 201.01] of the AICPA Rules of Conduct within the context of management advisory services.
b. Establish, under rule 204 [now rule 202] of the AICPA Rules of Conduct, other standards deemed appropriate for such services.

DEFINITIONS

.04 Certain terms are defined below for purposes of Statements on Standards for Management Advisory Servivces.

Management advisory services (MAS). The management consulting function of providing advice and technical assistance where the primary purpose is to help the client improve the use of its capabilities and resources to achieve its objectives.[4] For the purose of illustration, "helping the client improve the use of its capabilities and resources" may involve activities such as

a. Counseling management in its analysis, planning, organizing, operating, and controlling functions.
b. Conducting special studies,[5] preparing recommendations, proposing plans and programs, and providing advice and technical assistance in their implementation.
c. Reviewing and suggesting improvement of policies, procedures, systems, methods, and organization relationships.
d. Introducing new ideas, concepts, and methods to management.

MAS engagement. That form of MAS in which an analytical approach and process is applied in a study or project. It typically involves more than an incidental effort devoted to some combination of activities relating to determination of client objectives, fact-finding, opportunity or problem definition, evaluation of alternatives, formulation of proposed action, communication of results, implementation, and follow-up.

MAS consultation. That form of MAS based mostly, if not entirely, on existing personal

[4]Recommendations and comments prepared as a direct result of observations made while performing an audit, review, or compilation of financial statements or while providing tax services, including tax consultations, are not MAS as herein defined.

[5]Statement on Auditing Standards 30 [AU section 642], provides guidance on studies made for that purpose.

knowledge about the client, the circumstances, the technical matters involved, and the mutual intent of the parties. It generally involves advice or information given by a practitioner in a short time frame. Usually, information is received through discussions with the client and, by mutual agreement, is accepted by the practitioner as represented. The nature of an MAS consultation and the basis for the practitioner's response are generally communicated to the client orally. The practitioner's response may be definitive when existing personal knowledge is deemed adequate; otherwise, it may be qualified, in which case limitations are stated. A qualified response often reflects cost, time, scope, or other limitations imposed by the client's specific circumstances.

MAS practitioner. Any Institute member in the practice of public accounting while engaged in the performance of an MAS service for a client, or any other individual who is carrying out MAS for a client on behalf of any Institute member.[6]

STANDARDS FOR MAS PRACTICE

.05 The following general standards apply to both MAS engagements and MAS consultations. They are contained in rule 201 [ET section 201.01] of the AICPA Rules of Conduct and apply to all services performed in the practice of public accounting.[7]

Professional competence. A member shall undertake only those engagements which he or his firm can reasonably expect to complete with professional competence.

Due professional care. A member shall exercise due professional care in the performance of an engagement.

Planning and supervision. A member shall adequately plan and supervise an engagement.

Sufficient relevant data. A member shall obtain sufficient relevant data to afford a reasonable basis for conclusions or recommendations in relation to an engagement.

Forecasts. A member shall not permit his name to be used in conjunction with any forecast of future transactions in a manner that may lead to the belief that the member vouches for the achievability of the forecast. [Deleted from general standards, January 12, 1988]

.06 The following technical standards apply to MAS engagements, as

[6]A member shall not permit others to carry out on his behalf, either with or without compensation, acts which, if carried out by the member, would place him in violation of the rules of conduct (See ET section 91.02-.05).

[7]The use of the terms "MAS engagement" and "MAS consultation" to differentiate the two recognized forms of MAS is not intended to exclude MAS consultations from the meaning of the term "engagement" as it is used in rule 201 [ET section 201.01].

defined in paragraph .04. They are established under rule 204 [now rule 202] of the AICPA Rules of Conduct. Technical standards for MAS consultations, as defined in paragraph .04, may be established in future statements.

Role of MAS practitioner. In performing an MAS engagement, an MAS practitioner should not assume the role of management or take any positions that might impair the MAS practitioner's objectivity.[8]

Understanding with client. An oral or written understanding should be reached with the client concerning the nature, scope, and limitations of thte MAS engagement to be performed.

Client benefit. Since the potential benefits to be derived by the client are a major consideration in MAS engagements, such potential benefits should be viewed objectively and the client should be notified of reservations regarding them. In offering and providing MAS engagements, results should not be explicitly or implicitly guaranteed. When estimates of quantifiable results are presented, they should be clearly identified as estimates and the support for such estimates should be disclosed.

Communication of results. Significant information pertinent to the results of an MAS engagement, together with any limitations, qualifications, or reservations needed to assist the client in making its decision, should be communicated to the client orally or in writing.

EFFECTIVE DATE

.07 This statement is effective for MAS rendered after May 1, 1982.

MS Section 21

MAS Engagements

Effective for MAS
engagements undertaken
on or after May 1, 1983,
unless otherwise indicated

INTRODUCTION

.01 Statement on Standards for Management Advisory Services (SSMAS) No. 1 [section 11], *Definitions and Standards for MAS Practice,* categorizes management

[8]An Institute member or his employee might at times serve in the role of management for a client. The Statements on Standards for MAS do not apply to situations in which the member or his employee serve in that role, but, under rule 101 [ET section 101.01] of the Rules of Conduct and Statement on Standards for Accounting and Review Services no. 1 [AR section 100], independence might be impaired for the purpose of an audit, review, or compilation of financial statements.

advisory services (MAS) as MAS engagements or MAS consultations.[9] It defines an MAS engagement as

> That form of MAS in which an analytical approach and process is applied in a study or project. It typically involves more than an incidental effort devoted to some combinationn of activities relating to determination of client objectives, fact-finding opportunity or problem definition, evaluation of atlernatives, formulation of proposed action, communication of results, implementation, and follow-up.

.02 This statement provides guidance on the application of certain of the standards set forth in SSMAS No. 1 [section 11].

NATURE OF MAS ENGAGEMENTS

.03 MAS engagements generally involve gathering and analyzing appropriate information concerning the client's business, operating results, financial condition, systems and procedures, or other matters needed for the development of conclusions and recommendations to assist a client to achieve its objectives.

.04 Engagements performed by MAS practitioners vary widely in size, complexity, staffing and time requirements, and technical subject matter. An MAS engagement may require the joint participation of the MAS practitioner, the client, and other personnel with the skills required to achieve the engagement objectives.

.05 While performing an MAS engagement, a practitioner may be asked to respond to a client inquiry on an MAS matter that is not related to the engagement. The nature of the inquiry and the response in such circumstances may fall within the definition of an MAS consultation, in which case the standards for MAS consultations would apply.

PROFESSIONAL COMPETENCE IN MAS ENGAGEMENTS

.06 Professional competence in performing MAS engagements includes an ability to identify and define client needs, select and supervise appropriate staff, apply an analytical approach and process appropriate to the engagement, apply knowledge of the technical subject matter under consideration, communicate recommendations effectively, and, when required, assist in implementing recommendations.

.07 An MAS engagement may require more than one individual and diverse

[9]Recommendations and comments prepared as a direct result of observations made while performing an audit, review, or compilation of financial statements or while providing tax services, including tax consultations, are not MAS as defined in SSMAS No. 1 [section 11].

technical skills. The MAS practitioner should carefully assess the combined abilities, education, and experience of the individuals on his staff, or otherwise engaged by him, who are to participate in a specific MAS engagement. In deciding whether he or his firm can reasonably expect to complete the engagement with professional competence, the MAS practitioner may also give consideration to the skills, education, and experience of client personnel and personnel from other organizations who have assumed responsibility for tasks related to the engagement.

PLANNING AND SUPERVISION IN MAS ENGAGEMENTS

.08 The MAS practitioner should plan and supervise an MAS engagement in a manner that provides reasonable assurance that the work is conducted in accordnce with the understanding with the client and with the professional standards set forth in Statements on Standards for Management Advisory Services and the AICPA Rules of Conduct.

.09 If staff is needed, the MAS practitioner should determine that a sufficient number of persons with appropriate skills and experience are available to perform the work.

.10 A plan should be developed to guide the conduct, supervision, control, and completion of the engagement. The plan should be modified, if necessary, during the course of the engagement. Engagement planning should include consideration of the approach and tasks required to achieve the engagement objectives.

.11 Throughout an MAS engagement, the MAS practitioner should exercise professional judgment concerning the level of documentation and the amount of supervision required, based on the experience of the persons involved and the complexity and duration of the assignment.

.12 An MAS engagement should be directed by an individual who is competent to supervise the personnel assigned, evaluate the quality and completeness of the work performed, and accept responsibility for successful completion of the engagement.

SUFFICIENT RELEVANT DATA IN MAS ENGAGEMENTS

.13 The MAS practitioner should obtain sufficient relevant data to complete an MAS engagement in a manner consistent with the understanding with the client. Sufficient relevant data may be obtained by interview, observation, review of client documents, research, computation, and analysis. The nature and quantity of information that constitutes sufficient relevant data will vary with the scope and circumstances of each engagement. It normally consists of information needed to analyze the course of action that might be considered. Sufficient relevant data include information that supports conclusions or recommendations.

.14 The MAS practitioner should exercise professional judgment in determining the nature and quantity of information required to develop conclusions or recommendations that fulfill the objectives of the MAS engagement. In making this determination, the MAS practitioner should consider the objectives, nature, and scope of the engagement, the costs of data gathering versus the benefits of added data, the intended use of the engagement results, and related circumstances. The source, reliability, and completeness of the data, and any limitations thereof, should be considered in forming and reviewing conclusions and recommendations.

ROLE OF PRACTITIONER IN MAS ENGAGEMENTS

.15 A pervasive characteristic of the pracatitioner's role in an MAS engagement is that of being an objective adviser. In performing an MAS engagement, the practitioner should not assume the role of management.[10] Because of the various advisory services that may be performed by the MAS practitioner and the singular responsibility of the client to make all management decisions, the roles and responsibilities of all parties should be clearly defined in the understanding with the client.

.16 An MAS engagement should be structured to enable management to make decisions on matters requiring action by providing for review and approval of the engagement findings, conclusions, recommendations, and other results. The implementation of any course of action recommended during an MAS engagement must be authorized by management.

UNDERSTANDING WITH CLIENT IN MAS ENGAGEMENTS

.17 Prior to undertaking an MAS engagement, the practitioner should consider such matters as the following in reaching an appropriate understanding with the client:

[10]An institute member or his employee might at times serve in the role of management for a client. The Statements on Standards for MAS do not apply to situations in which the member or his employee serve in that role, but, under rule 101 of the AICPA Rules of Conduct [ET Section 101.01] and Statement on Standards for Accounting and Review Services No. 1 [AR section 100], independence might be impaired for the purpose of an audit, review, or compilation of financial statements.

- Engagement objectives.
- Nature of the services to be performed.
- Engagement scope, including areas of client operations to be addressesd and limitations or constraints, if any.
- Respective roles, responsibilities, and relationships of the MAS practitioner, the client, and other parties to the engagement.
- The anticipated engagement approach, including major tasks and activities to be performed and, if appropriate, methods to be used.
- The manner in which engagement status and results are to be communicated.
- Work schedule.
- Fee arrangements.

.18 The MAS practitioner should exercise professional judgment in determing the nature and extent of documentation appropriate in the circumstances. MAS engagements normally include a documented understanding with the client, which may be in the form of an accepted proposal letter, a confirmation letter, an engagement arrangement letter, a contract, or a file memorandum documenting an oral understanding.

.19 Written documentation of the understanding may not be appropriate in some situations. Client confidentiality requirements or other engagement circumstances might explicitly preclude such documentation.

.20 If circumstances require a significant change in the nature, scope, or limitations of the services to be performed, the MAS practitioner should modify his understanding with the client.

CLIENT BENEFIT IN MAS ENGAGEMENTS

.21 Before beginning an MAS engagement, the MAS practitioner should obtain an understanding of the possible benefits, both tangible and intangible, that the client wishes to achieve.

.22 The MAS practitioner should not guarantee results either explicitly or implicitly. The ultimate achievability of results will depend on the effectiveness of client management in implementing the MAS practitioner's recommendations and on client management's ability to address changes or uncertainties. The MAS practitioner should communicate to the client reservations concerning the achievability of the anticipated benefits.

.23 If potential benefits are quantified, they should be described as estimates, and the support for such estimates should be disclosed. If estimated benefits or estimated costs change significantly during an engagement, the client should be informed.

COMMUNICATION OF RESULTS IN MAS ENGAGEMENTS

.24 The principal findings, conclusions, recommendations, or other results of an MAS engagement, including the major facts and assumptions upon which results are based, should be communicated to the client, together with limitations, reservations, or other qualifications.

.25 During lengthy or complex engagements, interim client communciation is desirable. Interim communication encourages client involvement and decision-making and keeps the client informed of results and progress.

.26 Final reports to a client may be written or oral depending on factors such as

- The understanding with the client.
- The degree to which the engagement results are provided to the client as the engagement progresses.
- The intended use of engagement results.
- Sensitivity or significance of material covered.
- The need for a formal record of the engagement.

.27 When an MAS practitioner does not issue a written report to the client, a memorandum to the file should be considered, outlining matters such as results achieved and documentation provided to the client.

EFFECTIVE DATE

.28 This statement is effective for MAS engagements undertaken on or after May 1, 1983.

MS Section 31

MAS Consultations

Effective for MAS
consultations occurring
after May 1, 1983,
unless otherwise indicated

INTRODUCTION

.01 Statement on Standards for Management Advisory Services (SSMAS) No. 1 [section 11], *Definitions and Standards for MAS Practice,* categorizes advisory services (MAS) as MAS engagements or MAS consultations.[11] It defines an MAS consultation as

> That form of MAS based mostly, if not entirely, on existing personal knowledge about the client, the circumstances, the technical matters involved, and the mutual intent of the parties. It generally involves advice or information given by a practitioner in a short time frame. Usually, information is received through discussions with the client and, by mutual agreement, is accepted by the practitioner as represented. The nature of an MAS consultation and the basis for the practitioner's response are generally communicated to the client orally. The practitioner's response may be definitive when existing personal knowledge is deemed adequate; otherwise it may be qualified, in which case limitations are stated. A qualified response often reflects cost, time, scope, or other limitations imposed by the client's specific circumstances.

.02 This statement provides guidance on the application of certain of the general standards of the profession (see SSMAS No. 1 [section 11] to MAS consultations and establishes certain technical standards applicable to MAS consultations.

NATURE OF MAS CONSULTATIONS

.03 MAS consultations may occur concurrently with the performance of other professional services, such as audit, review, or compilation of financial statements, tax services, or an MAS engagement. MAS consultations also may be the only type of service provided to a client. They may entail advice concerning a single matter or continuing consultations on a wide variety of matters. MAS consultations may occur casually in telephone conversations, take place in nonbusiness settings, transpire during periodic meetings at the client's or practitioner's offices, or may entail specific written inquiries or responses.

[11] Recommendations and comments prepared as a direct result of observations while performing an audit, review, or compilation of financial statements or while providing tax services, incuding tax consultations, are not MAS as defined in SSMAS No. 1 [section 11].

.04 MAS consultations may constitute a significant portion of a practitioner's services to a client. Implicit and explicit understanding between the practitioner and the client form the basis for client reliance on the professional advice that is given. An MAS consultation generally is based on the practitioner's existing personal knowledge of the technical matters in question and those aspects of the client's financial, business, and, perhaps, personal affairs to which the inquiry applies. Depending on the inquiry, the practitioner's response may be immediate or may be made after reference to client file information and technical source materials, discussions with colleagues, or consideration of the advantages, disadvantages, and financial consequences of available alternatives.

.05 Examples of MAS consultations include: advice in the form of explicit recommendations, guidance on a suggested course of action or method of inquiry, limited analysis of options or the advantages and disadvantages of alternative actions, and fact finding in the form of limited technical research on a specific matter.

INTERPRETATIONS OF GENERAL STANDARDS

.06 The following paragraphs interpret general standards of the profession (see SSMAS No. 1 [section 11] as they apply to MAS consultations.

Due Professional Care in MAS Consultations

.07 In an MAS consultation, the practitioner should exercise professional care that

- The advice furnished is clearly communicated.
- The advice and the manner in which it is given do not generate a degree of reliance that is inappropriate in light of qualifications that apply to the advice.

Planning and Supervision in MAS Consultations

.08 The nature and extent of planning in an MAS consultation will vary with the complexity of the inquiry and the entity involved and usually will be entirely a mental process that includes the following steps:

- Understanding of the inquiry and nature of service requested by the client.
- Consideration of knowledge of the entity and the subject of the inquiry.
- Determination of steps to be taken to respond to the inquiry.

If staff is used, supervision required will depend upon their qualifications and experience.

Sufficient Relevant Data in MAS Consultations

.09 In an MAS consultation, the practitioner often is furnished with information by a client that is not verified, corroborated, or reviewed by the MAS practitioner. When this is the case, the client should be informed that the advice given is dependent upon the accuracy and completeness of the unverified client information.

.10 The MAS practitioner should consider whether the information provided is relevant to the matter at issue and whether it appears to be sufficient to provide a basis for a definitive response to the client. If the practitioner does not obtain sufficient relevant information for that purpose, the practitioner should consider whether a qualified response can be given or whether a response cannot be given without further study and analysis.

TECHNICAL STANDARDS FOR MAS CONSULTATIONS

.11 **The following technical standards apply to MAS consultations. They are established under rule 204 of the AICPA Rules of Conduct [now rule 202].**

Role of MAS practitioner. In performing an MAS consultation, an MAS practitioner should not assume the role of management or take any positions that might impair the MAS practitioner's objectivity.[12]

Understanding with client. An oral or written understanding should be reached with the client concerning the nature, scope, and limitations of the MAS consultation to be performed.

Client benefit. Since the potential benefits to be derived by the client are a major consideration in MAS consultations, such potential benefits should be viewed objectively and the client should be notified of reservations regarding them. In offering and providing MAS consultations, results should not be explicitly or implicitly guaranteed. When estimates of quantifiable results are presented, they should be clearly identifed as estimates, and the support for such estimates should be disclosed.

Communication of results. Significant information pertinent to the results of an MAS consultation, together with any limitations, qualifications, or reservations needed to assist the client in making its decision, should be communicated to the client orally or in writing.

[12]An Institute member or his employee might at times serve in the role of management for a client. The Statements on Standards for MAS do not apply to situations in which the member or his employee serve in that role, but, under rule 101 of the AICPA Rules of Conduct [ET section 101.01] and Statement on Standards for Accounting and Review Services No. 1 [AR section 100], independence might be impaired for the purpose of an audit, review, or compilation of financial statements.

Role of Practitioner in MAS Consultations

.12 In the conduct of an MAs consultation, the MAS practitioner often functions as a general business adviser presenting recommendations to a client faced with decisions to make. The circumstances under which the service is provided require the MAS practitioner to recognize and seek to minimize the possibiity that the client might erroneously conclude that the practitioner has

- Assumed responsibility for making the required decisions.
- Guaranteed, through his recommendations, the implicit or explicit benefits the client seeks.
- Predicated his advice on full consideration of all relevant information.

Client Understanding and Communication of Results in MAS Consultations

.13 In MAS consultations, the client inquiry, understanding between parties, and practitioner response often occur in the same conversation. In such an environment, the practitioner, the client, or both may presume that the other has a knowledge and understanding of pertinent matters that actually were not communicated to the other party. The MAS practitioner should recognize this possibility for misunderstanding and take reasonable steps to prevent it by giving attention to matters such as

- The specific or general nature of advice sought.
- The financial and operational significance of the advice given.
- The complexity of the inquiry, the advice, or the conditions or qualifications that might attach to the practitioner's response.

.14 The nature and form of communication with a client in an MAS consultation is a matter of professional judgment. In many cases, especially in connection with the practitioner's general advisory role, circumstances will dictate that the understanding with the client and practitioner response be oral; in some cases the combination of circumstances in an MAS consultation might justify written communication to the client.

EFFECTIVE DATE

.15 This statement is effective for MAS consultations occurring after May 1, 1983.

Appendix 3

Statements on Responsibilities in Tax Practice[1]

Statements on Responsibilities in Tax Practice are published for the guidance of members of the Institute and do not constitute enforceable standards. The statements have been approved by at least two-thirds of the members of the Responsibilities in Tax Practice Subcommittee and the Federal Taxation Executive Committee.

Statements containing recommended standards of responsibilities that are more restrictive than those established by the Internal Revenue Code, the Treasury Department, or the Institute's Code of Professional Conduct depend for their authority on the general acceptability of the opinions expressed. These statements are not intended to be retroactive.

TX Section 102

Introduction

Issue date, unless
otherwise indicated:
August, 1988

THE PROGRAM

0.1 The program contemplates publication and dissemination of a numbered series of Statements on Responsibilities in Tax Practice by the Institute's Federal Taxation Executive Committee.

THE SIGNIFICANCE OF THE STATEMENTS

.02 The series of statements constitutes a body of advisory opinion on what are appropriate standards of tax practice, outlining the extent of a CPA's responsibility to clients, the public, the government, and the profession. Each statement covers a particular aspect of tax practice. The statements take into account applicable legal requirements of tax practice as well as the Federal Taxation Executive Committee's opinions as to appropriate standards of responsibilities in tax practice.

[1] *AICPA Professional Standards*, vol. 2, TX Sections 102, 112, 122, 132, 142, 152, 162, 172, and 182. Copyright © 1989 by the American Institute of Certified Public Accountants, Inc.

THE OBJECTIVES

.03 The principal objectives of the program are—

a. To recommend appropriate standards of responsibilities in tax practice and to promote their uniform application by CPAs.
b. To encourage the development of increased understanding of the responsibilities of the CPA by the Treasury Department and Internal Revenue Service and to urge their officials to promote the application of commensurate standards of responsibilities by their personnel.
c. To foster increased public understanding of, compliance with, and confidence in our tax system through awareness of the recommended standards of responsibilities of CPAs in tax practice.

THE PROGRAM IN PERSPECTIVE

.04 There are numerous guides to help determine practice responsibilities. The CPA is required to follow the statutes, regulations, and rules governing practice before the Internal Revenue Service (for example, Treasury Department Circular 230). The Institute's Code of Professional Conduct requires the observance of high moral and ethical standards. These statements are published to clarify the CPA's dual responsibilities to the tax system as well as to clients.

.05 Although the CPA has no separate enforceable statement of standards of conduct relating solely to tax practice, the Institute's Code of Professional Conduct requires attitudes and habits of truthfulness and integrity in all of the CPA's practice, including tax practice. Rule 102 of the Code of Professional Conduct [ET section 201.01] states:

> In the performance of any professional service, a member shall maintain objectivity and integrity, shall be free of conflicts of interest, and shall not knowingly misrepresent facts or subordinate his or her judgment to others.

.06 The statements are not intended to establish a code of conduct in tax practice that is separate and apart from the general ethical precepts of the Institute's Code of Professional Conduct. That Code imposes upon individual members obligations to maintain high standards of technical competence and integrity in dealing with clients and the public in all phases of the professional activities of members, including tax practice.

.07 In this environment, the Federal Taxation Executive Committee concludes that while the Code of Professional Conduct is a major factor in molding the CPA's professional behavior, it is in the public interest and in the self-interest of the CPA to develop separate statements of recommended standards of responsibilities of CPAs in tax practice for the guidance of taxpayers and CPAs alike.

THE SCOPE AND PURPOSE OF THE STATEMENTS

.08 The statements generally are confined to discussions of the considerations relating to *federal income tax* practice, including the preparation of tax returns, tax planning, and representation before the Internal Revenue Service. The Federal Taxation Executive Committee will consider development of statements of responsibilities in other areas of tax practice in the future as part of its ongoing program to review, revise, and add statements as necessary or appropriate.

.09 The primary purpose of the program is educational. The statements do not have the force of authority, in contrast, for example, to the regulations contained in Treasury Department Circular 230, the Internal Revenue Code or its regulations, or the AICPA Code of Professional Conduct. Statements containing recommended standards of responsibilities that are more restrictive than those established by the Internal Revenue Code, the Treasury Department, or the AICPA Code of Professional Conduct are advisory opinions and CPAs should use them as guides.

AUTHORITY OF THE FEDERAL TAXATION EXECUTIVE COMMITTEE

.10 By resolution of the Institute's Council, the Federal Taxation Executive Committee is authorized to express opinions on matters of broad policy related to taxation including the issuance of Statements on Responsibilities in Tax Practice.

THE PROCEDURES

.11 The statements present the opinion of at least two-thirds of the members of the Responsibilities in Tax Practice Subcommittee and two-thirds of the Federal Taxation Executive Committee.

.12 Drafts of a proposed statement are given appropriate exposure before the Federal Taxation Executive Committee issues a statement.

.13 Details of the procedural aspects of issuing the statements can be found in the AICPA *Tax Division Administrative Manual.*

TX Section 112

Tax Return Positions

Issue date, unless otherwise indicated: August, 1988

INTRODUCTION

.01 This statement sets forth the standards a CPA should follow in recommending tax return positions and in preparing or signing tax returns including claims for refunds. For this purpose, a "tax return position" is (1) a position reflected on the tax return as to which the client has been specifically advised by the CPA or (2) a position as to which the CPA has knowledge of all material facts and, on the basis of those facts, has concluded that the position is appropriate.

STATEMENT

.02 With respect to the tax return positions, a CPA should comply with the following standards:

a. A CPA should not recommend to a client that a position be taken with respect to the tax treatment of any item on a return unless the CPA has a good faith belief that the position has a realistic possibility of being sustained administratively or judicially on its merits if challenged.
b. A CPA should not prepare or sign a return as an income tax return preparer if the CPA knows that the return takes a position that the CPA could not recommend under the standard expressed in paragraph .02*a*.
c. Notwithstanding paragraphs .02*a* and .02*b*, a CPA may recommend a position that the CPA concludes is not frivolous so long as the position is adequately disclosed on the return or claim for refund.
d. In recommending certain tax return positions and in signing a return on which a tax return position is taken, a CPA should, where relevant, advise the client as to the potential penalty consequences of the recommended tax return position and the opportunity, if any, to avoid such penalties through disclosure.

.03 The CPA should not recommend a tax return position that—

a. Exploits the Internal Revenue audit selection process, or
b. Serves as a mere "arguing" position advanced solely to obtain leverage

in the bargaining process of settlement negotiation with the Internal Revenue Service.

.04 A CPA has both the right and responsibility to be an advocate for the client with respect to any positions satisfying the aforementioned standards.

EXPLANATION

.05 Our self-assessment tax system can only function effectively if taxpayers report their income on a tax return that is true, correct, and complete. A tax return is primarily a taxpayer's representation of facts, and the taxpayer has the final responsibility for positions taken on the return.

.06 CPAs have a duty to the tax system as well as to their clients. However, it is well-established that the taxpayer has no obligation to pay more taxes than are legally owed, and the CPA has a duty to the client to assist in achieving that result. The aforementioned standards will guide the CPA in meeting responsibilities to the tax system and to clients.

.07 The standards suggested herein require that a CPA in good faith believe that the position is warranted in existing law or can be supported by a good faith argument for an extension, modification, or reversal of existing law. For example, the CPA may reach such a conclusion on the basis of well-reasoned articles, treatises, IRS General Counsel Memoranda, a General Explanation of a Revenue Act prepared by the staff of the Joint Committee on Taxation, and Internal Revenue Service written determinations (for example, private letter rulings), whether or not such sources are treated as "authority" under section 6661. A position would meet these standards even though, for example, it is later abandoned because of practical or procedural aspects of an Internal Revenue Service administrative hearing or in the litigation process.

.08 Where the CPA has a good faith belief that more than one position meets the standards suggested herein, the CPA's advice concerning alternative acceptable positions may include a discussion of the likelihood that each such position might or might not cause the client's tax return to be examined and whether the position would be challenged in an examination.

.09 In some cases, a CPA may conclude that a position is not warranted under the standard set forth in the preceding paragraph, .02*a*. A client may, however, still wish to take such a tax return position. Under such circumstances, the client should have the opportunity to make such an assertion, and the CPA should be able to prepare and sign the return provided the position is adequately disclosed on the return or claim for refund and the position is not frivolous. A "frivolous" position is one which is knowingly advanced in bad faith and is patently improper.

.10 The CPA's determination of whether information is adequately disclosed by the client is based on the facts and circumstances of the particular case. No detailed rules have been formulated, for purposes of this statement, to prescribe the manner in which information should be disclosed.

.11 Where the particular facts and circumstances lead the CPA to believe that a taxpayer penalty might be asserted, the CPA should so advise the client and should discuss with the client issues related to disclosure on the tax return. Although disclosure is not required if the position meets the standard in paragraph .02*a*, the CPA may nevertheless recommend that a client disclose a postion. Disclosure should be considered when the CPA believes it would mitigate the likelihood of claims of taxpayer penalties under the Internal Revenue Code or would avoid the possible application of the six-year statutory period for assessment under section 6501(e). Although the CPA should advise the client with respect to disclosure, it is the client's responsibility to decide whether and how to disclose.

TX Section 122

Answers to Questions on Returns

Issue date, unless
otherwise indicated:
August, 1988

INTRODUCTION

.01 This statement considers whether a CPA may sign the preparer's declaration on a tax return where one or more questions on the return have not been answered. The term "questions" includes requests for information on the return, in the instructions, or in the regulations, whether or not stated in the form of a question.

STATEMENT

.02 A CPA should make a reasonable effort to obtain from the client, and provide, appropriate answers to all questions on a tax return before signing as preparer.

EXPLANATION

.03 It is recognized that the questions on tax returns are not of uniform importance, and often they are not applicable to the particular taxpayer. Nevertheless, aside from administrative convenience to the Internal Revenue Service, there are at least two considerations which dictate that a CPA should be satisfied that a reasonable effort has been made to provide appropriate answers to the questions on the return which are applicable to the taxpayer:

a. A question may be of importance in determining taxable income or loss, or the tax liability shown on the return, in which circumstance the omission tends to detract from the quality of the return.

b. The CPA must sign the preparer's declaration stating that the return is true, correct, and complete.

.04 While an effort should be made to provide an answer to each question on the return that is applicable to the taxpayer, reasonable grounds may exist for omitting an answer. For example, reasonable grounds may include the following:

a. The information is not readily available and the answer is not significant in terms of taxable income or loss, or the tax liability shown on the return.

b. Genuine uncertainty exists regarding the meaning of the question in relation to the particular return.

c. The answer to the question is voluminous; in such cases, assurance should be given on the return that the data will be supplied upon examination.

.05 The fact that an answer to a question might prove disadvantageous to the client does not justify omitting an answer.

.06 Where reasonable grounds exist for omission of an answer to an applicable question, a CPA is not required to provide on the return an explanation of the reason for the omission. In this connection, the CPA should consider whether the omission of an answer to a question may cause the return to be deemed incomplete.

TX Section 132

Certain Procedural Aspects of Preparing Returns

Issue date, unless
otherwise indicated:
August, 1988

INTRODUCTION

.01 This statement considers the responsibility of the CPA to examine or verify certain supporting data or to consider information related to another client when preparing a client's tax return.

STATEMENT

.02 In preparing or signing a return, the CPA may in good faith rely without verification upon information furnished by the client or by third parties. However, the CPA should not ignore the implications of information furnished and should make reasonable inquiries if the information furnished appears to be incorrect, incomplete, or inconsistent either on its face or on the basis of other facts known to the CPA. In this connection, the CPA should refer to the client's returns for prior years whenever feasible.

.03 Where the Internal Revenue Code or income tax regulations impose a condition with respect to deductibility or other tax treatment of an item (such as taxpayer maintenance of books and records or substantiating documentation to support the reported deduction or tax treatment), the CPA should make appropriate inquiries to determine to his or her satisfaction whether such condition has been met.

.04 The individual CPA who is required to sign the return should consider information actually known to that CPA from the tax return of another client when preparing a tax return if the information is relevant to that tax return, its consideration is necessary to properly prepare that tax return, and use of such information does not violate any law or rule relating to confidentiality.

EXPLANATION

.05 The preparer's declaration on the income tax return states that the information contained therein is true, correct, and complete to the best of the preparer's knowledge and belief "based on all information of which the preparer has any knowledge." This reference should be understood to relate to information furnished by the client or by third parties to the CPA in connection with the preparation of the return.

.06 The preparer's declaration does not require the CPA to examine or verify supporting data. However, a distinction should be made between (1) the need to either determine by inquiry that a specifically required condition (such as maintaining books and records or substantiating documentation) has been satisfied, or to obtain information when the material furnished appears to be incorrect or incomplete, and (2) the need for the CPA to examine underlying information. In fulfilling his or her obligation to exercise due diligence in preparing a return, the CPA ordinarily may rely on informaiton furnished by the client unless it appears to be incorrect, incomplete, or inconsistent. Although the CPA has certain responsibilities in exercising due diligence in preparing a return, the client has ultimate responsibility for the contents of the return. Thus, where the client presents unsupported data in the form of lists of tax information, such as dividends and interest received, charitable contributions, and medical expenses, such information may be used in the preparation of a tax return without verification unless it appears to be incorrect, incomplete, or inconsistent either on its face or on the basis of other facts known to the CPA.

.07 Even though there is no requirement to examine underlying documentation, the CPA should encourage the client to provide supporting data where appropriate. For example, the CPA should encourage the client to submit underlying documents for use in tax return preparation to permit full consideration of income and deductions arising from security transactions and from pass-through entities such as estates, trusts, partnerships, and S corporations. This should reduce the possibility of misunderstanding, inadvertent errors, and administrative problems in the examination of returns by the Internal Revenue Service.

.08 The source of information provided to the CPA by a client for use in preparing the return is often a pass-through entity, such as a limited partnership, in which the client has an interest but is not involved in management. In some instances, it may be appropriate for the CPA to advise the client to ascertain the nature and amount of possible exposure to tax deficiencies, interest, and penalties, by contact with management of the pass-through entity. However, the CPA need not require the client to do so and may accept the information provided by the pass-through entity without further inquiry, unless there is reason to believe it is incorrect, incomplete, or inconsistent, either on its face or on the basis of other facts known to the CPA.

.09 The CPA should make use of the client's prior years' returns in preparing the current return whenever feasible. Reference to prior returns and discussion of prior year tax determinations with the client should provide information as to the client's general tax status, avoid the omission or duplication of items, and afford a basis for the treatment of similar or related transactions. As with the examination of information supplied for the current year's return, the extent of comparison of the details of income and deduction between years depends upon the particular circumstances.

TX Section 142

Use of Estimates

Issue date, unless otherwise indicated:
August, 1988

INTRODUCTION

.01 This statement considers the CPA's responsibility in connection with the CPA's use of the taxpayer's estimates in the preparation of a tax return. The CPA may advise on estimates used in the preparation of a tax return, but responsibility for estimated data is that of the client, who should provide the estimated data. Appraisals or valuations are not considered estimates for purposes of this statement.

STATEMENT

.02 A CPA may prepare tax returns involving the use of the taxpayer's estimates if it is impracticable to obtain exact data, and the estimated amounts are reasonable under the facts and circumstances known to the CPA. When the taxpayer's estimates are used, they should be presented in such a manner as to avoid the implications of greater accuracy than exists.

EXPLANATION

.03 Accounting requires the exercise of judgment and, in many instances, the use of approximations based on judgment. The application of such accounting judgments, as long as not in conflict with methods set forth in the Internal Revenue Code, is acceptable and expected. These judgments are not estimates within the purview of this statement. For example, the income tax regulations provide that if all other conditions for accrual are met, the exact amount of income or expense need not be known or ascertained at year end if the amount can be determined with reasonable accuracy.

.04 In the case of transactions involving small expenditures, accuracy in recording some data may be difficult to achieve. Therefore, the use of estimates by the taxpayer in determining the amount to be deducted for such items may be appropriate.

.05 In other cases where all of the facts relating to a transaction are not accurately known, either because records are missing or because precise information is not available at the time the return must be filed, estimates of the missing data may be made by the taxpayer.

.06 Estimated amounts should not be presented in a manner which provides a misleading impression as to the degree of factual accuracy.

.07 Although specific disclosure that an estimate is used for an item in the return is not required in most instances, there are unusual circumstances where such disclosure is needed to avoid misleading the Internal Revenue Service regarding the degree of accuracy of the return. Some examples of unusual circumstances include the following:

a. The taxpayer has died or is ill at the time the return must be filed.
b. The taxpayer has not received a K–1 form for a flow-through entity at the time the tax return is to be filed.
c. There is litigation pending (for example, a bankruptcy proceeding) which bears on the return.
d. Fire or computer failure destroyed the relevant records.

TX Section 152

Departure From a Position Previously Concluded in an Administrative Proceeding or Court Decision

Issue date, unless
otherwise indicated:
August, 1988

INTRODUCTION

.01 This statement discusses whether a CPA may recommend a tax return position that departs from the treatment of an item as concluded in an administrative proceeding or a court decision with respect to a prior return of the taxpayer. For this purpose, a "tax return position" is (1) a position reflected on the tax return as to which the client has been specifically advised by the CPA, or (2) a position about which the CPA has knowledge of all material facts and, on the basis of those facts, has concluded that the position is appropriate.

.02 For purposes of this statement, "administrative proceeding" includes an examination by the Internal Revenue Service or an appeals conference relating to a return or a claim for refund.

.03 For purposes of this statement, "court decision" means a decision by any federal court having jurisdiction over tax matters.

STATEMENT

.04 The recommendation of a position to be taken concerning the tax treatment of an item in the preparation or signing of a tax return should be based upon the facts and the law as they are evaluated at the time the return is prepared or signed by the CPA. Unless the taxpayer is bound to a specified treatment in the later year, such as by a formal closing agreement, the treatment of an item as part of concluding an administrative proceeding or as part of a court decision does not restrict the CPA from recommending a different tax treatment in a later year's return. Therefore, if the CPA follows the standards in SRTP (1988 Rev.) No. 1 [section 112], the CPA may recommend a tax return position, prepare, or sign a tax return that departs from the treatment of an item as concluded in an administrative proceeding or a court decision with respect to a prior return of the taxapyer.

EXPLANATION

.05 A CPA usually will recommend a position with respect to the tax treatment of an item that is the same as was consented to by the taxpayer for a similar item as a result of an administrative proceeding or that was subject to a court decision concerning a prior year's return of the taxpayer. The question is whether the CPA is required to do so. Considerations include the following:

a. The Internal Revenue Service tends to act consistently with the manner in which an item was disposed of in a prior administrative proceeding, but is not bound to do so. Similarly, a taxpayer is not bound to follow the tax treatment of an item as consented to in an earlier administrative proceeding.

b. An unfavorable court decision does not prevent a taxpayer from taking a position contrary to the earlier court decision in a subsequent year.

c. The consent in an earlier administrative proceeding and the existence of an unfavorable court decision are factors that the CPA should consider in evaluating whether the standards in SRTP (1988 Rev.) No. 1 are met.

d. The taxpayer's consent to the treatment in the administrative proceeding or the court's decision may have been caused by a lack of documentaiton, whereas supporting data for the later year is adequate.

e. The taxpayer may have yielded in the administrative proceeding for settlement purposes or not appealed the court decision even though the position met the standards in SRTP (1988 Rev.) No. 1.

f. Court decisions, rulings, or other authorities that are more favorable to the taxpayer's current position may have developed since the prior administrative proceeding was concluded or the prior court decision was rendered.

TX Section 162

Knowledge of Error: Return Preparation

Issue date, unless
otherwise indicated:
August, 1988

INTRODUCTION

.01 This statement considers the responsibility of a CPA who becomes aware of an error in a client's previously filed tax return or of the client's failure to file a required tax return. As used herein, the term "error" includes an omission. However, for purposes of this statement, the term "error" does not include (1) a position taken by the client which, at the time the return was filed, satisfied the standards in SRTP (1988 Rev.) No. 1 [section 112]; (2) an item that has no more than an insignificant effect on the client's tax liability; or (3) an erroneous method of accounting continued in a prior year under circumstances believed to require the permission of the Internal Revenue Service to effect a change in the manner of reporting the item involved.[2]

.02 This statement applies whether or not the CPA prepared or signed the return that contains the error.

STATEMENT

.03 The CPA should inform the client promptly upon becoming aware of an error in a previously filed return or upon becoming aware of a client's failure

[2]Future statements will address (1) the appropriate standards to be considered by a CPA when a client's tax return for a prior year is affected by a law, regulation, or court decision having retroactive effect and (2) whether the standards in SRTP (1988 Rev.) No. 1 [section 112] are satisfied when a client continues an erroneous method of accounting in the current year's return.

to file a required return. The CPA should recommend the measures to be taken. Such recommendation may be given orally. The CPA is not obligated to inform the Internal Revenue Service, and the CPA may not do so without the client's permission, except where required by law.

.04 If the CPA is requested to prepare the current year's return and the client has not taken appropriate action to correct an error in a prior year's return, the CPA should consider whether to withdraw from preparing the return and whether to continue a professional relationship with the client. If the CPA does prepare such current year's return, the CPA should take reasonable steps to ensure that the error is not repeated.

EXPLANATION

.05 While performing services for a client, a CPA may become aware of an error in a previously filed return or may become aware that the client failed to file a required return. The CPA should advise the client of the error (as required by Treasury Department Circular 230) and the measures to be taken. It is the client's responsibility to decide whether to correct the error. In appropriate cases, particularly where it appears that the Internal Revenue Service might assert the charge of fraud or other criminal misconduct, the client should be advised to consult legal counsel before taking any action. In the event that the client does not correct an error, the CPA should consider whether to continue a professional relationship with the client.[3]

.06 If the CPA decides to continue a professional relationship with the client and is requested to prepare a tax return for a year subsequent to that in which the error occurrred, then the CPA should take reasonable steps to ensure that the error is not repeated.

.07 Whether an error has no more than an insignificant effect on the client's tax liability is left to the judgment of the individual CPA based on all the facts and circumstances known to the CPA.

.08 Where the CPA becomes aware of the error during an engagement which does not involve tax return preparation, the responsibility of the CPA is to advise the client of the existence of the error and to recommend that the error be discussed with the client's tax return preparer.

[3]The CPA shluld consider consulting his or her own legal counsel before deciding upon recommendations to the client and whether to continue a professional relationship with the client. The potential for violating AICPA Rule 301 [ET section 301.01] (relating to the CPA's confidential client relationship), the Internal Revenue Code and income tax regulations, or state laws on privileged communications and other considerations may create a conflict between the CPA's interests and those of the client.

TX Section 172

Knowledge of Error: Administrative Proceedings

Issue date, unless
otherwise indicated:
August, 1988

INTRODUCTION

.01 This statement considers the responsibility of a CPA who becomes aware of an error in a return that is the subject of an administrative proceeding, such as an examination by the IRS or an appeals conference relating to a return or a claim for refund. As used herein, the term "error" includes an omission. However, the term "error" does not include (1) the position taken by the client which, at the time the return was filed, satisfied the standards in SRTP (1988 Rev.) No. 1 [Section 112], (2) an item that has no more than an insignificant effect on the client's tax liability, or (3) an erroneous method of accounting continued in the year of the administrative proceeding under circumstances believed to require the permission of the Internal Revenue Service to effect a change in the manner of reporting the item involved.[4]

.02 This statement applies whether or not the CPA prepared or signed the return that contains the error; it does not apply where a CPA has been engaged by legal counsel to provide assistance in a matter relating to the counsel's client.

STATEMENT

.03 When the CPA is representing a client in an administrative proceeding with respect to a return which contains an error of which the CPA is aware, the CPA should inform the client promptly upon becoming aware of the error. The CPA should recommend the measures to be taken. Such recommendation may be given orally. The CPA is neither obligated to inform the Internal Revenue Service nor is he or she permitted to do so without the client's permission, except where required by law.

.04 The CPA should request the client's agreement to disclose the error to the Internal Revenue Service. Lacking such agreement, the CPA should consider whether to withdraw from representing the client in the administrative proceeding and whether to continue a professional relationship with the client.

[4]Future statements will address the appropriate standards to be considered by a CPA when a client's tax return which is the subject of an administrative proceeding (1) is affected by a law, regulation, or court decision having retroactive effect, or (2) includes an erroneous accounting method.

EXPLANATION

.05 When the CPA is engaged to represent the client before the Internal Revenue Service in an administrative proceeding with respect to a return containing an error of which the CPA is aware, the CPA should advise the client to disclose the error to the Internal Revenue Service. It is the client's responsibility to decide whether to disclose the error. In appropriate cases, particularly where it appears that the Internal Revenue Service might assert the charge of fraud or other criminal misconduct, the client should be advised to consult legal counsel before taking any action. If the client refuses to disclose or permit disclosure of an error, the CPA should consider whether to withdraw from representing the client in the administrative proceeding and whether to continue a professional relationship with the client.[5]

.06 Once disclosure is agreed upon, it should not be delayed to such a degree that the client or CPA might be considered to have failed to act in good faith or to have, in effect, provided misleading information. In any event, disclosure should be made before the conclusion of the administrative proceeding.

.07 Whether an error has an insignificant effect on the client's tax liability should be left to the judgment of the individual CPA based on all the facts and circumstances known to the CPA.

TX Section 182

Form and Content of Advice to Clients

Issue date, unless otherwise indicated: August, 1988

INTRODUCTION

.01 This statement discusses certain aspects of providing tax advice to a client and considers the circumstances in which the CPA has a responsibility to communicate with the client when subsequent developments affect advice previously provided. The statement does not, however, cover the CPA's responsibilities when it is expected that the advice rendered is likely to be relied upon by parties other than the CPA's client.[6]

[5]The CPA should consider consulting his or her own legal counsel before deciding upon recommendations to the client and whether to continue a professional relationship with the client. The potential for violating AICPA Rule 301 [ET section 301.01] (relating to the CPA's confidential client relationship), the Internal Revenue Code and income tax regulations, or state laws on privileged communications and other considerations may create a conflict between the CPA's interests and those of the client.

[6]The CPA's responsibilities when providing advice that will be relied upon by third parties will be addressed in a future statement.

STATEMENT

.02 In providing tax advice to a client, the CPA should use judgment to ensure that the advice given reflects professional competence and appropriately serves the client's needs. The CPA is not required to follow a standard format or guidelines in communicating written or oral advice to a client.

.03 In advising or consulting with a client on tax matters, the CPA should assume that the advice will affect the manner in which the matters or transactions considered ultimately will be reported on the client's tax returns. Thus, for all tax advice the CPA gives to a client, the CPA should follow the standards in SRTP (1988 Rev.) No. 1 [section 112] relating to tax return positions.

.04 The CPA may choose to communicate with a client when subsequent developments affect advice previously provided with respect to significant matters. However, the CPA cannot be expected to have assumed responsibility for initiating such communication except while assisting a client in implementing procedures or plans associated with the advice provided or when the CPA undertakes this obligation by specific agreement with the client.

EXPLANATION

.05 Tax advice is recognized as a valuable service provided by CPAs. The form of advice may be oral or written and the subject matter may range from routine to complex. Because the range of advice is so extensive and because advice should meet specific needs of a client, neither a standard format nor guidelines for communicating advice to the client can be established to cover all situations.

.06 Although oral advice may serve a client's needs appropriately in routine matters or in well-defined areas, written communications are recommended in important, unusual, or complicated transactions. In the judgment of the CPA, oral advice may be followed by a written confirmation to the client.

.07 In deciding on the form of advice provided to a client, the CPA should exercise professional judgment and should consider such factors as the following:

a. The importance of the transaction and amounts involved.
b. The specific or general nature of the client's inquiry.
c. The time available for development and submission of the advice.
d. The technical complications presented.
e. The existence of authorities and precedents.
f. The tax sophistication of the client and the client's staff.
g. The need to seek legal advice.

.08 The CPA may assist a client in implementing procedures or plans associated with the advice offered. During this active participation, the CPA continues to advise and should review and revise such advice as warranted by new developments and factors affecting the transaction.

.09 Sometimes the CPA is requested to provide tax advice but does not assist in implementing the plans adopted. While developments such as legislative or administrative changes or further judicial interpretations may affect the advice previously provided, the CPA cannot be expected to communicate later developments that affect such advice unless the CPA undertakes this obligation by specific agreement with the client. Thus, the communication of significant developments affecting previous advice should be considered an additional service rather than a implied obligation in the normal CPA-client relationship.

.10 The client should be informed that advice reflects professional judgment based on an existing situation and that subsequent developments could affect previous professional advice. CPAs should use precautionary language to the effect that their advice is based on facts as stated and authorities that are subject to change.

Appendix 4

Standards of Ethical Conduct for Management Accountants[1]

Management accountants have an obligation to the organizations they serve, their profession, the public, and themselves to maintain the highest standards of ethical conduct. In recognition of this obligation, the National Association of Accountants has promulgated the following standards of ethical conduct for management accountants. Adherence to these standards is integral to achieving the *Objectives of Management Accounting.*[2] Management accountants shall not commit acts contrary to these standards nor shall they condone the commission of such acts by others within their organizations.

COMPETENCE

Management accountants have a responsibility to:

- Maintain an appropriate level of professional competence by ongoing development of their knowledge and skills.
- Perform their professional duties in accordance with relevant laws, regulations, and technical standards.
- Prepare complete and clear reports and recommendations after appropriate analyses of relevant and reliable information.

CONFIDENTIALITY

Management accountants have a responsibility to:

- Refrain from disclosing confidential information acquired in the course of their work except when authorized, unless legally obligated to do so.
- Inform subordinates as appropriate regarding the confidentiality of information acquired in the course of their work and monitor their activities to assure the maintenance of that confidentiality.
- Refrain from using or appearing to use confidential information acquired in the course of their work for unethical or illegal advantage either personally or thorugh third parties.

[2]National Association of Accountants, *Statements on Management Accounting: Objectives of Management Accounting*, Statement No. 1B, New York, N.Y., June 17, 1982.

INTEGRITY

Management accountants have a responsibility to:

- Avoid actual or apparent conflicts of interest and advise all appropriate parties of any potential conflict.
- Refrain from engaging in any activity that would prejudice their ability to carry out their duties ethically.
- Refuse any gift, favor, or hospitality that would influence or would appear to influence their actions.
- Refrain from either actively or passively subverting the attainment of the organization's legitimate and ethical objectives.
- Recognize and communicate professional limitations or other constraints that would preclude responsible judgment or successful performance of an activity.
- Communicate unfavorable as well as favorable information and professional judgments or opinions.
- Refrain from engaging in or supporting any activity that would discredit the profession.

OBJECTIVITY

Management accountants have a responsibility to:

- Communicate information fairly and objectively.
- Disclose fully all relevant information that could reasonably be expected to influence an intended user's understanding of the reports, comments, and recommendations presented.

RESOLUTION OF ETHICAL CONFLICT

In applying the standards of ethical conduct, management accountants may encounter problems in identifying unethical behavior or in resolving an ethical conflict. When faced with significant ethical issues, management accountants should follow the established policies of the organization bearing on the resolution of such conflict. If these policies do not resolve the ethical conflict, management accountants should consider the following courses of action:

- Discuss such problems with the immediate superior except when it appears that the superior is involved, in which case the problem should be presented initially to the next higher managerial level. If satisfactory resolution cannot be achieved when the problem is initially presented, submit the issues to the next higher managerial level.

If the immediate superior is the chief executive officer, or equivalent, the acceptable reviewing authority may be a group such as the audit committee, executive committee, board of directors, board of trustees, or owners. Contact with levels above the immediate superior should be initiated only with the superior's knowledge, assuming the superior is not involved.

- Clarify relevant concepts by confidential discussion with an objective advisor to obtain an understanding of possible courses of action.
- If the ethical conflict still exists after exhausting all levels of internal review, the management accountant may have no other recourse on significant matters than to resign from the organization and to submit an informative memorandum to an appropriate representative of the organization.

Except where legally prescribed, communication of such problems to authorities or individuals not employed or engaged by the organization is not considered appropriate.

Appendix 5

Code of Ethics of Financial Executives Institute[1]

To be eligible for active membership in Financial Executives Institute, applicants must possess those personal attributes such as character, personal integrity and business ability that will be an asset to the Institute. They must also meet pre-established criteria indicating a high degree of participation in the formulation of policies for the operation of the enterprises they represent and in the administration of the financial functions. Members of the Institute are expected to follow this Code of Ethics.

As a member of Financial Executives Institute, I will:

- Conduct my business and personal affairs at all times with honesty and integrity.
- Provide complete, appropriate and relevant information in an objective manner when reporting to management, stockholders, employees, government agencies, other institutions and the public.
- Comply with rules and regulations of federal, state, provincial, and local governments, and other appropriate private and public regulatory agencies.
- Discharge duties and responsibilities to my employer to the best of my ability, including complete communication on all matters within my jurisdiction.
- Maintain the confidentiality of information acquired in the course of my work except when authorized or otherwise legally obligated to disclose. Confidential information acquired in the course of my work will not be used for my personal advantage.
- Maintain an appropriate level of professional competence through continuing development of my knowledge and skills.
- Refrain from committing acts discreditable to myself, my employer, FEI or fellow members of the Institute.

Appendix 6

The Institute of Internal Auditors Code of Ethics[1]

PURPOSE

A distinguishing mark of a profession is acceptance by its members of responsibility to the interests of those it serves. Members of The Institute of Internal Auditors (Members) and Certified Internal Auditors (CIAs) must maintain high standards of conduct in order to effectively discharge this responsibility. The Institute of Internal Auditors (Institute) adopts this *Code of Ethics* for Members and CIAs.

APPLICABILITY

This *Code of Ethics* is applicable to all Members and CIAs. Membership in The Institute and acceptance of the "Certified Internal Auditor" designation are voluntary actions. By acceptance, Members and CIAs assume an obligation of self-discipline above and beyond the requirements of laws and regulations.

The standards of conduct set forth in this *Code of Ethics* provide basic principles in the praactice of internal auditing. Members and CIAs should realize that their individual judgment is required in the application of these principles.

CIAs shall use the "Certified Internal Auditor" designation with discretion and in a dignified manner, fully aware of what the designation denotes. The designation shall also be used in a manner consistent with all statutory requirements.

Members who are judged by the Board of Directors of The Institute to be in violation of the standards of conduct of the *Code of Ethics* shall be subject to forfeiture of their membership in The Institute. CIAs who are similarly judged also shall be subject to forfeiture of the "Certified Internal Auditor" designation.

STANDARDS OF CONDUCT

I. Members and CIAs shall exercise honesty, objectivity, and diligence in the performance of their duties and responsibilities.

II. Members and CIAs shall exercise loyalty in all matters pertaining to the affairs of their organization or to whomever they may be rendering a service. However, Members and CIAs shall not knowingly be a party to any illegal or improper activity.

III. Members and CIAs shall not knowingly engage in acts or activities which are discreditable to the profession of internal auditing or to their organization.

IV. Members and CIAs shall refrain from entering into any activity which may be in conflict with the interest of their organization or which would prejudice their ability to carry out objectively their duties and responsibilities.

V. Members and CIAs shall not accept anything of value from an employee, client, customer, supplier, or business associate of their organization which would impair or be presumed to impair their professional judgment.

VI. Members and CIAs shall undertake only those services which they can reasonably expect to complete with professional competence.

VII. Members and CIAs shall adopt suitable means to comply with the *Standards for the Professional Practice of Internal Auditing.*

VIII. Members and CIAs shall be prudent in the use of information acquired in the course of their duties. They shall not use confidential information for any personal gain nor in any manner which would be contrary to law or detrimental to the welfare of their organization.

IX. Members and CIAs, when reporting on the results of their work, shall reveal all material facts known to them which, if not revealed, could either distort reports of operations under review or conceal unlawful practices.

X. Members and CIAs shall continually strive for improvement in their proficiency, and in the effectiveness and quality of their service.

XI. Members and CIAs, in the practice of their profession, shall be ever mindful of their obligation to maintain the high standards of competence, morality and dignity promulgated by The Institute. Members shall abide by the *Bylaws* and uphold the objectives of The Institute.

Appendix 7

Statement of Responsibilities of Internal Auditing[1]

The purpose of this statement is to provide in summary form a general understanding of the role and responsibilities of internal auditing. For more specific guidance, readers should refer to the *Standards for the Professional Practice of Internal Auditing.*

NATURE

Internal auditing is an independent appraisal activity established within an organization as a service to the organization. It is a control which functions by examining and evaluating the adequacy and effectiveness of other controls.

OBJECTIVE AND SCOPE

The objective of internal auditing is to assist members of the organization in the effective discharge of their responsibilities. To this end, internal auditing furnishes them with analysis, appraisals, recommendations, counsel, and information concerning the activities reviewed. The audit objective includes promoting effective control at reasonable cost.

The scope of internal accounting encompasses the examination and evaluation of the adequacy and effectiveness of the organization's system of internal control and the quality of performance in carrying out assigned responsibilities. The scope of internal auditing includes:

- Reviewing the reliability and integrity of financial and operating information and the means to identify, measure, classify, and report such information.
- Reviewing the systems established to ensure compliance with those policies, plans, procedures, laws, and regulations which could have a significant impact on operations and reports, and determining whether the organization is in compliance.
- Reviewing the means of safeguarding assets and, as appropriate, verifying the existence of such assets.
- Appraising the economy and efficiency with which resources are employed.
- Reviewing operations or programs to ascertain whether results are consistent with established objectives and goals and whether the operations or programs are being carried out as planned.

RESPONSIBILITY AND AUTHORITY

Internal auditing functions under the policies established by management and the board. The purpose, authority and responsibility of the internal auditing department should be defined in a formal written document (charter), approved by management, and accepted by the board. The charter should make clear the purposes of the internal auditing department, specify the unrestricted scope of its work, and declare that auditors are to have no authority or responsibility for the activities they audit.

The responsibility of internal auditing is to serve the orgnaization in a manner that is consistent with the *Standards for the Professional Practice of Internal Auditing* and with professional standards of conduct such as the *Code of Ethics* of The Institute of Internal Auditors, Inc. This responsibility includes coordinating internal audit activities with others so as to best achieve the audit objectives and the objectives of the organization.

INDEPENDENCE

Internal auditors should be independent of the activities they audit. Internal auditors are independent when they can carry out their work freely and objetively. Independence permits internal auditors to render the impartial and unbiased judgments essential to the proper conduct of audits. It is achieved through organizational status and objectivity.

Organizational status should be sufficient to assure a broad range of audit coverage, and adequate consideration of and effective action on audit findings and recommendations.

Objectivity requires that internal auditors have an independent mental attitude, and an honest belief in their work product. Drafting procedures, designing, installing, and operating systems are not audit functions. Performing such activities is presumed to impair audit objectivity.

Appendix 8

Standards for the Professional Practice of Internal Auditing[1]

100 INDEPENDENCE—*INTERNAL AUDITORS SHOULD BE INDEPENDENT OF THE ACTIVITY THEY AUDIT.*

110 Organizational Status—*The organizational status of the internal auditing department should be sufficient to permit the accomplishment of its audit responsibilities.*

120 Objectivity—*Internal auditors should be objective in performing audits.*

200 PROFESSIONAL PROFICIENCY—*INTERNAL AUDITS SHOULD BE PERFORMED WITH PROFICIENCY AND DUE PROFESSIONAL CARE.*

The Internal Auditing Department

210 Staffing—*The internal auditing department should provide assurance that the technical proficiency and educational background of internal auditors are appropriate for the audits to be performed.*

220 Knowledge, Skills, and Disciplines—*The internal auditing department should possess or should obtain the knowledge, skills, and disciplines needed to carry out its audit responsibilities.*

230 Supervision—*The internal auditing department should provide assurance that internal audits are properly supervised.*

240 Compliance with Standards of Conduct—*Internal auditors should comply with professional standards of conduct.*

250 Knowledge, Skills, and Disciplines—*Internal auditors should possess the knowledge, skills, and disciplines essential to the performance of internal audits.*

260 Human Relations and Communications—*Internal auditors should be skilled in dealing with people and in communicating effectively.*

270 Continuing Education—*Internal auditors should maintain their technical competence through continuing education.*

280 Due Professional Care—*Internal auditors should exercise due professional care in performing internal audits.*

300 SCOPE OF WORK—*THE SCOPE OF THE INTERNAL AUDIT SHOULD ENCOMPASS THE EXAMINATION AND EVALUATION OF THE ADEQUACY AND EFFECTIVENESS OF THE ORGANIZATION'S SYSTEM OF INTERNAL CONTROL AND THE QUALITY OF PERFORMANCE IN CARRYING OUT ASSIGNED RESPONSIBILITIES.*

310 Reliability and Integrity of Information—*Internal auditors should review the reliability and integrity of financial and operating information and the means used to identify, measure, classify, and report such information.*

320 Compliance with Policies, Plans, Procedures, Laws, and Regulations—*Internal auditors should review the systems established to ensure compliance with those policies, plans, procedures, laws, and regulations which could have a signifi-*

cant impact on operations and reports and should determine whether the organization is in compliance.

330 Safeguarding of Assets—*Internal auditors should review the means of safeguarding assets and, as appropriate, verify the existence of such assets.*

340 Economical and Efficient Use of Resources—*Internal auditors should appraise the economy and efficiency with which resources are employed.*

350 Accomplishment of Established Objectives and Goals for Operations or Programs—*Internal auditors should review operations or programs to ascertain whether results are consistent with established objectives and goals and whether the operations or programs are being carried out as planned.*

400 PERFORMANCE OF AUDIT WORK—*AUDIT WORK SHOULD INCLUDE PLANNING THE AUDIT, EXAMINING AND EVALUATING INFORMATION, COMMUNICATING RESULTS, AND FOLLOWING UP.*

410 Planning the Audit—*Internal auditors should plan each audit.*

420 Examining and Evaluating Information—*Internal auditors should collect, analyze, interpret, and document information to support audit results.*

430 Communicating Results—*Internal auditors should report the results of their audit work.*

440 Follow Up—*Internal auditors should follow up to ascertain that appropriate action is taken on reported audit findings.*

500 MANAGEMENT OF THE INTERNAL AUDITING DEPARTMENT—*THE DIRECTOR OF INTERNAL AUDITING SHOULD PROPERLY MANAGE THE INTERNAL AUDITING DEPARTMENT.*

510 Purpose, Authority, and Responsibility—*The director of internal auditing should have a statement of purpose, authority, and responsibility for the internal auditing department.*

520 Planning—*The director of internal auditing should establish plans to carry out the responsibilities of the internal auditing department.*

530 Policies and Procedures—*The director of internal auditing should provide written policies and procedures to guide the audit staff.*

540 Personnel Management and Development—*The director of internal auditing should establish a program for selecting and developing the human resources of the internal auditing department.*

550 External Auditors—*The director of internal auditing should coordinate internal and external audit efforts.*

560 Quality Assurance—*The director of internal auditing should establish and maintain a quality assurance program to evaluate the operations of the internal auditing department.*

Appendix 9

Association of Government Accountants Code of Ethics[1]

Introduction

The Association of Government Accountants is a national professional organization devoted to exellence in financial management at all levels of government. In has 13,000 in 85 chapters located in 39 states, the District of Columbia and several U.S. territories. Individually, members are dedicated financial managers, accountants, auditors, budget analysts or financial planners at the federal, state and municipal levels. Together, the members proudly serve government and its people with vitality and, above all, an unswerving commitment to quality.

The Association of Government Accountants' major program objectives are to:

- Unite professional financial managers in government service to perform more efficiently for their own development and thereby for the benefit of the government and society.
- Encourage and provide an effective means for interchange of work-related and professional ideas.
- Aid in improving financial management and accounting and auditing techniques and concepts.
- Improve financial management education in all levels of government and universities.

Purpose

To foster the highest professional standards and behavior, and to provide exemplary service to the government, this Code of Ethics has been developed to guide members of the Association of Government Accountants and for the information of their employers.

Definitions

When reference is made to a member, it is intended to include all classes of membership. Reference made to employer applies to a government agency as an entity and to a nongovernment organization to the extent the principle is considered applicable.

Explanations

To better define each ethical principle, an explanation is included.

[1]AGA Bylaws, Article I, Section 3.

ETHICAL PRINCIPLES

Personal Behavior

1. A member shall not engage in acts or be associated with activities which are contrary to the public interest or bring discredit to the Association of Government Accountants.
   This principle cautions members to avoid actions which adversely affect the public interest and the professional image of the association.
2. A member shall not engage in private employment or act as an independent practitioner for remuneration except with the employer's consent.
   This principle identified a restriction against private earnings which result from the use of a member's professional qualifications without the employer's expressed approval.
3. A member shall not purposefully transmit or use confidential information obtained in professional work for personal gain or other advantage.
   This principle prohibits the improper use of official position or office for strictly personal purposes, monetary or otherwise.
4. A member shall adhere to all employer-generated Standards of Conduct.
   This principle endorses the commitment of employees to recognize the Standards of Conduct prescribed by their employers.

Professional Competence and Performance

5. A member shall strive to fulfill all work-related responsibilities and supervise the work of subordinates with the highest degree of professional care.
   This principle emphasizes the requirement that a member give special attention to the professional aspects of work and not condone substandard performance at any level.
6. A member shall continually seek to increase professional knowledge and skills and to improve service to employers, associates and fellow members.
   This principle stresses the importance of professional development and skills in contributing to the profession as a whole.
7. A member shall render opinions, observations or conclusions for official purposes only after appropriate professional consideration of the pertinent facts.
   This principle underscores the importance of avoiding unsupported opinions involving professional judgments which would cause inappropriate official actions.
8. A member shall exercise diligence, objectivity and honesty in professional activities and be aware of the responsibility to disclose any and all improprieties that may arise.
   This principle places the responsibility upon a member to exercise moral and independent judgment and to disclose to appropriate authorities those illegal, improper or unethical practices noted in the course of work.

9. A member shall be aware of and strive to apply work-related requirements and standards prescribed by employers.
   This principle recognizes that special professional criteria may be required by employers in certain assignments.

Responsibility to Others

10. In the performance of any assignment, a member shall consider the public interest to be paramount.
    This principle stresses that a member's foremost concern must be the public interest in any work situation involving competing interests.
11. A member shall not engage in any activity or establish any relationship which creates or gives the appearance of a conflict with employer-related responsibilities.
    This principle cautions against becoming involved in situations in which a member's official or personal activities appear to be inconsistent with prescribed employer responsibilities.
12. In speaking engagements or writings for publication, a member shall identify personal opinions which may differ from official, employer-related positions.
    This principle underscores the need to avoid inappropriate interpretations by the public from speeches or articles by members which reflect their personal viewpoints rather than the official positions of their employers.

Appendix 10

Summary of Statement on Government Auditing Standards[1]

I. Introduction

A. Purpose

1. This statement contains standards for audits of government organizations, programs, activities, and functions, and of government funds received by contractors, nonprofit organizations, and other nongovernment organizations.
2. The standards are to be followed by auditors and audit organizations when required by law, regulation, agreement or contract, or policy.

II. Types of Government Audits

A. Purpose

1. This chapter describes the types of audits that government and nongovernment audit organizations conduct, and that government organizations arrange to have conducted. This description is not intended to limit or require the types of audits that may be conducted or arranged.
2. In conducting these types of audits, auditors should follow the applicable standards included and incorporated in this statement.

B. Financial Audits

1. Financial statement audits determine (a) whether the financial statements of an audited entity present fairly the financial position, results of operations, and cash flows or changes in financial position in accorance with generally accepted accounting principles, and (b) whether the entity has complied with laws and regulations for those transactions and events that may have a material effect on the financial statements.
2. Financial related audits include determining (a) whether financial reports and related items, such as elements, accounts, or funds are fairly presented, (b) whether financial information is presented in accorance with established or stated critiera, and (c) whether the entity has adhered to specific financial compliance requirements.

C. Performance Audits

1. Economy and efficiency audits include determining (a) whether the entity is acquiring, protecting, and using its resources (such as personnel, property, and space) economically and efficiently, (b) the causes of inefficiencies or uneconomical practices, and (c) whether the entity has complied with laws and regulations concerning matters of economy and efficiency.
2. Program audits include determining (a) the extent to which the desired results or benefits established by the legislature or other authorizing body

[1]Comptroller General of the United States, *Government Auditing Standards,* 1988 Revision (United States General Accounting Office, 1988).

are being achieved, (b) the effectiveness of organizations, programs, activities, or functions, and (c) whether the entity has complied with laws and regulations applicable to the program.

D. Understanding the Audit Objectives and Scope

1. Audits may have a combination of financial and performance audit objectives, or may have objectives limited to only some aspects of one audit type.
2. Auditors should follow the appropriate standards in this statement that are applicable to the individual objectives of the audit.

E. Other Activities of An Audit Organization

1. Services other than audits: The head of the audit organization should establish policy on which audit standards from this statement should be followed by the auditors in performing such services. However, as a minimum, auditors should collectively possess adequate professional proficiency and exercise due professional care for the service being performed.
2. Investigative work: The head of the audit organization should establish policy on whether the audit standards in this statement, or some other appropriate standards, are to be followed by the employees performing this work.
3. Nonaudit activities: The head of the audit organization should establish policy on what standards in this statement are to be followed, or whether some other appropriate standards are to be followed, by the employees in performing this type of work.

III. General Standards

A. Qualifications: The staff assigned to conduct the audit should collectively possess adequate professional proficiency for the tasks required.

B. Independence: In all matters relating to the audit work, the audit organization and the individual auditors, whether government or public, should be free from personal and external impairments to independence, should be organizationally independent, and should maintain an independent attitude and appearance.

C. Due Professional Care: Due professional care should be used in conducting the audit and in preparing related reports.

D. Quality Control: Audit organizations conducting government audits should have an appropriate internal quality control system in place and participate in an external quality control review program.

IV. Field Work Standards for Financial Audits

A. Relationship to AICPA Standards

1. The standards of field work for government financial audits incorporate the AICPA standards of field work for financial audits, and prescribes supplemental standards of field work needed to satisfy the unique needs of government financial audits.
2. The field work standards of the AICPA and the supplemental standards

in chapter 4 of this statement apply to both financial statement audits and financial related audits.

B. Planning:

1. **Supplemental planning field work standards for government financial audits are:**
   a. Audit Requirements for all Government Levels: Planning should include consideration of the audit requirements of all levels of government.
   b. Legal and Regulatory Requirements: A test should be made of compliance with applicable laws and regulations.
      (1) In determining compliance with laws and regulations:
         (a) The auditor should design audit steps and procedures to provide reasonable assurance of detecting errors, irregularities, and illegal acts that could have a direct and material effect on the financial statement amounts or the results of financial related audits.
         (b) The auditor should also be aware of the possibility of illegal acts which could have an indirect and material effect on the financial statements or results of financial related audits.

C. Evidence (Working papers)

1. The AICPA field work standards and this statement require that: A record of the auditors' work be retained in the form of working papers.
2. Supplemental working paper requirements for financial audits are that working papers should:
   a. Contain a written audit program cross-referenced to the working papers.
   b. Contain the objectives, scope, methodology and results of the audit.
   c. Contain sufficient information so that supplementary oral explanations are not required.
   d. Be legible with adequate indexing and cross-referencing, and include summaries and lead schedules, as appropriate.
   e. Restrict information included to matters that are materially important and relevant to the objectives of the audit.
   f. Contain evidence of supervisory reviews of the work conducted.

D. Internal Control

1. The AICPA field work standards and this statement require that: A sufficient understanding of the internal control structure is to be obtained to plan the audit and to determine the nature, timing, and extent of tests to be performed.

V. Reporting Standards for Financial Audits

A. Relationship to AICPA Standards

1. The standards of reporting for governmental financial audits incorporate the AICPA standards of reporting for financial audits, and prescribes supplemental standards of reporting needed to satisfy the unique needs of government financial audits.

2. The reporting standards of the AICPA and the supplemental standards in chapter 5 of this statement apply to both financial statement audits and financial related audits.

B. Supplemental reporting standards for government financial audits are:

1. Statement on Auditing Standards: A statement should be included in the auditors' report that the audit was made in accordance with generally accepted government auditing standards (AICPA standards require that public accountants state that the audit was made in accordance with generally accepted auditing standards. In conducting government audits, public accountants should also state that their audit was conducted in accordance with the standards set forth in chapters 3, 4, and 5.)
2. Report on Compliance: The auditors should prepare a written report on their tests of compliance with applicable laws and regulations. This report, which may be included in either the report on the financial audit or a separate report, should contain a statement of positive assurance on those items which were tested for compliance and negative assurance on those items not tested. It should include all material instances of noncompliance, and all instances or indications of illegal acts which could result in criminal prosecution.
3. Report on Internal Controls: The auditors should prepare a written report on their understanding of the entity's internal control structure and the assessment of control risk made as part of a financial statement audit, or a financial related audit. This report may be included in either the auditor's report on the financial audit or a separate report. The auditor's report should include as a minimum: (a) the scope of the auditor's work in obtaining an understanding of the internal control structure and in assessing the control risk, (b) the entity's significant internal controls or control structure including the controls established to ensure compliance with laws and regulations that have a material impact on the financial statements and the results of the financial related audit, and (c) the reportable conditions, including the identification of material weaknesses, identified as a result of the auditors work in understanding and assessing the control risk.
4. Reporting on Financial Related Audits: Written audit reports are to be prepared giving the results of each financial related audit.
5. Privileged and Confidential Information: If certain information is prohibited from general disclosure, the report should state the nature of the information omitted and the requirement that makes the omission necessary.
6. Report Distribution: Written audit reports are to be submitted by the audit organization to the appropriate officials of the organization audited and to the appropriate officials of the organizations requiring or arranging for the audits, including external funding organizations, unless legal restrictions, ethical considerations, or other arrangements prevent it. Copies of the reports should also be sent to other officials who have legal

oversight authority or who may be responsible for taking action and to others authorized to receive such reports. Unless restricted by law or regulation, copies should be made available for public inspection.

VI. Field Work Standards for Performance Audits

A. Planning: Work is to be adequately planned.

B. Supervision: Staff are to be properly supervised.

C. Legal and Regulatory Requirements: An assessment is to be made of compliance with applicable requirements of laws and regulations when necessary to satisfy the audit objectives.

1. Where an assessment of compliance with laws and regulations is required: Auditors should design the audit to provide reasonable assurance of detecting abuse or illegal acts that could significantly affect the audit objectives.
2. In all performance audits: Auditors should be alert to situations or transactions that could be indicative of abuse or illegal acts.

D. Internal Control: An assessment should be made of applicable internal controls when necessary to satisfy the audit objectives.

E. Evidence: Sufficient, competent, and relevant evidence is to be obtained to afford a reasonable basis for the auditors' judgments and conclusions regarding the organization, program, activity, or function under audit. A record of the auditors' work is to be retained in the form of working papers. Working papers may include tapes, films, and discs.

VII. Reporting Standards for Performance Audits

A. Form: Written audit reports are to be prepared communicating the results of each government audit.

B. Timeliness: Reports are to be issued promptly so as to make the information available for timely use by management and legislative officials, and by other interested parties.

C. Report Contents

1. Objectives, Scope, and Methodology: The report should include a statement of the audit objectives and a description of the audit scope and methodology.
2. Audit Findings and Conclusions: The report should include a full discussion of the audit findings, and where applicable, the auditor's conclusions.
3. Cause and Recommendations: The report should include the cause of problem areas noted in the audit, and recommendations for actions to correct the problem areas and to improve operations, when called for by the audit objectives.
4. Statement on Auditing Standards: The report should include a statement that the audit was made in accordance with generally accepted government auditing standards and disclose when applicable standards were not followed.
5. Internal Controls: The report should identify the significant internal

controls that were assessed, the scope of the auditor's assessment work, and any significant weaknesses found during the audit.

6. Compliance With Laws and Regulations: The report should include all significant instances of noncompliance and abuse and all indications or instances of illegal acts that could result in criminal prosecution that were found during or in connection with the audit.
7. Views of Responsible Officials: The report should include the pertinent views of officials of the organization, program, activity, or function audited concerning the auditors' findings, conclusions, and recommendations, and what corrective action is planned.
8. Noteworthy Accomplishments: The report should include a description of any significant noteworthy accompalishments, particularly when management improvements in one area may be applicable elsewhere.
9. Issues Needing Further Study: The report should include a listing of any significant issues needing further study and consideration.
10. Privileged and Confidential Information: The report should include a statement about any pertinent information that was omitted because it was deemed privileged or confidential. The nature of such information should be described, and the basis under which it is withheld should be stated.

D. Report Presentation: The report should be complete, accurate, objective, and convincing, and be as clear and concise as the subject matter permits.

E. Report Distribution: Written audit reports are to be submitted by the audit organization to the appropriate officials of the organization audited, and to the appropriate officials of the organizations requiring or arranging for the audits, including external funding organizations, unless legal restrictions, ethical considerations, or other arrangements prevent it. Copies of the reports should also be sent to other officials who may be responsible for taking action on audit findings and recommendations and to others authorized to receive such reports. Unless restricted by law or regulation, copies should be made available for public inspection.

VIII. AICPA Generally Accepted Auditing Standards

A. General Standards

1. The examination is to be performed by a person or persons having adequate technical training and proficiency as an auditor.
2. In all matters relating to the assignment, an independence in mental attitude is to be maintained by the auditor or auditors.
3. Due professional care is to be exercised in the performance of the examination and the preparation of the report.

B. Standards of Field Work

1. The work is to be adequately planned and assistants, if any, are to be properly supervised.
2. A sufficient understanding of the internal control structure is to be

obtained to plan the audit and to determine the nature, timing, and extent of tests to be performed.

3. Sufficient competent evidential matter is to be obtained through inspection, observation, inquiries, and confirmations to afford a reasonable basis for an opinion regarding the financial statements under examination.

C. Standards of Reporting

1. The report shall state whether the financial statements are presented in accordance with generally accepted accounting principles.
2. The report shall identify those circumstances in which such principles have not been consistenty observed in the current period in relation to the preceding period.
3. Informative disclosures in the financial statements are to be regarded as reasonably adequate unless otherwise stated in the report.
4. The report shall either contain an expression of opinion regarding the financial statements, taken as a whole, or an assertion to the effect that an opinion cannot be expressed. When an overall opinion cannot be expressed, the reasons therefor should be stated. In all cases where an auditor's name is associated with financial statements, the report should contain a clear-cut indication of the character of the auditor's examination, if any, and the degree of responsibility he is taking.

Appendix 11

American Bar Association Statement of Policy Regarding Lawyers' Responses to Auditors' Requests for Information[1]

NOTE: This document, in the form herein set forth, was approved by the Board of Governors of the American Bar Association in December 1975, which official action permitted its release to lawyers and accountants as the standard recommended by the American Bar Association for the lawyer's response to letters of audit inquiry.

PREAMBLE

The public interest in protecting the confidentiality of lawyer-client communications is fundamental. The American legal, political and economic systems depend heavily upon voluntary compliance with the law and upon ready access to a respected body of professionals able to interpret and advise on the law. The expanding complexity of our laws and governmental regulations increases the need for prompt, specific and unhampered lawyer-client communication. The benefits of such communication and early consultation underlie the strict statutory and ethical obligations of the lawyer to preserve the confidences and secrets of the client, as well as the long-recognized testimonial privilege for lawyer-client communication.

Both the Code of Professional Responsibility and the cases applying the evidentiary privilege recognize that the privilege against disclosure can be knowingly and voluntarily waived by the client. It is equally clear that disclosure to a third party may result in loss of the "confidentiality" essential to maintain the privilege. Disclosure to a third party of the lawyer-client communication on a particular subject may also destroy the privilege as to other communications on that subject. Thus, the mere disclosure by the lawyer to the outside auditor, with due client consent, of the substance of communications between the lawyer and client may significantly impair the client's ability in other contexts to maintain the confidentiality of such communications.

Under the circumstances a policy of audit procedure which requires clients to give consent and authorize lawyers to respond to general inquiries and disclose information to auditors concerning matters which have been communicated in confidence is essentially destructive of free and open communication and early consultation between lawyer and client. The institution of such a policy would inevitably discourage management from discussing potential legal problems with counsel for fear that such discussion might become public and precipitate a loss to or possible liability of the business enterprise and its stockholders that might otherwise never materialize.

[1]*The Business Lawyer,* vol. 31, No. 3, April 1976, pp. 1709–1715. Reprinted by permission of the American Bar Association.

It is also recognized that our legal, political and economic systems depend to an important extent on public confidence in published financial statements. To meet this need the accounting profession must adopt and adhere to standards and procedures that will command confidence in the auditing process. It is not, however, believed necessary, or sound public policy, to intrude upon the confidentiality of the lawyer-client relationship in order to command such confidence. On the contrary, the objective of fair disclosure in financial statements is more likely to be better served by maintaining the integrity of the confidential relationship between lawyer and client, thereby strengthening corporate management's confidence in counsel and encouraging its readiness to seek advice of counsel and to act in accordance with counsel's advice.

Consistent with the foregoing public policy considerations, it is believed appropriate to distinguish between, on the one hand, litigation which is pending or which a third party has manifested to the client a present intention to commence and, on the other hand, other contingencies of a legal nature or having legal aspects. As regards the former category, unquestionably the lawyer representing the client in a litigation matter may be the best source for a description of the claim or claims asserted, the client's position (e.g., denial, contest, etc.), and the client's possible exposure in the litigation (to the extent the lawyer is in a position to do so). As to the latter category, it is submitted that, for the reasons set forth above, it is not in the public interest for the lawyer to be required to respond to general inquiries from auditors concerning possible claims.

It is recognized that the disclosure requirements for enterprises subject to the reporting requirements of the Federal securities laws are a major concern of managements and counsel, as well as auditors. It is submitted that compliance therewith is best assured when clients are afforded maximum encouragement, by protecting lawyer-client confidentiality, freely to consult counsel. Likewise, lawyers must be keenly conscious of the importance of their clients being competently advised in these matters.

STATEMENT OF POLICY

NOW, THEREFORE, BE IT RESOLVED that it is desirable and in the public interest that this Association adopt the following Statement of Policy regarding the appropriate scope of the lawyer's response to the auditor's request, made by the client at the request of the auditor, for information concerning matters referred to the lawyer during the course of his representation of the client:

(1) *Client Consent to Response.* The lawyer may properly respond to the auditor's requests for information concerning loss contingencies (the term and concept established by Statement of Financial Accounting Standards No. 5, promulgated by the Financial Accounting Standards Board in March 1975 and discussed in Para-

graph 5.1 of the accompanying Commentary), to the extent hereinafter set forth, subject to the following:

(a) Assuming that the client's initial letter requesting the lawyer to provide information to the auditor is signed by an agent of the client having apparent authority to make such a request, the lawyer may provide to the auditor information requested, without further consent, unless such information discloses a confidence or a secret or requires an evaluation of a claim.

(b) In the normal case, the initial request letter does not provide the necessary consent to the disclosure of a confidence or secret or to the evaluation of a claim since that consent may only be given after full disclosure to the client of the legal consequences of such action.

(c) Lawyers should bear in mind, in evaluating claims, that an adverse party may assert that any evaluation of potential liability is an admission.

(d) In securing the client's consent to the disclosure of confidences or secrets, or the evauation of claims, the lawyer may wish to have a draft of his letter reviewed and approved by the client before releasing it to the auditor; in such cases, additional explanation would in all probability be necessary so that the legal consequences of the consent are fully disclosed to the client.

(2) *Limitation on Scope of Response.* It is appropriate for the lawyer to set forth in his response, by way of limitation, the scope of his engagement by the client. It is also appropriate for the lawyer to indicate the date as of which information is furnished and to disclaim any undertaking to advise the auditor of changes which may thereafter be brought to the lawyer's attention. *Unless the lawyer's response indicates otherwise, (a) it is properly limited to matters which have been given substantive attention by the lawyer in the form of legal consultation and, where appropriate, legal representation since the beginning of the period or periods being reported upon, and (b) if a law firm or a law department, the auditor may assume that the firm or department has endeavored, to the extent believed necessary by the firm or department, to determine from lawyers currently in the firm or department who have performed services for the client since the beginning of the fiscal period under audit whether such services involved substantive attention in the form of legal consultation concerning those loss contingencies referred to in Paragraph 5(a) below but, beyond that, no review has been made of any of the client's transactions or other matters for the purpose of identifying loss contingencies to be described in the response.***

(3) *Response May Be Limited to Material Items.* In response to an auditor's request for disclosure of loss contingencies of a client, it is appropriate for the lawyer's response to indicate that the response is limited to items which are considered individually or collectively material to the presentation of the client's financial statements.

(4) *Limited Responses.* Where the lawyer is limiting his response in accordance with this Statement of Policy, his response should so indicate (see Paragraph 8). If in any

*As contemplated by Paragraph 8 of this Statement of Policy, this sentence is intended to be the subject of incorporation by reference as therein provided.

other respect the lawyer is not undertaking to respond to or comment on particular aspects of the inquiry when responding to the auditor, he should consider advising the auditor that his response is limited, in order to avoid any inference that the lawyer has responded to all aspects; otherwise, he may be assuming a responsibility which he does not intend.

(5) *Loss Contingencies.* When properly requested by the client, it is appropriate for the lawyer to furnish to the auditor information concerning the following matters if the lawyer has been engaged by the client to represent or advise the client professionally with respect thereto and he has devoted substantive attention to them in the form of legal representation or consultation:

(a) *overtly threatened or pending litigation,* whether or not specified by the client;

(b) a *contractually assumed obligation* which the client has specifically identified and upon which the client has specifically requested, in the inquiry letter or a supplement thereto, comment to the auditor;

(c) *an unasserted possible claim or assessment* which the client has specifically identifed and upon which the client has specifically requested, in the inquiry letter or a supplement thereto, comment to the auditor.

With respect to clause (a), overtly threatened litigation means that a potential claimant has manifested to the client an awareness of and present intention to assert a possible claim or assessment unless the likelihood of litigation (or of settlement when litigation would normally be avoided) is considered remote. With respect to clause (c), where there has been no manifestation by a potential claimant of an awareness of and present intention to assert a possible claim or assessment, consistent with the considerations and concerns outlined in the Preamble and Paragraph 1 hereof, the client should request the lawyer to furnish information to the auditor only if the client has determined that it is probable that a possible claim will be asserted, that there is a reasonable possibility that the outcome (assuming such assertion) will be unfavorable, and that the resulting liability would be material to the financial condition of the client. Examples of such situations might (depending in each case upon the particular circumstances) include the following: (i) a catastrophe, accident or other similar physical occurrence in which the client's involvement is open and notorious, or (ii) an investigation by a government agency where enforcement proceedings have been instituted or where the likelihood that they will not be instituted is remote, under circumstances where assertion of one or more private claims for redress would normally be expected, or (iii) a public disclosure by the client acknowledging (and thus focusing attention upon) the existence of one or more probable claims arising out of an event or circumstance. In assessing whether or not the assertion of a possible claim is probable, it is expected that the client would normally employ, by reason of the inherent uncertainties involved and insufficiency of available data, concepts parallel to those used by the lawyer (discussed below) in assessing whether or not an unfavorable outcome is probable; thus, assertion of a possible claim would be considered probable only when the prospects of its being asserted seem reasonably certain (i.e., supported by extrinsic evidence strong enough to establish a presumption that it will happen) and the prospects of non-assertion seem slight.

It would not be appropriate, however, for the lawyer to be requested to furnish information in response to an inquiry letter or supplement thereto if it appears that (a) the client has been required to specify unasserted possible claims without regard to the standard suggested in the preceding paragraph, or (b) the client has been required to specify all or substantially all unasserted possible claims as to which legal advice may have been obtained, since, in either case, such a request would be in substance a general inquiry and would be inconsistent with the intent of this Statement of Policy.

The information that lawyers may properly give to the auditor concerning the foregoing matters would include (to the extent appropriate) an identification of the proceedings or matter, the stage of proceedings, the claim(s) asserted, and the position taken by the client.

In view of the inherent uncertainties, the lawyer should normally refrain from expressing judgments as to outcome except in those relatively few clear cases where it appears to the lawyer that an unfavorable outcome is either "probable" or "remote"; for purposes of any such judgment it is appropriate to use the following meanings:

(i) *probable*—an unfavorable outcome for the client is probable if the prospects of the claimant not succeeding are judged to be extremely doubtful and the prospects for success by the client in its defense are judged to be slight.

(ii) *remote*—an unfavorable outcome is remote if the prospects for the client not succeeding in its defense are judged to be extremely doubtful and the prospects of success by the claimant are judged to be slight.

If, in the opinion of the lawyer, considerations within the province of his professional judgment bear on a particular loss contingency to the degree necessary to make an informed judgment, he may in appropriate circumstances communicate to the auditor his view that an unfavorable outcome is "probable" or "remote," applying the above meanings. No inference should be drawn, from the absence of such a judgment, that the client will not prevail.

The lawyer also may be asked to estimate, in dollar terms, the potential amount of loss or range of loss in the event that an unfavorable outcome is not viewed to be "remote." In such a case, the amount or range of potential loss will normally be as inherently impossible to ascertain, with any degree of certainty, as the outcome of the litigation. Therefore, it is appropriate for the lawyer to provide an estimate of the amount or range of potential loss (if the outcome should be unfavorable) only if he believes that the probability of inaccuracy of the estimate of the amount or range of potential loss is slight.

The considerations bearing upon the difficulty in estimating loss (or range of loss) where pending litigation is concerned are obviously even more compelling in the case of unasserted possible claims. In most cases, the lawyer will not be able to provide any such estimate to the auditor.

As indicated in Paragraph 4 hereof, the auditor may assume that all loss contingencies specified by the client in the manner specified in clauses (b) and (c) above have received comment in the response, unless otherwise therein indicated. The lawyer should not be asked, nor need the lawyer undertake, to furnish information to the auditor concerning loss contingencies except as contemplated by this Paragraph 5.

(6) *Lawyer's Professional Responsibility.* Independent of the scope of his response to the auditor's request for information, the lawyer, depending upon the nature of the matters as to which he is engaged, may have as part of his professional responsibility to his client an obligation to advise the client concerning the need for or advisability of public disclosure of a wide range of events and circumstances. The lawyer has an obligation not knowingly to participate in any violation by the client of the disclosure requirements of the securities laws. In appropriate circumstances, the lawyer also may be required under the Code of Professional Responsibility to resign his engagement if his advice concerning disclosures is disregarded by the client. The auditor may properly assume that whenever, in the course of performing legal services for the client with respect to a matter recognized to involve an unasserted possible claim or assessment which may call for financial statement disclosure, the lawyer has formed a professional conclusion that the client must disclose or consider disclosure concerning such possible claim or assessment, the lawyer, as a matter of professional responsibility to the client, will so advise the client and will consult with the client concerning the question of such disclosure and the applicable requirements* of FAS 5.

(7) *Limitation on Use of Response. Unless otherwise stated in the lawyer's response, it shall be solely for the auditor's information in connection with his audit of the financial condition of the client and is not to be quoted in whole or in part or otherwise referred to in any financial statements of the client or related documents, nor is it to be filed with any governmental agency or other person, without the lawyer's prior written consent.† Notwithstanding such limitation, the response can properly be furnished to others in compliance with court process or when necessary in order to defend the auditor against a challenge of the audit by the client or a regulatory agency, provided that the lawyer is given written notice of the circumstances at least twenty days before the response is so to be furnished to others, or as long in advance as possible if the situation does not permit such period of notice.†*

(8) *General.* This Statement of Policy, together with the accompanying Commentary (which is an integral part hereof), has been developed for the general guidance of the legal profession. In a particular case, the lawyer may elect to supplement or modify the approach hereby set forth. If desired, this Statement of Policy may be incorporated by reference in the lawyer's response by the following statement: "This response is limited by, and in accordance with, the ABA Statement of Policy Regarding Lawyers' Responses to Auditors' Requests for Information (December 1975); without limiting the generality of the foregoing, the limitations

*Under FAS 5, when there has been no manifestation by a potential claimant of an awareness of a possible claim or assessment, disclosure of an unasserted possible claim is required only if the enterprise concludes that (i) it is probable that a claim will be asserted, (ii) there is a reasonable possibility, if the claim is in fact asserted, that the outcome will be unfavorable, and (iii) the liability resulting from such unfavorable outcome would be material to its financial condition.

†As contemplated by Paragraph 8 of this Statement of Policy, this sentence is intended to be the subject of incorporation by reference as therein provided.

set forth in such Statement on the scope and use of this response (Paragraphs 2 and 7) are specifically incorporated herein by reference, and any description herein of any 'loss contingencies' is qualified in its entirety by Paragraph 5 of the Statement and the accompanying Commentary (which is an integral part of the Statement)."

NOTE: An extensive Commentary accompanies this Statement of Policy and is an integral part of it. Those interested in using this Appendix should consult it in conjunction with the Commentary.

INDEX

A

D

E

T

U

W